Commercial General
Liability Coverage

Property and Casualty Continuing Education Course

At press time, this edition contains the most complete and accurate information currently available. Owing to the nature of license examinations, however, information may have been added recently to the actual test that does not appear in this edition. Please contact the publisher to verify that you have the most current edition.

This publication is designed to provide accurate and authoritative information in regard to the subject matter covered. It is sold with the understanding that the publisher is not engaged in rendering legal, accounting, or other professional services. If legal advice or other expert assistance is required, the services of a competent professional should be sought.

To submit comments or suggestions, please send an email to errata@kaplan.com.

Published by DF Institute, Inc., d/b/a Kaplan Financial Education.

Printed in the United States of America.

ISBN: 1-4195-3999-X

PPN: 5932-8501

10 11 12 10 9 8 7 6 5 4 3
J   F   M   A   M J J A S O N D

Contents

Introduction

WHO SHOULD STUDY THIS COURSE

Commercial General Liability Coverage is designed for insurance personnel involved in commercial liability functions.

OBJECTIVES OF THIS COURSE

In this course, you will analyze the coverages provided by the commercial general liability (CGL) occurrence and claims-made forms. The course also addresses popular endorsements and several single-purpose coverage forms.

Before studying this course, you need a basic understanding of general insurance principles and commercial insurance concepts. The course assumes you have no knowledge of general liability insurance and begins at this level of understanding.

After completing the course, you will be able to:

- explain the legal basis for liability;

- differentiate between various types of liability;

- explain the purposes of liability insurance;

- explain the commercial package policy concept and how the commercial general liability coverage part is integrated;

- define and use the special terms of the CGL coverage forms;

- explain the coverage provided by the CGL occurrence and claims-made coverage forms, including their differences, by using the forms as a reference; and

- describe the purposes of various CGL endorsements and single-purpose coverage forms

HOW TO USE THIS COURSE

Programmed Instruction

As you proceed through each unit of *Commercial General Liability Coverage*, you will have the opportunity to interact with the study material and check your progress. This method of learning is called **programmed instruction**. Each step in programmed instruction is numbered for your easy reference. Each of these numbered steps is called a **frame**, and a series of frames composes a **unit**.

To learn more about how programmed instruction works, read the frames that follow and respond as requested.

1. Three of the basic principles of programmed instruction are:

    1. The material is presented step-by-step, in logical groupings.

    2. After you have read an increment of information, you are asked to demonstrate your comprehension and retention of what you've learned by answering questions, selecting the correct answer from a number of options or by responding to the information in some other way.

    3. You receive immediate confirmation of your response. The answers and suggestions provided in the textbook are located immediately below the frame exercise.

    Now, try this exercise.

    Each of the following statements corresponds to one of the three principles we just listed. Mark a **1, 2** or **3** in front of each statement to match it to the principle it represents.

    _____ A. Throughout the course, you will apply what you have learned by answering questions.

    _____ B. You will know each step of the way whether you have understood the material up to that point.

    _____ C. The text takes you through the material step-by-step, in logical groupings.

    Answer: 2 A.; 3 B.; 1 C.

2. You should check your answer after completing each frame in the text.

    If your answer matches the printed answer that immediately follows the exercise, go to the next frame. If it does not match, review the material in the frame, then respond differently. Check that response. You may need to follow this procedure more than once in a single frame. If the correct response still escapes you, read the material again from the beginning. Such review is more likely to be necessary if there has been a prolonged interruption in your study.

    If the response you have made does not match the response that appears after the exercise, you should first

    A. go on to the next frame

    B. go back several frames and start over

    C. review the material in the frame and select a different response

    Answer: C is correct.

3. Once you understand the material in a frame, go to the next frame and repeat the study-respond-verify cycle.

    Arrange the following steps in the correct sequence by writing a number in the blank beside each statement to indicate how to proceed through a programmed instruction text. Write **1** for the first step, **2** for the second step, and so on.

    _____ A. Check your response.

    _____ B. Read the material in the frame.

    _____ C. Go to the next frame.

    _____ D. Answer the question asked in the frame.

    _____ E. Repeat the previous steps until you understand, reading the prior material again if necessary.

    Answer: 3 A.; 1 B.; 5 C.; 2 D.; 4 E.

Other Features of Programmed Instruction

4. Programmed instruction incorporates some other features that will make your study even more effective:

    - **Illustrations:** The course includes illustrations, charts, and graphics to stimulate your interest in what you are studying, make concepts easier to understand, and promote retention of what you have learned.

    - **Key Words:** Pay special attention to terms that are in **boldface** type. It is important that you know the meanings of these key words.

    - **Job Builders:** Occasionally, the Notes column on a page will contain instructions for you to perform some job-related activity. These activities may help you directly relate what you have learned to your job. Although your supervisor may review the results of those activities, you will *not* be tested on them on the examination you will take when you have completed this course.

■ **Job Aid:** At the end of the text, you will find a tear-out Checklist that contains guidelines for underwriting new applicants for general liability insurance.

Which of the following statements concerning programmed instruction are correct?

A. Illustrations are often used to explain certain concepts more effectively.

B. It is important that you know the meaning of key words printed in boldface type.

C. The course exam includes questions on the results of Job Builder activities.

D. All of the above

Answer: B and C are correct.

When you're ready, begin your study with Unit One.

1

Introduction to Legal Liability

CRIMINAL AND CIVIL LAW

1. Before you can begin to analyze a liability policy, you must understand the fundamentals of legal liability. Law is divided into two broad categories: **criminal law** and **civil law**. Here is a simplified illustration of the primary differences between criminal and civil law.

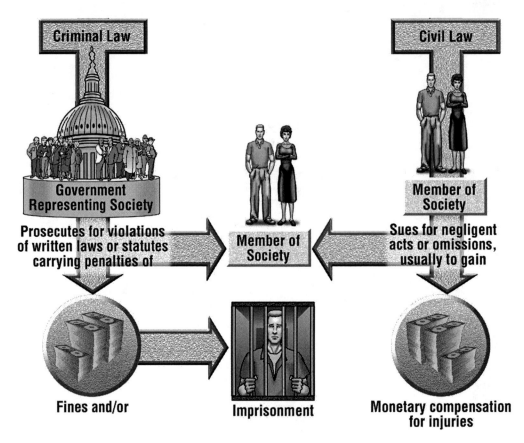

The phrase government representing society refers to government at any level—national, state, municipal, and so forth. And, in both criminal and civil law, the phrase *member of society* can refer to a single individual, several individuals, or even a corporation or other business entity.

Indicate whether each situation described below is an example of a criminal offense or a civil offense by writing either **CR** for criminal or **CV** for civil.

A. A store owner is stabbed by a thief who is later arrested for stealing $15,000 worth of retail goods.

B. Consolidated Cupric sues a supplier for failing to deliver a contracted order of copper wire.

C. A customer takes legal action against National Bank after the bank's escalator malfunctioned, pitching the customer backward and injuring him.

D. Vincent is arrested for poisoning his wealthy aunt to hasten his inheritance of her business.

Answer: CR A; CV B; CV C; CR D

2. In some cases, an act might be subject to both criminal and civil law. For example, an individual might operate a car in a wantonly careless manner, causing the death of another person. This driver would be subject to criminal prosecution for auto homicide and might also be sued, under civil law, for wrongful death damages by the victim's family.

   Answer these questions concerning the differences between criminal and civil law.

   A. Legal action taken by the state in the interest of society involves (criminal/civil) _____ law, while legal action taken by members of society against others involves (criminal/civil) _____ law.

   B. Which type of law involves fines or imprisonment? _____

   C. Which type of law involves negligent acts or omissions for which monetary compensation is sought? _____

   D. An act might fall under criminal law or under civil law, but never both.   ( ) True   ( ) False

   Answer: A. criminal, civil; B. Criminal; C. Civil; D. False. Some acts may be subject to both criminal and civil actions.

DIVISIONS OF CIVIL LAW

Contract Law and Tort Law

3. As a student of liability insurance, you will want to be aware of what criminal law is, but you will not normally be involved in these cases. Civil law, on the other hand, directly involves liability insurance. This illustration shows the two types of civil law.

Contract Law
- Written or stated agreement
- Between two or more parties
- For a specific promise of action

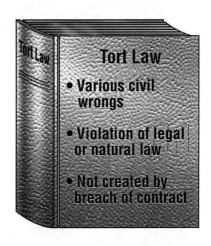
Tort Law
- Various civil wrongs
- Violation of legal or natural law
- Not created by breach of contract

Here is an example of contract law: Rigoro Paper Company executive Sherman Vale signs a written contract to deliver six loads of paper stock to Paley's Printers within a six-week deadline, but fails to do so. As a result, Paley's loses two valuable customers and sues Rigoro and Vale for the loss. Since this was a valid contractual agreement, Rigoro and Vale are held legally responsible for Vale's specific promise of action.

Here is an example of tort law: Pedestrians have a legal and natural right to cross city streets at designated crossings without being struck intentionally by the driver of a vehicle. If a pedestrian is struck by a car while legally crossing the street, the driver of the car commits a tort, making the driver a **tortfeasor**, and can be held liable for the pedestrian's injuries.

In front of each situation described below, write in a **C** if it is an example of contract law or a **T** if it is an example of tort law.

_____ A. A business owner fails to repair a faulty parking brake on his fork-lift. The forklift rolls down a ramp in his warehouse and strikes a person who is visiting the business premises.

_____ B. Warren becomes angry during a business meeting and punches his business partner in the nose.

_____ C. Patricia decides to move her business to another state. She ignores the lease on her business property and moves away without telling the landlord.

_____ D. A traveling salesman signs for a credit card with a major oil company. The company revokes the card when the salesman fails to pay his bill for three months in a row.

Answer: T A; T B; C C; C D

4. Under the principles of our legal system, a person owes a duty to others to refrain from deliberately doing anything to injure another person or another's property. In addition, a person owes a duty to others to exercise care to avoid causing unintentional injury or damage.

An individual who commits a tort and is judged liable for actions taken while committing the tort normally must pay damages to the party who was injured or wronged. Liability insurance does not usually apply to an insured's intentional torts, even though the wronged party may have a legal right to sue for damages for those intentional acts. On the other hand, liability insurance usually does apply to an insured person's unintentional torts.

A. Legal principles stipulate that a person owes a duty to others regarding

   1. intentional actions that may cause harm

   2. unintentional actions that may cause harm

   3. both 1 and 2

B. Liability insurance typically applies to an individual's

   1. intentional torts

   2. unintentional torts

   3. both 1 and 2

Answer: A. 3 is correct; B. 2 is correct.

TYPES OF TORTS

Intentional Tort

5. There are three types of actions that constitute tort violations:

    ■ intentional torts;

    ■ absolute liability; and

    ■ negligence.

    An **intentional tort** is an action taken with the deliberate intent to harm another. Suppose Gordon becomes enraged with his employer for refusing to raise Gordon's salary. Gordon slashes the tires on his boss' car, committing an intentional tort. It is likely Gordon will be held liable for the damage.

    Which one of the following is an example of an intentional tort?

    A. Jane knows a board on the front porch step of her grocery store is loose, but she doesn't repair it. One day, a delivery person falls through the step and is injured.

    B. Hillsdale keeps her valuable coin collection in her store, Coin Collector's Community. For protection, she keeps two vicious watchdogs in the store at night. During the day, one of the dogs escapes and injures a customer.

    C. An irate customer makes an insulting remark to Mitchell, a clerk in a hardware store. Mitchell angrily throws a handful of nails at the customer, injuring the customer's eye.

    Answer: C is correct.

Absolute Liability

6. In some cases, a person may be liable on the basis of **absolute liability.** This type of liability may be imposed as a matter of law, by court decision, by statute, or by any combination of the three. This type of liability without fault may result when an individual deliberately acts in a way that is *potentially* hazardous, even though there was no *intent* to harm others. Answer choice B in the previous exercise illustrates this principle because keeping vicious dogs is potentially hazardous even without the intent to cause harm.

Absolute liability is most frequently applied when dangerous materials, hazardous operations, or animals are involved, regardless of the skills or precautions used to prevent harm from occurring. For example, a construction company that uses blasting materials is absolutely liable for any damage to others resulting from blasting activities, no matter how carefully they are performed.

Which of the following are examples of absolute liability?

A. When a vat of hydrochloric acid overflows at Creative Chemical Company, an acre of land owned by a neighboring business is damaged.

B. Lola keeps seven cobra snakes in a cage at her pet store. One escapes and injures a young boy in the store.

C. Hobie places a freezer in the open bed of his pickup truck for delivery to a purchaser. As Hobie drives along the highway, the rope holding the freezer breaks. The freezer topples off the truck and hits an automobile, injuring its passengers.

Answer: A and B are correct. These situations involve absolute liability because of the inherent danger of the chemicals and poisonous snakes.

Negligence

7. The third area of tort law is **negligence**, the most commonly evoked area in tort law. Negligence is defined as:

Failure to use the care that is required to protect others from unreasonable chance of harm.

When negligence exists, an individual can be held legally liable for damages. Answer choice C in the previous exercise is an example of negligence because Hobie failed to use appropriate care in securing the freezer so others would not be harmed.

In attempting to clarify the concept of negligence, courts have established that everyone is expected to behave as a **reasonable person** would behave, following the ordinary considerations that guide human affairs.

Which of the following are examples of negligence?

A. Although Ken, a delivery driver for a large supermarket chain, has not slept for 58 hours, he decides to make one more delivery before going home. He falls asleep at the wheel of his truck and crashes into a gasoline station, injuring the attendant.

B. Demetrius breaks a soft drink bottle on his driveway but does not clean it up before he leaves for work. During his absence, the newspaper carrier cuts her foot on the glass while delivering papers.

C. Early one morning, a supermarket customer drops an overripe plum onto the floor and leaves without mentioning it. Later that day, another customer slips on the plum and is injured.

Answer: A, B and C all illustrate a lack of reasonable care to prevent harm to others and therefore, are examples of negligence.

Establishing Negligence

Legal Duty Owed

8. Four conditions must exist for a charge of negligence to be established. There must be:

   ■ a legal duty owed;

   ■ a breach of that duty;

   ■ actual damage sustained; and

   ■ evidence that the breach of legal duty is the proximate cause of loss.

   We will look at each of these conditions separately.

   First, there must be a legal **duty owed** by the wrongdoer to the claimant. It is everyone's duty to take reasonable care to protect the rights and property of others. For example, it is your duty to resist punching your neighbor when you are angry, just as it is your duty to drive carefully. Sometimes, however, allegations of negligence are not accepted because there is no legal duty owed by one party to another.

   Suppose Madeline White was responsible for an auto accident in which she and another party were injured. When Clayton White read about the accident in the newspaper, he mistakenly thought that it was his sister Madeline who was involved. Highly upset, Clayton hyperventilated, then fainted, and was injured as a result. His attempt to recover loss from the stranger, Madeline White, was unsuccessful because there was no duty owed by Madeline to Clayton.

   A. List the four requirements for establishing negligence.

      1. _____

      2. _____

      3. _____

      4. _____

   B. In which of the following cases of alleged negligence is there **no** legal duty owed?

      1. Sharma is having a walkway at her business replaced, and there are several large, unfilled holes. A postal carrier steps in one of these holes and sprains his ankle. He charges Sharma's business for his injury.

      2. Jill purchases crabapple jam from a gourmet jam company. She later claims damages from the company for severe stomach pain after eating the jam.

3. Steve is restoring an antique auto at his garage. Colin passes by the garage, slows down to admire the car, and strikes a wall. Colin charges Steve for damages.

Answer: A. (In any order) 1. Legal duty owed; 2. Breach of legal duty owed; 3. Actual damage; 4. Proximate cause (or direct causal relationship between breach of legal duty owed and damage); B. 3 is correct.

Breach of Legal Duty

9. The second element necessary for negligence to be substantiated is that the legal duty owed must be violated—that is, there is a **breach of duty**.

    Tony stops for breakfast at a roadside restaurant. He parks his car on an incline in the restaurant's parking lot but fails to set the parking brake. While Tony is inside enjoying his meal, his car rolls backward into the highway, causing a chain reaction collision of passing cars. Is there a breach of legal duty owed?   ( ) Yes   ( ) No   Why? _____
    _____

Answer: Yes. It is Tony's legal duty to park his car safely; since he did not, he has breached that duty.

Actual Damage

10. Another requirement for establishing negligence is that **actual damage** is sustained by the party claiming harm.

    As an example, Jay Eversoll races his motorcycle around neighborhood streets, and on several occasions has nearly driven over the lawn at Dickerson's auto business. Dickerson wants to prevent the damage he fears is inevitable because of Jay's recklessness, so he brings suit against Jay. Dickerson cannot collect because no actual damage has occurred.

    In which one of the following situations has actual damage been sustained?

    A. Lavonia Nelson's husband dies as the result of the negligence of a coworker on his construction crew. Although Lavonia is employed and her income exceeded that of her deceased husband, she sues for damages.

    B. While eating lunch at the City Diner, Beth notices a rock in her tuna salad sandwich before biting into it. The waiter quickly replaces the sandwich with a fresh one. Although she experiences no ill effects from the experience, Beth sues the diner.

    C. Allie Taylor is a passenger in a car driven by Maxwell Byrd. Maxwell swerves off the road and into a field to avoid striking a child. Although she sustains no bodily injury, Allie makes a claim against Maxwell for inconvenience as a result of the incident.

Answer: A is correct.

Proximate Cause

11. The final requirement for a charge of negligence to be established is that there be a **direct causal relationship** between the breach of legal duty and the damage that is sustained. When this is the case, the negligent act is said to be the **proximate cause** of the loss.

    The proximate cause of a loss is an action that, in a natural and continuous sequence, produced the loss. This sequence is unbroken by any other factors or events, and the loss would not have occurred without this proximate cause.

    Sometimes several events occur between the initial event causing the loss and the loss itself. However, the proximate cause relationship remains **as long as these events occur in a type of chain reaction with no other causal element interrupting the sequence.**

    A small fire in a control unit at a manufacturing company causes a short circuit in the electrical wiring. The short circuit causes a machine that regulates another machine to shut down. The second machine goes out of control and flips a flywheel off its shaft, badly damaging adjacent equipment. Would the fire be considered the proximate cause of the damage to the equipment?   ( ) Yes   ( ) No   Explain._____

    _____

    _____

    Answer: Yes. This chain reaction sequence had no other intervening causal relationship between the fire and the final damage to the equipment.

12. When intervening events occur between the negligent act and the final damage, the negligent party is not liable because the proximate cause requirement is missing.

    Because Curt Hansell does not repair faulty wiring in the structure housing his business, a fire destroys the premises. Just after the fire, a stranger named Sam Mills is one of several curious people who are investigating the rubble of the building. Mills trips on some debris and is injured. Is Hansell likely to be held liable for Mills' injuries?   ( ) Yes   ( ) No   Why?

    _____

    _____

    _____

    _____

    Answer: No. There was no direct causal relationship between Hansell's negligence and Mills' injury. The proximate cause of Mills' injury was his own actions, not Hansell's negligent act of not repairing the wiring.

Gross Negligence

13. Individuals or businesses are guilty of negligence when they fail to use *ordinary* care. If they fail to use even *slight* care, the result is:

Gross negligence involves:

■ total disregard for the safety of others;

■ reckless, wanton, and willful misconduct; and

■ flagrant breach of the standard of due care of a reasonably prudent person.

Which of the following illustrate gross negligence?

A. Annabelle is driving several friends home from work when she encounters a dense fog. Although she slows down, she is unable to see a stalled truck ahead, and strikes it in the rear. Annabelle's passengers are injured.

B. Excited about his new sports car, Antoine takes his friend Bryan for a demonstration ride. Speeding to impress his friend, Antoine loses control of the car when he attempts to turn a corner without reducing speed. Bryan is injured.

C. Corinne invites a group of friends over for a pool party in her new swimming pool. After several martinis, Corinne decides to experiment with diving techniques. She jumps off the board while holding a beach umbrella and strikes several people in the water, injuring them.

Answer: B and C are correct.

DEFENSES AGAINST NEGLIGENCE

Contributory Negligence

14. Negligence is an important ingredient in determining liability in many legal cases. However, there are several defenses in the area of negligence that may influence a finding of liability.

Sometimes, both parties involved in a damage claim acted negligently to cause the injury. This situation is called contributory liability or, more commonly, **contributory negligence**, and can prevent either party from collecting for damages.

The following illustration shows how contributory negligence occurs. Here, Party A's degree of care for his own safety falls below the required standard of care and, interacting with Party B's negligence, contributes to his own injury. When both factors contribute to the damage, contributory negligence exists.

Standard of Care
_____

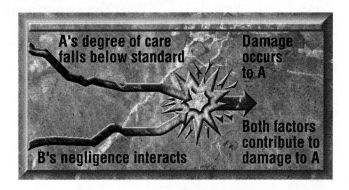

A. While a driver is making a U-turn on an interstate highway, his car is struck by a pickup truck traveling far in excess of the speed limit. Is the driver of the car guilty of contributory negligence?   ( ) Yes   ( ) No
Why? _____
_____

B. Would the driver of the car be likely to collect any damages from the truck driver in this case?   ( ) Yes   ( ) No

Answer: A. Yes. By making a U-turn on an interstate highway, the driver has allowed his degree of care to fall below the required standard; B. No

Comparative Negligence

15. To counter the harshness of contributory negligence, which allows no recovery for the injured parties, many states consider the **comparative negligence** of each party. According to this principle, recovery for damages may be more or less depending upon the degree of liability in each instance.

_____
Ask your supervisor or trainer whether your state uses contributory or comparative negligence to determine damages when more than one party's negligence contributes to a loss.
_____

If the injured party was more negligent than the person against whom the claim is made, the injured party may not collect for damages at all, or may collect less for damages.

Study this illustration, and then answer the following questions.

A. Whose degree of negligence is greater, Party A or Party B? _____

_____

B. If Party B is the injured party, is Party B likely to collect for damages from Party A? ( ) Yes ( ) No   Explain your answer. _____

_____

Answer: A. Party B; B. No. Comparatively, A's negligence was less than B's.

Assumption of Risk

16. When people willfully and knowingly expose themselves to the possibility of injury, this is known as **assumption of risk**.

   Assumption of risk exists when *all* of the fault for injury lies with the person who suffers the loss. Under the law, a person who consents to becoming involved in a potentially hazardous situation may have difficulty collecting for any resulting loss.

   Rosemary accepts a ride home from a party with Leland, even though she knows Leland has been drinking alcoholic beverages steadily for four consecutive hours. Leland drives the wrong way down a one-way street, crashing into an oncoming vehicle. Rosemary is injured. Might Rosemary be barred from recovering any damages from Leland? ( ) Yes ( ) No Explain your answer. _____

_____

Answer: Yes. Rosemary knowingly exposed herself to a hazardous situation.

Avoidable Consequences

17. Another defense against negligence comes into play *after* a loss actually occurs. The law assumes that when a reasonable person experiences a loss, she will take every precaution to prevent any further damages. If that

person does *not* take such precautions and further loss occurs, the principle of **avoidable consequences** is introduced.

The essence of avoidable consequences is that a person should not recover for an injury that results because the individual failed to take appropriate action to avoid further injury.

Wally's garage roof is damaged by fire as a result of Tom's negligence. The roof remains unrepaired during the next three weeks while Wally negotiates a settlement with Tom. During that time, a priceless antique auto that Wally keeps in the garage is damaged in a hailstorm.

A. Could Wally probably collect from Tom for the loss to the *garage?*
( ) Yes   ( ) No

B. Could Wally probably collect from Tom for the loss to the antique auto?   ( ) Yes   ( ) No

C. Explain your answers. _____

_____

_____

_____

Answer: A. Yes; B. No; C. Wally could collect for the garage damage since Tom was negligent. However, under the principle of avoidable consequences, Wally could have avoided the loss to the car if he had repaired the roof or moved the car.

RESPONSIBILITY OF PROPERTY OWNERS

Invitees

18. In considering negligence, some special concepts apply to the **responsibility of property owners** to others who may visit the property. Whether or not a property owner is responsible for injury to a visitor to the property depends on the purpose of the visit.

    We will discuss three different types of visitors to the property and how these types affect the owner's responsibility. The three types are:

    ■ invitees;

    ■ licensees; and

    ■ trespassers.

    Note: In some states, the law does not make distinctions between invitees, licensees, and trespassers. In these states, all visitors are considered invitees.

First, let's consider **invitees**. An invitee is a person who is

■ invited onto the premises

■ for some purpose involving potential benefit to the owner of the property

■ whether the invitation is expressed or implied.

A property owner owes an invitee the duty of keeping the premises in a reasonably safe condition. The owner must also warn the invitee of any hidden defects in the property of which the invitee is not aware.

Which one of the following situations best illustrates the invitee relationship?

A. While Carmelita is standing outside a department store waiting for a bus, it begins to rain, so she steps inside the doors of the store to wait. When she sees the bus approaching, she rushes through the doors, drops a package, trips over the package, and is injured.

B. A pedestrian takes a shortcut through a parking lot and accidentally stumbles into a delivery truck.

C. BDB Corporation hosts an annual event during which potential customers are invited into the building to attend a new product showing that BDB hopes will attract new purchasers. During the event, diesel fumes from a semi-trailer truck unloading company products onto a loading dock escape into the meeting room. Several customers become ill.

Answer: C is correct because the visitors are at BDB for the potential benefit of BDB.

Licensees

19. Another type of visitor is a **licensee**, which is a person who is:

■ on the premises with the owner's or occupant's consent; but

■ for the sole benefit of the visitor.

The duty owed to a licensee is less than that owed to an invitee. The property owner or occupant is expected to use ordinary care in maintaining the property, but the licensee takes it as he finds it. Licensees expose themselves to the same dangers to which the owner is exposed, but the owner is still expected to use reasonable care.

In the previous exercise, answer choice A illustrates the licensee relationship because Carmelita was inside the store for her own benefit. Based on what you just read, would the store owner be held liable for the injuries she sustained?   ( ) Yes   ( ) No   Explain your answer. _____

_____

_____

Answer: No. The injury did not result from any failure on the part of the store owner to take reasonable care of the property.

Trespassers

20. The third type of party visiting the property of another is a **trespasser.** A trespasser is one who is:

■ on the premises:

■ without permission, either express or implied, from the property owner.

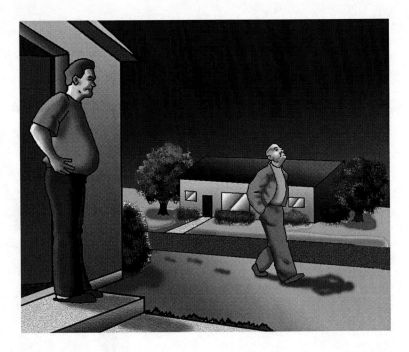

Although a property owner does not owe a duty to keep the premises safe for trespassers, he must use reasonable care for a trespasser's safety after realizing a trespasser is present. A property owner cannot deliberately attempt to harm a trespasser.

Suppose that every evening, cowboy Collins takes a horseback ride across neighbor Neville's lower pasture. Neville complains to Collins that this disturbs Neville's cattle, but Collins continues. Neville installs a series of thin wires across Collins' usual path. The horse trips on a wire, throwing Collins off and injuring him. Collins sues Neville.

A. Is Collins a trespasser?   ( ) Yes   ( ) No

B. Is it likely that Collins can collect damages from Neville for his injuries?   ( ) Yes   ( ) No   Why? _____

_____

Answer: A. Yes; B. Yes. Even though Collins is a trespasser, Neville has no right to willfully attempt to harm him.

Attractive Nuisance Doctrine

21. We mentioned earlier that a property owner does not owe a duty to keep the premises safe for trespassers. This principle is modified if the trespasser is a child—usually a person under age 14.

    A property owner must use ordinary care to protect trespassing children from an **attractive nuisance.** An attractive nuisance is:

    ■ An artificial structure or condition, rather than a naturally occurring part of the land or property,

    ■ Especially attractive to children,

    ■ Capable of resulting in injury to children.

Which one of the following fits the description of an attractive nuisance?

A. Parker, the proprietor of an antique store located in a rural area, has several bad-tempered geese that have taken up residence on the store's property. These birds sometimes chase and bite children who try to play with them.

B. Symes, a plumber, leaves scrap pipe from his work in the back lot of his business. Over the years, the pipe has accumulated into piles of various shapes and sizes. Occasionally, passing elementary school children have been injured playing on the pipes.

C. A bait and tackle shop has a large natural pond on its business property. Customers' children are often attracted to the pond while their parents shop.

Answer: B is correct. In A and C, the conditions described were not artificially created.

This completes your introduction to the principles of legal liability. In the next unit, you'll learn how insurance is used to handle legal liability exposures.

UNIT

2

The Liability Exposure

FIRST, SECOND, AND THIRD PARTIES

1. We have discussed some common legal principles behind the concept of holding individuals and businesses liable for their actions. Now, we will address the role of insurance in handling that liability. First, consider why insurance might be needed.

   When people are judged liable for a loss, they usually are required to pay money as compensation to the party who was wronged. Liability insurance can provide that money, and when it does, the insurer essentially becomes one of the parties in the legal framework involving liability losses.

   Insurance language identifies the parties involved like this:

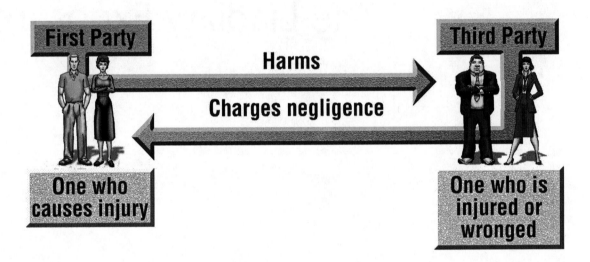

   A. According to the illustration, the person or entity that is wronged is the (first/third) _____ party.
   B. The person or entity responsible for causing injury to another is the (first/third) _____ party.

   Answer: A. third; B. first

2. Because a liability judgment against the first party can be very expensive, most people transfer all or a portion of the burden of their liability exposure to an insurance company by purchasing a liability insurance policy. A liability policy promises to pay, on behalf of the insured first party, judgments for which the first party is legally liable. Here is how the insurer and the liability policy fit into the picture:

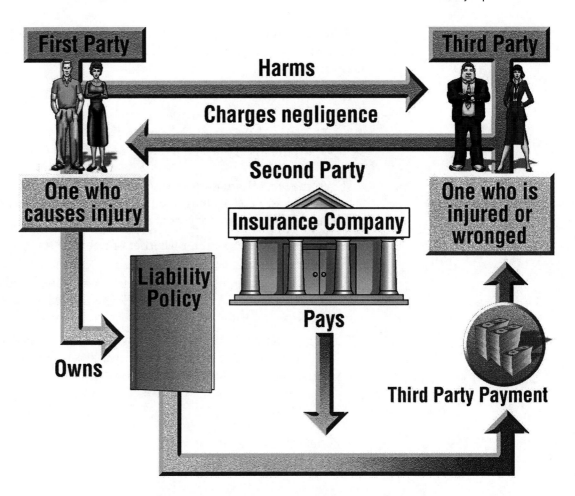

Tawanda Kegley purchases a liability insurance policy from XYZ Insurance Company. Three months later, Kegley is judged liable for injuries to Michael Crosby. The insurer pays the amount of the judgment to Crosby. Using the illustration as a guide, answer these questions.

A. Who is the first party?_____

B. Who is the second party?_____

C. Who is the third party?_____

D. The payments the insurer makes to the injured party are called _____
    _____ party payments.

Answer: A. Tawanda Kegley; B. XYZ Insurance Company; C. Michael Crosby; D. third

3. Before an insurer will pay for a liability loss, it must determine that the insured is actually legally liable. This is accomplished in either of the following ways.

    1. A court of law determines that the insured has committed a tort and is liable.

    2. The facts of the event indicate to the insurer that if the case went to court, the insured would likely be found liable.

    When the second situation exists, an insurer might agree to make payment before the case goes to court to eliminate court costs and possibly limit the amount of payment to the person seeking damages.

    A. What is one criterion for whether or not an insurer will pay for a liability loss? _____

    B. The only way an insurer will decide to pay a loss based on legal liability is when a court of law finds the insured is liable.
        ( ) True   ( ) False

    C. An insurer might decide, based upon the facts available, that an insured will be found liable if the case goes to court, so the insurer might make payment before that happens.   ( ) True   ( ) False

    Answer: A. Whether the insured is legally liable for the loss; B. False; the facts may indicate that if the case went to court, the insured would likely be found liable; C. True

THE THREE LIABILITY EXPOSURES

4. **Liability exposure** is the possibility of financial loss due to a claim by a third party. There are three categories of liability exposure:

    ■ personal;

    ■ professional; and

    ■ business.

    The first category of exposure is **personal** liability, which is the possibility of claims by a third party arising from an individual's personal activities, such as participation in sports, the use of an automobile, or owning a home.

    The second category, **professional** exposure, is the possibility of claims by a third party arising from the conduct of a profession, such as medicine, insurance, law, or accounting.

    The third category is **business** exposure, which is the possibility of claims by a third party arising from the conduct of a business, such as steel erection, well drilling, appliance maintenance, candy manufacturing, operating a retail store, or any of hundreds of types of businesses.

We'll take a look at each category in more detail, but first, match the category of liability exposure listed in the left-hand column that exists for each situation described in the right-hand column.

1. Personal   _____ A. Dr. Proctor and her husband go for a leisurely drive every Sunday afternoon.

2. Professional _____ B. While removing an opera star's tonsils, surgeon Balinski accidentally nicks the star's vocal cords.

3. Business   _____ C. Arlene has just finished digging a hole in her side yard in which she'll have a tree planted tomorrow.

   _____ D. Kim has leased a vacant lot from a friend in order to raise a garden.

   _____ E. Porteus is constructing a four-story medical center building that will be occupied by a group of doctors.

   _____ F. A crane operated by Porteus fell over and blocked the entrance to a neighboring department store.

   _____ G. Captain Blythe, a retired sailor, owns a marina where he sells and services boats.

Answer: 1 A; 2 B; 1 C; 1 D; 3 E; 3 F; 3 G

Personal Liability Exposure

5. Although **personal liability** is not covered as part of commercial general liability coverage, you should be knowledgeable about this topic so you can see its relationship to liability exposures in general.

An individual faces many of the same liability exposures as a businessperson, although these are hazards for which the individual is *personally* responsible, aside from any business liability. Personal liability can arise from an individual's:

■ ownership, maintenance, or use of a home;

■ ownership, maintenance, or use of an automobile;

■ personal activities, such as participation in sports or interacting with other people; or

■ indirect, or vicarious, responsibility for the actions of others, such as children or pets.

For each of the following situations, identify the type of personal liability as one of those stated in the preceding list.

A. While playing baseball in his backyard, young Timmy hit a home run into a neighbor's window. _____

B. Shereen accidentally dropped her bowling ball on the foot of the top bowler on her team, breaking two of his toes. _____

C. While visiting the Ferellis, a guest tripped over a magazine rack and broke his ankle. _____

D. Leonard swerved his car to avoid a chuckhole and knocked over a street sign. _____

Answer: A. Vicarious responsibility; B. Personal activities; C. Home; D. Auto

Professional Liability Exposure

6. Like personal liability, the **professional liability** exposure is not covered as part of commercial general liability coverage, but a basic understanding of its context is important to your study of liability coverages.

The professional liability exposure is the possibility of claims arising from the pursuit of a profession. This exposure is common to persons such as dentists, doctors and other medical practitioners, insurance professionals, accountants, attorneys, architects, and engineers. These claims typically arise from one of two aspects of conducting a profession:

- **rendering services** of a professional nature; or

- **failing to render** services.

The critical elements in the professional liability exposure are:

- Did the action (or failure to take action) occur while the individual was acting in a professional capacity?

- Were the acts involved of a professional nature (a surgeon performing surgery, for example, rather than merely driving down the street like any other citizen)?

Which of the following situations could involve the professional liability exposure?

A. An insurance producer forgets to add a requested endorsement to a client's policy.

B. An art store employee inadvertently sprays black paint on a customer's priceless portrait.

C. Dr. Cass drops his boat anchor on a fisherman's foot.

D. A Mercury Messenger Service employee drops an expensive vase entrusted to her for delivery.

E. A&E Engineering Analysis Corporation mistakenly furnishes erroneous results of tests on aircraft engine components.

F. Dentist Sheila Drake's patient slips and falls on Drake's highly buffed waiting room floor.

G. Accountant Donaldson knocks over a fireplug while driving to work.

H. Architect Elaine Morgan fails to follow her client's instructions.

I. While installing a gas fireplace in a customer's home, a C&C Contracting Company employee sets fire to the house.

J. A nurse accidentally injects a patient with the wrong medication.

Answer: A, E, H, and J are correct.

Business Liability Exposure

7. Commercial general liability insurance covers the **business liability exposure.**

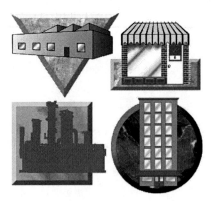

This exposure arises from the conduct of business, including:

■ the ownership, maintenance, or use of business premises, such as stores, warehouses, plants, and offices;

■ necessary or incidental operations performed away from the premises, such as taking the day's receipts to the bank;

■ the ownership, maintenance, or use of automobiles in the course of business operations (must be covered under a Commercial Auto policy rather than as a commercial general liability coverage);

■ indirect, or vicarious, responsibilities resulting from the actions of employees, agents or subcontractors;

■ assuming another's liability exposure through a contractual liability agreement;

■ defects in manufactured products; or

■ defects from completed operations, such as a problem that arises after all of the work is completed in a structure built by a contractor.

Label each situation below according to the type of business liability exposure that exists.

A. To obtain a construction contract, the owner of a construction company signs an agreement to be responsible for any damages that may be caused by the electrical subcontractor he hired. _____

_____

B. An employee of the insured's gift-wrapping service accidentally jabs a pair of scissors into a customer's hand. _____

C. A company vice president has an auto accident while driving a company car on company business. _____

_____

D. A customer in a department store is injured when the glass display case he is leaning on suddenly cracks and breaks. _____

_____

E. A hundred dozen cream-filled pastries were prepared using spoiled ingredients. When consumed by attendees at a large convention, the pastries make everyone ill. _____

Answer: A. Contractual liability; B. Vicarious liability; C. Automobile liability (not covered by commercial general liability insurance); D. Business premises; E. Manufactured products

PURPOSE OF LIABILITY INSURANCE

8. You have seen the various types of liability exposures to which people and organizations are exposed, and which can cause financial loss to those involved. Here is where liability insurance enters the picture.

   The purpose of liability insurance is to protect an insured from financial loss arising out of liability claims by transferring the burden of financial loss from an insured to an insurance company.

   What is the basic purpose of liability insurance?
   A. Transfer the legal liability for damages from the insured to the insurance company
   B. Protect the insured from financial loss by shifting the burden of financial loss from the individual to the insurance company
   C. Assume the responsibility for the insured's negligence
   D. Protect the insured from legal liability by transferring the burden of financial loss from the insured to the company

   Answer: B is correct.

LIABILITY COVERAGES OUTSIDE THE GENERAL LIABILITY AREA

9. While the broad category of commercial general liability insurance includes many types of liability coverage, there are other forms of liability insurance that are *not* considered part of this general category.

Workers' Compensation and Employers Liability policies are not a part of general liability insurance. **Workers' compensation** insurance involves specific benefits payable to an employee by an employer, *without regard to liability*, in case of injury, disability, or death. The payments are required by state laws.

Employers liability insurance provides coverage against the common law liability of an employer for injuries to employees. Thus, these coverages are related specifically to **employer-employee liability** and are not *general* liability.

The category of commercial general liability insurance also does *not* include the liability portions of:

■ auto policies; and

■ aviation policies.

In other words, when you think of general liability insurance, you should not consider the liability portions of auto or aviation policies as being a part of this category. These coverages may be purchased through *separate* policies designed for these specific categories of risk.

List four liability coverages that do not fall under the category of commercial general liability insurance.

1. _____

2. _____

3. _____

4. _____

Answer: (In any order) 1. Workers' Compensation; 2. Employers Liability; 3. The liability portion of an auto policy; 4. The liability portion of an aviation policy

In these first two units, we have looked specifically at the legal boundaries of liability and broadly at the entire area of general liability. Even though the bulk of this course deals with and analyzes commercial general liability coverage, it was important first to see how general liability fits into the broad picture of commercial insurance coverage. Later units narrow the focus of this course to the coverage provided by the Commercial General Liability Coverage Part. The foundation we have laid here will help you better understand this policy, which is available to cover many business exposures of commercial insureds.

3

The Commercial Package Policy and Commercial General Liability

THE COMMERCIAL PACKAGE POLICY

1. The commercial general liability coverage part is just one of several policies that may be included in the **commercial package policy**, or **CPP**. In this unit, we will examine how the CPP is organized and, specifically, how commercial general liability coverage fits into that package.

    Now let's look at the CPP, which was developed as part of ISO's Commercial Lines Simplification Project to:

    ■ reduce the number of repetitive forms;

    ■ standardize format and assembly;

    ■ use the same forms in both monoline and package policies; and

    ■ streamline the entire commercial lines operation.

    Which of these are reasons ISO developed the CPP?

    A. Ease of policy packaging
    B. Avoiding duplication
    C. Standardization of forms
    D. Elimination of coverages

    Answer: A, B, and C are correct.

Coverage Parts

2. A coverage part is the standard element of any commercial lines policy. A coverage part includes all the forms and endorsements of a specific line of insurance needed to provide the desired coverage.

 EXAMPLE   For the commercial general liability line of insurance, the coverage part includes any mandatory and optional forms and endorsements that provide exactly the coverages agreed upon between the insured and the insurance company. In a CPP, there might be coverage parts for commercial general liability, commercial property, and other commercial lines of insurance.

The term that refers to the combination of forms and endorsements for a specific line of insurance is called a_____.

Answer: coverage part

Monoline Versus Multiline Policies

3. While a commercial lines policy may be either a **monoline** or **multiline** policy, the CPP refers solely to the multiline **commercial package policy.**

    A policy containing a *single* coverage part, or one line of insurance, is a monoline policy. A commercial policy containing **two or more** coverage parts or **two or more lines of insurance** is a commercial package policy.

    Label each illustration as either a monoline policy or a CPP.

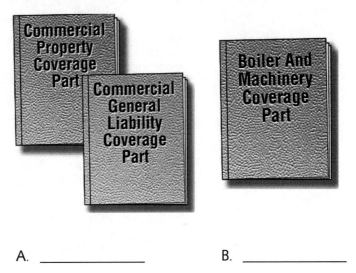

A. _____   B. _____

Answer: A. CPP; B. Monoline

Required and Common Parts in the CPP

4. Typically, there are several items common to all CPPs.

    ■ **Common policy conditions** include the terms on which the contract is issued.

    ■ **Common policy declarations** contain information about *who* is insured, *when* he is insured, and *how* he is insured.

    ■ **Line of insurance declaration pages** normally contain one or more pages that tell the line or lines of insurance coverage purchased in addition to the information on the common policy declarations.

    ■ **Line of insurance coverage forms** contain one or more forms that describe the coverage applicable to the line or lines of insurance purchased.

    ■ **Line of insurance general conditions forms** normally contain one or more forms that tell about the specific terms of the line or lines of insurance purchased.

- **Endorsements** modify the policy in some way. They may provide additional coverage or restrict or change the terms of the policy. **Interline** endorsements may be used for two or more lines of insurance. **Line of insurance** endorsements modify one or more coverage forms within a single line of insurance. Some endorsements might be mandatory, while others are optional.

The same forms may be used to write either a monoline policy or a CPP.

A. Name the item that contains information regarding who is insured, when he is insured, and how he is insured. _____

B. What is included in a policy's conditions form? _____ _____

C. What item modifies the policy in some way, either by providing additional coverage or restricting or changing the terms of the policy? _____

Answer: A. Common policy declarations; B. The terms upon which the policy is issued; C. Endorsement

5. With the package policy approach, many items common to all or most of the coverage parts need to be included only once. For example, the common policy declarations and common policy conditions are included only once even though the CPP may include many different lines of insurance.
    Suppose an insured's CPP includes a:

- commercial general liability Coverage part;

- commercial property coverage part; and

- crime and fidelity coverage part.

A. How many different lines of insurance are represented? _____

B. How many common policy declarations must be included in the CPP? _____

C. How many common policy conditions must be included? _____

Answer: A. Three; B. One; C. One

COMMON POLICY DECLARATIONS

6. Samples of the forms and endorsements used to write commercial general liability insurance are included with this course. If you are using the print version of this course, the forms and endorsements are at the end of this book. If you are using the online version of this course, there is a separate

link for these documents in the course's Table of Contents section. You will be referring to these sample forms during the analysis of policy coverage.

The **Forms and Endorsements** include a sample **common policy declarations**. This sample form is representative of declarations pages commonly in use.

The declarations form contains information about:

■ who is insured;

■ when he is insured; and

■ how he is insured.

Refer to the sample declarations form as we discuss each item. The declarations describe who is insured by showing the:

■ name and mailing address of the insured; and

■ description of the insured's business.

A. In the sample declarations, who is the named insured? _____
_____

B. What is the mailing address of the insured? _____
_____

C. What is the description of the insured's business? _____
_____

Answer: A. Jay's Jewelry Manufacturing Company; B. 1110 Wishingwell Road, Indianapolis, Indiana 46222; C. Manufacturing of gold and diamond jewelry

7. **The period of time when** the insured is covered is described in the declarations as the **policy period**. This is very precisely defined in terms of the effective date and time.

A. According to the sample Declarations, what is the exact policy period for Jay's Jewelry Manufacturing Company?
From:_____
To:_____

B. Standard time in this case refers to the time at what location? _____
_____
_____

C. If the named insured on the sample declarations suffers a loss in California at 11:30 pm Standard time, February 1, 2003, would there be coverage since Indianapolis is on EST.?   ( ) Yes   ( ) No

Why?_____
_____
_____
_____

Answer: A. From 12:01 am Standard time February 2, 2002, to 12:01 am Standard time, February 2, 2003; B. At the insured's mailing address shown in the declarations; C. No. The policy would expire at 12:01 am EST February 2, 2003, 2 hours and 29 minutes before the loss since the policy period begins and ends at 12:01 am Standard time at the mailing address shown.

8. **How** the insured is covered is described in the declarations by listing the coverage parts purchased and their premiums. A coverage part has been purchased when a dollar amount appears as the premium. According to the sample declarations page, what coverages has Jay's Jewelry Manufacturing Company purchased? _____

_____

Answer: (In any order) crime and fidelity, commercial general liability, commercial property

9. Any forms required to be used with *all* coverage parts in the CPP are listed as "Forms Applicable to all Coverage Parts." Find this section of the sample declarations, and list the forms that apply to all coverage parts in this commercial package policy. _____

_____

Answer: (In either order) Common Policy Conditions-IL 00 17 11 98; Common Policy Declarations-IL DS 00 07 02

COMMON POLICY CONDITIONS

Cancellation

10. Locate the **common policy conditions** in your Forms and Endorsements. The first condition deals with **cancellation**. Read **Part A, Cancellation**.

These conditions specify the procedures that must be followed by the first named insured or the company when canceling a policy. The first named insured, upon requesting cancellation, must mail or deliver some advance written notice of cancellation to the insurance company. Note that no specific time notification requirements apply when the *insured* cancels.

The insurer, on the other hand, must give a specified number of days' notice to an insured when canceling an insured's policy:

■ 10 days' notice for cancellation due to nonpayment of premium

■ 30 days' notice for any other reason

Suppose the owner of Glenn's Manufacturing has not paid the premium on her insurance policy for two months, and Eveready Insurance Company is going to cancel the policy. According to the cancellation condition, how many days' notice must Eveready give the insured? _____

Answer: 10

11. When a policy is canceled before the expiration date, the insurer has not yet earned the entire prepaid premium. A portion of the *unearned* premium is then returned to the insured as indicated in the cancellation condition.

If the *insurer* cancels the policy, the premium earned is computed on a **pro rata** basis, which means that the company is due only the exact proportion of the annual premium earned as of the cancellation date. Any remaining prepaid premium is refunded to the insured.

However, if the *insured* cancels, the insurer normally is permitted to keep a portion of premium in excess of earned premium—that is, part of the unearned premium goes to the insured and part goes to the insurer. This is often referred to as a **short rate** return.

The insurance company cancels Jay's Jewelry Manufacturing Company's policy after 197 days of coverage. Will Jay's Jewelry forfeit the entire prepaid premium to the insurance company?   ( ) Yes   ( ) No
Why? _____

_____

Answer: No, because the premium will be prorated and Jay's Jewelry will be refunded the unearned premium.

Changes

12. Read **Part B, Changes** in the common policy conditions before continuing.

    This condition emphasizes that only the first named insured—no other insured—may make changes in the policy, and then only with the insurer's consent as indicated by an endorsement the insurer issues. These requirements ensure that the insurance company and the first named insured are the only ones who may officially make a policy change.

    According to the changes condition, the terms of a policy may be changed

    A. by agreement of the producer that the change should be made.

    B. by policy endorsement authorized by the first named insured and the insurer.

    C. through a written request to the company specifying the changes to be made.

    Answer: B is correct.

Examination of Your Books and Records

13. Read **Part C, Examination of Your Books and Records,** and then study the following illustration to see how this condition applies.

Insurer's Right to Examine
Insured's Records

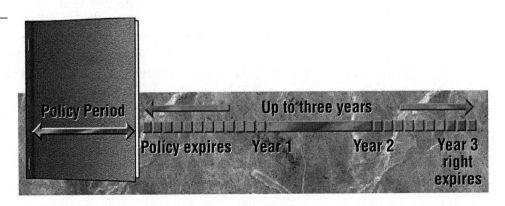

Doright Insurance Company asks to review Jay's Jewelry Manufacturing Company books and records three and one-half years after the policy period. This (is/is not) _____ allowed under the terms of the policy because_____
_____.

Answer: is not because the insurer may review books and records only up to three years after the policy expires

Inspections and Surveys

14. Read **Part D, Inspections and Surveys.**

This condition stresses that inspections and surveys relate only to insurability and premiums and may be made at any time. Safety inspections are not a part of this condition.

According to what you have just read, which of the following are correct?

A. The insurer is required under this provision to conduct inspections and surveys.

B. When an inspection or survey of the insured's operations is made, the insurer warrants that the operations are safe.

C. The insurer has the right to inspect the named insured's property and operations at any time.

D. If mandated by state or municipal laws, the insurer may be obligated to inspect boilers, pressure vessels, or elevators.

Answer: C and D are correct.

Premiums

15. Read the next condition, **Part E, Premiums.**

A. Suppose father and daughter Mike and Michelle Murphy buy a joint insurance policy for their business, Murphy & Murphy, Inc. Mike is the first named insured, and Michelle is the second named insured. Who is responsible for paying premiums?_____
Why?_____
_____

B. This same person (will/will not) _____ receive any unearned premiums returned.

Answer: A. Mike Murphy, because the condition specifies the first named insured is responsible for paying premiums; B. will

Transfer of Your Rights and Duties Under This Policy

16. Read the final condition, **Part F, Transfer of Your Rights and Duties Under This Policy.**

    No assignment of interest is binding *without the insurer's written consent* except in the event of death when all rights and duties are transferred to the named insured's legal representative. However, until a representative is appointed, anyone who properly has temporary custody of the property also has the named insured's rights and duties with respect to that property.

    Which of these situations will the insurer recognize as binding?

    A. The insured notifies the insurer in writing that he is transferring his rights and duties to his daughter, who is taking control of the business.

    B. An insured requests that her rights and duties be transferred to her brother, who will take charge of her business while she is out of the country for two years. The company notifies her in writing that this is acceptable.

    C. When the insured dies, his estate executor assumes his rights and duties under the policy.

    D. The insured's business succumbs to a hostile takeover by International Conglomerates, Inc., which then assumes the insured's rights and duties under the policy.

    Answer: B and C are correct.

17. A legal representative does not necessarily have to be an attorney, but could be the operating manager of a business, or a trustee or executor of the deceased's estate. The point is that the insurance applies to the legal representative as long as he is operating within the normal scope of a legal representative's duties, *but not otherwise*.

EXAMPLE

Susan Silvester, who operates a dry cleaning plant, happens to be the legal representative of an ice cream shop that she also manages due to the death of the named insured. If Susan is sued for something resulting from the operation of the dry cleaning plant, the liability insurance on the ice cream shop will not apply because she was not acting within the scope of her duties as the legal representative of that business.

John Casper is the legal representative of the Unique Boutique and also operates his own barber shop next door. John supervises the stacking of glass bottles to be sold in the boutique. Later, a customer is injured

when the stack collapses. Does the boutique's liability insurance apply?
( ) Yes   ( ) No   Why? _____

_____

_____

Answer: Yes, because John was acting within the scope of his duties.

PRICING THE COMMERCIAL PACKAGE POLICY

18. The following illustrates the initial steps in pricing a typical commercial package policy. This example assumes the CPP includes the coverage parts shown. Naturally, individual CPPs will vary as to the actual coverage parts included.

Step 1

Compute the **premium for each coverage part** based on the rules and rates for the particular line.

Step 2

Determine the **policywriting minimum premium** shown in the rules for each particular line.

	Computed Premium	Policywriting Minimum Premium
Commercial Property Coverage Part	$ 6,000	$100
Commercial General Liability Coverage Part	$10,500	$100
Boiler & Machinery Coverage Part	$ 2,000	$250
	$18,500	$450

Step 3

Separately total the **computed premiums** and the **minimum premiums**.

The sum of the policywriting minimum premiums for each coverage part included is the minimum premium permitted for the particular **CPP**. The *larger* of the computed premium or the minimum premium is the premium actually charged.

A. For the CPP in our illustration, what is the minimum premium?
$_____

B. What premium will be charged for this CPP? $_____

Answer: A. $450; B. $18,500

19. In the previous example, the amounts of the computed premium and the policywriting minimum premium are considerably different. However, for a very small business, the minimum for the CPP could become significant in some situations, as indicated here:

	6-Month Computed Premium	Policywriting Minimum Premium
Property	$ 98	$100
Liability	100	100
Boiler & Machinery	100	250
Totals	$298	$450

The minimum premium for *this* CPP is the (computed/policywriting minimum) _____ premium, which is $_____
_____.

Answer: policywriting minimum, $450

Package Modification Factor

20. The premium for a commercial package policy may be reduced if it is eligible for a **package modification factor**, or **PMF**. The PMF that is used depends on the type of coverage and what kind of risk is insured, such as an apartment, mercantile, or contractor risk.

EXAMPLE

Suppose the insured from our earlier example with the $18,500 premium is a mercantile risk. Here is a typical example of what happens when a PMF is applied:

Computed Premium		x	PMF	=	Adjusted Premium
Property:	$ 6,000	x	.95	=	$ 5,700
Commercial Liability:	10,500	x	.95	=	9,975
Boiler & Machinery:	2,000	x	.90	=	1,800
					$17,475

In this example, the insured will save over a thousand dollars as the result of having a commercial package policy that qualifies for a _____ _____.

Answer: package modification factor, or PMF

21. To qualify for the PMF, a CPP *must* include:

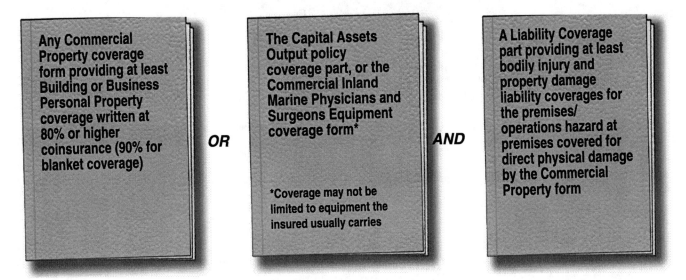

Any Commercial Property coverage form providing at least Building or Business Personal Property coverage written at 80% or higher coinsurance (90% for blanket coverage)

OR

The Capital Assets Output policy coverage part, or the Commercial Inland Marine Physicians and Surgeons Equipment coverage form*

*Coverage may not be limited to equipment the insured usually carries

AND

A Liability Coverage part providing at least bodily injury and property damage liability coverages for the premises/operations hazard at premises covered for direct physical damage by the Commercial Property form

Check any of the following illustrations that qualify for a package modification factor.

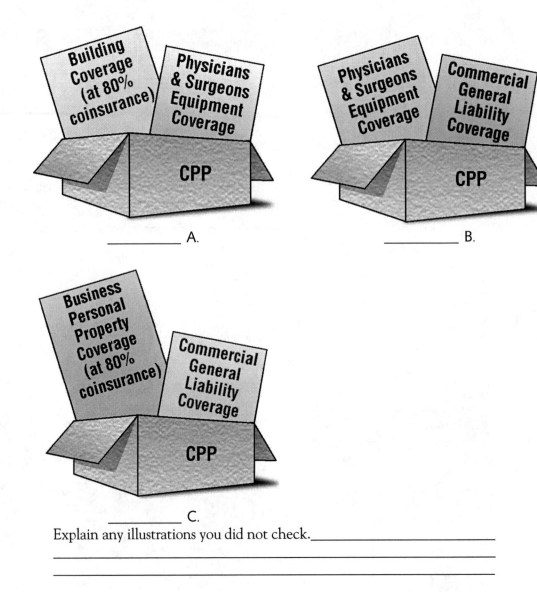

_____ A.

_____ B.

_____ C.

Explain any illustrations you did not check._____

_____

_____

Answer: B and C qualify. Choice A does not qualify because the required liability coverage part is missing.

INCORPORATING COMMERCIAL GENERAL LIABILITY IN THE CPP

22. You have learned that commercial general liability (CGL) may be one of the coverage parts in a CPP. The CGL coverage part includes the common policy declarations and the common policy conditions. Other items that make up the CGL coverage part are the:

- commercial general liability declarations;

- commercial general liability coverage form; and

- mandatory and optional endorsements.

Let's first consider the special CGL declarations, which is included in your Forms and Endorsements. The CGL declarations form is similar to the common policy declarations because it spells out the *who, when,* and *how* information of the policy. The first part of this form asks for the named insured, the mailing address, and the policy period. It is similar to the first part of the common policy declarations, so we won't discuss this section again. If you need to review these items, return to the **common policy declarations** section in this unit.

The limits of insurance section in the CGL declarations lists the amount of insurance coverage desired. A more detailed explanation of these items and limits appears later in the course.

Under the limits of insurance section, you'll see the retroactive date section of the declarations, which is applicable only to a **claims-made** insurance policy. Claims-made policies and an explanation of retroactive dates are discussed in more detail in a later unit. For now, you just need to know that either a specific date or the word "None" must be listed in this space on the declarations.

A. Under the limits of insurance section of the CGL declarations, dollar amounts will appear for

  1. every type of coverage shown.

  2. only the coverages the insured wants to purchase.

B. A retroactive date will appear in this section of the declarations for

  1. claims-made policies only.

  2. all CGL policies.

Answer: A. 2 is correct; B. 1 is correct.

23. In the description of business section, the declarations require information about the type of business and a business description. Note this section on the sample CGL declarations.

The next page of the declarations asks for the location of the business. Then the form requests additional information needed to determine the premium. This information appears in ISO's commercial lines manual and is combined with other insurer data to arrive at the proper premiums.

For this course, you don't need to know how to determine the premium, but you should know where to locate the required information. What manual is available for locating information needed to calculate a CGL policy premium?_____

Answer: ISO's Commercial Lines Manual

Occurrence and Claims-Made Coverage Forms

24. The heart of CGL coverage is one of two **commercial general liability coverage forms**. These are called the **occurrence** and **claims-made** forms. Not all states have approved the use of the claims-made form.

Ask your supervisor or trainer whether the claims-made CGL form is approved in the states your company serves.

We will discuss the precise provisions of each of these forms in later units. At this point, we just want to introduce you to the fact that two different versions of the CGL coverage form exist.

The primary difference between the two versions is what activates or *triggers* coverage. The **occurrence** form coverage is triggered by injury or damage that occurs **during the policy period**. The **claims-made** coverage is triggered when a **claim is first made against the insured during the policy period**, even if the actual injury or damage occurred at another time. There are some restrictions to this general rule, which you'll learn when we discuss the claims-made form in detail.

A. The CGL coverage form triggered by injury occurring during the policy period is called the (occurrence/claims-made) _____ _____ form.

B. The form under which coverage is triggered when a claim is first made during the policy period is the (occurrence/claims-made) _____ _____ form.

Answer: A. occurrence; B. claims-made

25. You may wonder why there are two types of CGL coverage forms available. While the occurrence form has the longer history, over the years a need has arisen for the claims-made form.

In many liability situations, the occurrence form fits the needs of both the insured and the insurer. Under this form, when injury or damage occurs, a claim is filed against the insured and the insurer pays the claim. All of this may occur within a short span of time. But consider the following situation.

Suppose an individual worked eight hours a day, six days a week with a lead-based spray paint from 1961–1971. In 2002, that person is diagnosed as having developed lead poisoning from exposure to the lead-based paint. This worker may be able to recover damages from the paint manufacturer under every occurrence policy the manufacturer has owned between 1961 and 1971. How much each policy pays may be subject to several interpretations. However, the bottom line is that the loss reserves insurers have set aside to pay future claims and the premium charged for the coverage may be inadequate to handle claims of this type. Many insurers find the uncertainties in writing coverage of this type are too financially risky.

To alleviate the situation, the claims-made trigger was developed. Under this type of policy, coverage applies only if a claim is made during the time the policy is in effect. The insurer does not have the burden of adequately calculating reserves for unreported claims as in an occurrence policy, and will be better able to establish rates and reserves.

Claims-made policies are attractive to many insurers because

A. they do not have to establish reserves to handle unreported claims

B. higher premiums are required for claims-made policies

C. the insurer is better able to establish rates and reserves

D. both A and C

Answer: D is correct.

26. You've learned that the CGL coverage part will include the CGL declarations and either the occurrence or claims-made coverage forms. The Nuclear Energy Liability Exclusion Endorsement (Broad Form) endorsementalso must be included.

Note that additional endorsements may be desired or required. The endorsement just mentioned is discussed in more detail in a later unit.

Some states require various mandatory endorsements. Check with your supervisor or trainer concerning the states where your company operates.

Optional endorsements may be used to change coverage in various ways, such as adding, eliminating, or modifying coverage. Several commonly used endorsements will be discussed later.

Which of the following are *always* included in the commercial general liability coverage part?

A. Optional endorsements

B. Nuclear Energy Liability Exclusion Endorsement (Broad Form)

C. Commercial general liability declarations

D. Common policy conditions

Answer: B and C are correct.

This concludes our discussion of the CPP and the CGL coverage part. In the next unit, you'll begin analyzing the CGL coverage forms.

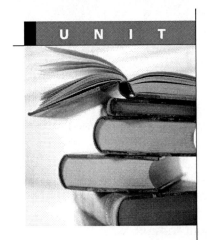

U N I T

4

Policy Definitions

INTRODUCTION

1. The commercial general liability coverage forms include a definitions section where the precise meanings of certain words and phrases used in the forms are defined. Defined terms are easily identifiable because they are enclosed in quotation marks.

   These terms are listed in alphabetical order at the end of each CGL form—Section V of the occurrence form and Section VI of the claims-made form. You will study these definitions now, before analyzing the forms, but you may refer to them as needed throughout the course.

   Both the occurrence and claims-made forms contain the same definitions, and they have the same meanings in both forms. You will refer to the definitions in the occurrence form in this unit.

   A. How will you know whether a word or phrase is specifically defined in the CGL forms? _____

   _____

   B. The occurrence and claims-made CGL forms include (the same/different) _____ definitions.

   Answer: A. The word or phrase is enclosed in quotation marks; B. the same

POLICY DEFINITIONS

Auto

2. Locate Section V—Definitions in the CGL occurrence form. Because some of the definitions are interrelated, this unit explains them in a different order than they appear in the form. Read the second definition, **auto**.

   The important point of this definition is that an auto may be one of many different types of land vehicles that are:

   ■ intended for travel on public roads; or

   ■ subject to compulsory or financial responsibility laws or other motor vehicle laws.

   It does not, however, include mobile equipment, which has its own definition and will be discussed shortly.

   Which of the following are autos according to the policy definition?

   A. A company's limousine

   B. An all-terrain vehicle

   C. A transit-mix concrete mixer

D. A swamp buggy

E. A motorboat that uses an automobile engine for power

F. A motorcycle

G. An inter-city bus

Answer: A, C, F, and G are correct. B and D are not correct because their major purpose is not travel on public roads. E is not a land vehicle.

Mobile Equipment

3. Now let's skip over to definition 12, **mobile equipment**. We'll look at the definition of mobile equipment in three steps. For now, read only through Item 12.d.(2).

   An important point to remember is that mobile equipment is different from an auto as defined, and both definitions have specific limitations. Careful reading of both definitions is needed to understand the coverage.

   Refer to the section you just read to decide which of the following pieces of equipment owned and operated by General Construction Company are mobile equipment as defined in the policy.

   A. A truck used to transport personnel to construction sites

   B. A power crane used to lift lumber and other materials from railroad cars on the railroad's property onto trucks for storage

   C. A road construction grader

   D. A helicopter used for surveying and lifting light loads

   E. A bulldozer

   F. A lawn tractor

   G. A barge-mounted crane

   Answer: B, C, E, and F are correct. A is not correct because this type of truck is subject to motor vehicle registration, so it is considered an auto under the policy. D and G are not correct because neither is a land vehicle.

4. Now study all of Item e.

   Jay Sahara contracts with Romley Orchard to pick the fruit on an acre of apple trees. Jay uses a trailer, to which cherry pickers are permanently attached and then hitched to his truck, to transport workers to the orchard to do the work. Does the equipment described illustrate the definition of mobile equipment?   ( ) Yes   ( ) No   Explain your answer.

   _____

   _____

   _____

Answer: Yes. A trailer (a vehicle that is not self-propelled) is used with a truck to transport the permanently attached cherry pickers.

5. Read the final part of the mobile equipment definition, Item f.

The first paragraph of this item indicates that other vehicles might be considered mobile equipment if their purpose is primarily something other than transporting people or cargo. Then, the item goes on to describe at length certain self-propelled vehicles that are considered to be autos rather than mobile equipment, even if certain equipment is permanently attached.

The final paragraph reiterates that land vehicles that are subject to compulsory or financial responsibility laws or other motor vehicle laws are considered autos, not mobile equipment.

Which one of the following fits the definition of mobile equipment?

A. A truck with a permanently attached street sweeper

B. An army tank

C. A truck with a hydraulic lift

D. A four-wheel drive vehicle with a permanently attached snow shovel

Answer: B is correct. All of the other choices are autos.

Bodily Injury

6. The third definition is **bodily injury.** Read this definition now.

Bodily injury to an individual is not limited to traumatic injury, but also includes sickness, disease, and death.

Which of the following is considered bodily injury as defined in the policy?

A. A tank car containing chlorine gas developed a leak and lost some of its deadly contents while parked overnight near a small town. Seventy cattle died as a result of inhaling the fumes.

B. During construction of a new skyscraper, a brick falls from the 125th floor and strikes a pedestrian in the head. He later dies from his injury.

Answer: B is correct. A is not correct because the injury was sustained by animals, not people.

Temporary Worker

7. Now go to definition 19, **temporary worker.** We will discuss this definition and definition 10, **leased worker,** now because they are important to your understanding of another definition.

Read definition 19, **temporary worker.**

Who of the following are temporary workers as defined in the policy?

A. Joanie is a temporary worker for Quick-Temp Services. She is assigned to Temple Industries to fill in for a secretary who is on a two-month maternity leave. After the secretary returns from her leave, Joanie's assignment is terminated.

B. Roxanne is employed by Betty's Temporaries. Betty's sends her to Fred's Fine Clothing to help run the cash register during the busy Christmas season. Her assignment ends shortly after the new year.

C. Vernon is the permanent, full-time office manager at the law firm of Brice, Smith, and Jones.

Answer: A and B are correct.

Leased Worker

8. Read definition 10, **leased worker.**

Who of the following are leased workers as defined in the policy?

A. Chang is hired as a stock clerk at a local department store.

B. Janelle is working as an electrical engineer on a special project for Mitchell Industries. Janelle is actually an employee of Hutchings Personnel, who contracted with Mitchell Industries to provide leased workers to Mitchell Industries for the project.

C. Betty answers a newspaper advertisement for seasonal help at a nearby vegetable canning factory. She is hired as a canner on a temporary basis.

Answer: B is correct.

Employee

9. Now that you understand how the CGL defines temporary and leased workers, read definition 5, **employee.**

The definition of employee includes

A. leased worker.

B. temporary workers

C. both leased and temporary workers

Answer: A is correct.

Volunteer Worker

10. One more type of worker is defined in the CGL. Read definition 20, **volunteer worker**.

Which of the following describe a volunteer worker?

A. Receives compensation for work performed

B. Donates his work

C. Acts at the direction of the insured

D. Is considered an employee

Answer: B and C are correct.

Executive Officer

11. Read definition 6, **executive officer.**

To be considered an executive officer as defined in the CGL, a person must

A. be named as an executive officer in the declarations.

B. hold an officer position created by the insured's charter, constitution, or other governing document.

Answer: B is correct.

Hostile Fire

12. Now read definition 7, **hostile fire.**

A hostile fire is one that has escaped from the place it was intended to be or is uncontrolled. In contrast, a friendly fire is one that was intentionally kindled and remains confined in the intended place.

Which of the following are hostile fires according to the definition?

A. A fire contained in the insured's boiler

B. A fire that breaks out of the insured's fireplace and ignites the carpeting

C. A fire that starts in the insured's incinerator but catches some nearby newspapers on fire

D. A fire that starts in the insured's gas stove and spreads throughout the kitchen

Answer: B, C, and D are correct.

Impaired Property

13. Read the definition of **impaired property**.

   This definition deals with **tangible property** other than the named insured's products or work. It is property that is less useful because of possible defects in incorporated work or products or in failure to fulfill a contract.

   GBS Gas Gauge Company, the insured, is a supplier of gas gauges to small aircraft. Because a faulty gas gauge registers a full tank of fuel when, in fact, there is nearly none, a plane carrying a cargo of computers crashes, destroying both the aircraft and its cargo. Also, other small aircraft using these gas gauges cannot operate until all gauges are checked. The gauges are found to be faulty and must be replaced, but there has been no damage to other planes that are using the gas gauges.

   The planes grounded because of the faulty gas gauges (do/do not) _____ illustrate impaired property because _____

   _____

   _____.

   Answer: do, because the defective gas gauges the insured supplied are incorporated in the planes.

Insured Contract

14. The next definition, **insured contract**, is divided into two general parts:

   ■ What an insured contract *is*, and

   ■ What an insured contract *is not*.

   Read the first part of this definition, the six paragraphs numbered 9.a through 9.f.

   Because some types of contractual liability are *not* covered by the CGL policy, this item intends to clearly define which types *are* covered. Notice that the form does not specify that these contracts or agreements must be written, so oral agreements could be covered as well.

   Refer to the definition as needed to complete the following.

   A. An easement agreement involving construction within 25 feet of a railroad (is/is not) _____ an insured contract.

   B. The insured contractor has an agreement to perform work for the city, under which the insured assumes the city's tort liability for third-party injury. Is this an insured contract?   ( ) Yes   ( ) No

   C. Which of the following are examples of an insured contract?

   1. To get permission to hang a sign over the public sidewalk, Ajax Drugstore's owners signed an agreement with the city assuming liability for damages if the sign falls.

2. J.J. Construction has leased the vacant lot next door to a construction site for storing equipment used in its current construction project.

3. Vandu Graff Elevator Service signed a contract agreeing to keep the elevators in Avante Department Store properly maintained.

Answer: A. is not; B. Yes; C. 1, 2, and 3 are all correct.

15. The remainder of Item 9 describes what an insured contract does *not* include. Read only Item f.(1).

Suppose the insured has contracted with B&B Railroad Systems for B&B to perform demolition within 50 feet of railroad property. As a result, property damage occurs to a nearby railroad trestle. The insured has an agreement to indemnify for such damage if it occurs. Is this an insured contract as defined by the CGL?   ( ) Yes   ( ) No   Explain your answer.

_____
_____
_____

Answer: No. The form specifically states that an insured contract does not include any agreement to indemnify a railroad under the circumstances described.

16. Read Items f.(2) and (3) of the definition of insured contract.

These items specifically exclude as an insured contract any agreements arising from the professional liability exposure of architects, engineers, and surveyors. While this type of professional liability can be covered by endorsement to the CGL, it is not included as part of the insured contract provision.

Suppose General Construction, the insured, contracts with Superior Engineering to locate underground pipes at a proposed construction site. After two days at the site, General Construction asks Superior to abandon the job of locating the pipes and locate underground cable instead. Superior then spends two more days locating the cable. Because of the extra number of days required to find the cable, Superior fails to complete another job contracted with Arway Construction at another site. Arway sues Superior Engineering. Under the CGL owned by General Construction, does an insured contract exist under which General would indemnify Superior for any loss? ( ) Yes   ( ) No   Why?_____

_____
_____
_____

Answer: No. This is the type of situation specifically indicated as not representing an insured contract under the CGL.

Loading or Unloading

17. Now read definition 11, **loading or unloading**.

Which of the following situations correctly describe loading or unloading as defined in the policy?

A. A trucker uses his semi-truck to deliver 500 boxes of computer parts to a purchaser. While a forklift operator is unloading the boxes, one falls to the ground and its contents are damaged.

B. Alice Parks takes three cartons of fragile antique dishes to the home of her friend Jacquelyn Cole for Cole to deliver to Andy's Antique Market the next day. While Parks is unloading the cartons of dishes onto a hand cart to put them in Cole's car, a carton pops open and a valuable dish shatters on the driveway.

C. While carrying a cargo of insecticide in his small plane for delivery to farmers in a rural area, Blaine Hawkins asks his copilot to rearrange the cargo by hand because several boxes of the insecticide have fallen and broken open.

Answer: B and C are correct. Choice A is not correct because a mechanical device (a forklift) was used—a situation excluded under this definition.

Occurrence

18. Read definition 13, **occurrence**.

In some types of insurance, an occurrence must be a *sudden* event, but this is not true with CGL insurance. Instead, the meaning includes exposure to essentially the same conditions *over a period of time*, resulting in harm. What is really important here is whether or not the insured could have anticipated the bodily injury or property damage that takes place—that is, whether or not the event is an **accident**.

Which of the following fit the definition of an occurrence?

A. The ice cream case at the Cool-n-Crisp Delicatessen leaks water onto the floor. A customer slips on the wet floor and breaks her ankle.

B. On a bitterly cold night, the insured florist, acting unscrupulously, shuts off the heat supply to a greenhouse owned by a competitor, causing the loss of $6,800 worth of flowers.

C. An out-of-control trash fire at CLM Construction Corporation results in the destruction of an apartment building nearby.

D. A person who lives near a dry cleaning firm becomes ill from repeated exposure to chemical fumes and sues the dry cleaners.

Answer: A, C, and D are correct. B is not correct because the event is not accidental.

Advertisement

19. Now turn to the beginning of the definitions section and read the first definition, **advertisement.** This definition relates closely to the one you'll study next.

    To constitute advertising, a notice has to be broadcast or published. An advertisement can include anything from the insured's logo on a T-shirt to an advertisement on the Internet. In addition, the notice has to go out to the general public or specific market segments. Personal promotions, such as personal correspondence or an individual sales presentation, would not be considered advertisements.

    According to the definition, which of the following are advertisements?

    A. A radio announcement about the insured's product
    B. A magazine advertisement about the insured's product
    C. A private meeting about the insured's product at a prospect's office
    D. A banner advertisement on the Internet about the insured's product
    E. A personal letter to a prospective customer about the insured's product
    F. An email about the insured's product sent to potential customers

    Answer: A, B, D, and F are correct.

Personal and Advertising Injury

20. Let's look at **personal and advertising injury,** definition 14. Read the first paragraph and Items a, b, and c.

    The terms used in Items a, b, and c of this definition are straightforward in meaning, although they may have certain nuances under the law if a claim reaches the lawsuit stage. For the most part, however, you can interpret them literally.

    Let's take a close look at the first paragraph, which describes two kinds of personal and advertising injuries.

One is injury that arises out of the listed offenses, such as false arrest, malicious prosecution, wrongful eviction, and invasion of privacy. For example, some consequences of personal and advertising injury might include illness, discomfort, humiliation, loss of income, or loss of business.

The other type of injury described in the first paragraph is any bodily injury that results as a consequence of the listed offenses. For example, suppose that someone suffers a broken arm while being falsely detained by a store's security guard. The broken arm is a consequential bodily injury.

Which of the following are examples of personal and advertising injury?

A. In a scheme to take control of Larson's business, Crawford has Larson detained against his will in the basement of Crawford's business while a meeting of Larson's stockholders is taking place.

B. Continuing with the previous example, Larson is severely beaten by his captors when he attempts to escape from the basement.

C. Dabny Torson enters the home of Schuyler Antz, who leases the property from Torson. Torson refuses to leave in spite of Antz's objections.

D. After Hillary Thompson failed to pay her rent for three months in a row, her landlord serves her notice and later evicts her.

Answer: A, B, and C are correct.

21. Now return to the definition of personal and advertising injury and read Item d.

This part of the definition uses some *undefined* terms that are explained in the following illustration.

Slander is defamation in spoken form.

Libel is defamation in written form.

Disparagement, either spoken or written, is untrue or misleading statements about goods, products, or services.

Here's an example. Carolyn Utz, a nutritionist, is the guest speaker at a meeting of Toledo business people. Carolyn represents a new diet and nutritional product line called Herbaldiet, which she is extolling to the group during her presentation. Carolyn compares her product with another diet product, Make-U-Slim, telling the group Make-U-Slim is a complete sham and that it contains harmful ingredients. Coincidentally, several people at the meeting have been using Make-U-Slim, have lost weight, and feel great as a result of using the product. Angry about Carolyn's tirade, one person calls the manufacturer of Make-U-Slim and reports Carolyn's remarks.

According to the CGL definition, could Carolyn have caused personal and advertising injury to the manufacturer of Make-U-Slim? ( ) Yes ( ) No Why?_____

_____

Answer: Yes. Carolyn made slanderous and disparaging oral statements about the product.

22. Now read Item e of the definition. This item addresses the violation of a person's right of privacy orally or in writing.

    Suppose the Bank of Maryville is a new and growing institution in that city. In the local newspaper, the bank ran a series of advertisements depicting the city's popular mayor endorsing the bank. When the mayor reads the advertisements, he is shocked to see they contain his likeness and quotes attributed to him without his knowledge or permission.

    In this situation, the mayor may have cause to sue the Bank of Maryville. Why?_____

    _____

    Answer: Without the mayor's permission, the Bank of Maryville's use of the image and quotations quite likely violates the right of privacy.

23. Refer again to Items d and e under the definition of personal and advertising injury. The phrase **"in any manner"** includes all forms of publication, even email and Website material.

    What types of personal and advertising injury you just studied might involve Internet and electronic publications?

    _____

    _____

    Answer: Slander, libel, disparagement, and publication of material that violates a person's right of privacy

24. Items f and g of the definition address the use of advertising ideas and copyright infringement. Read these items now.

An example of **use of another's advertising idea in your advertisement** is the practice of imitating an already successful and well-known product by using a similar packaging shape, size, label, or general appearance with the intent to mislead the public into thinking it is the same or a very similar product.

In some cases, an insured's advertisements may be **infringing upon another's copyright, trade dress, or slogan**. The *undefined* term **trade dress** means the total appearance and image of a product as well as the techniques for advertising and marketing its sale. Practicing the kind of deception described in this item is a type of personal and advertising injury.

Both Items e and f apply specifically to the insured's advertisements, as defined earlier, not to the insured's business activities in general.

The manufacturers of Jeans Plus observe that the designer jeans Zanadeau are selling extremely well. Jeans Plus duplicates the Zanadeau jeans as closely as possible, puts a false Zanadeau label on the back pocket and sells the jeans for $20 less than the genuine Zanadeau jeans.

According to Items e and f of the personal and advertising injury definition, Jeans Plus (is/is not) _____ likely to be found guilty of personal and advertising injury in regard to Zanadeau.

Answer: is

Coverage Territory

25. Carefully read the definition of **coverage territory**.

Of particular interest is paragraph c, which expands the territory to provide worldwide coverage for products, provided they were sold or made in the paragraph a. territory. Worldwide coverage also applies in two other situations: when injuries or damages arise from the activities of people who are away from the territory on a business trip for the insured; and when personal and advertising injury offenses take place on the Internet or in another form of electronic communication.

Regardless of where injuries or damages arise, all original suits under a CGL form must be filed within the territory described in paragraph a.

A. Sally Salsa, who lives and works in Baton Rouge, is a sales representative for a shrimp packer in Louisiana. While on a business trip to Guatemala, she serves samples of the company's canned shrimp to conventioneers. Ray Small, who eats the shrimp, becomes ill. When he returns to his home in Mississippi, Ray files suit against the shrimp packer. Do these circumstances describe events in the coverage territory as defined?   ( ) Yes   ( ) No

B. Does an off-shore drilling operation lying outside the territorial limits of the United States fall under the definition of coverage territory? ( ) Yes   ( ) No   Explain. _____

C. Enrique Manual, the owner of Exotic Imports of Puerto Rico, is in Italy on business for three days. While entertaining business clients in his hotel suite, he trips while carrying a tray of cocktails. The glasses fall onto a table near a client, scattering glass shards everywhere. The client suffers severe cuts on his arms and hands, and decides to sue for damages. The suit for damages must be filed in (Italy/Puerto Rico)

_____.

D. Suppose that Chico Ban, president of Chico Bananas, writes a disparaging email about his competitor, Top Banana, Inc. Instead of sending the remarks to one of his vice presidents, he mistakenly sends the message to his entire customer mailing list, spanning several countries. If Top Banana sues for libel, would the case of the "email gone global" be considered an event within the coverage territory? ( ) Yes   ( ) No

Answer: A. Yes. This fits the situation described in paragraph c; B. Yes. International waters are covered in the definition, subject to certain provisions under paragraph b; C. Puerto Rico, which is in the territory described in paragraph a; D. Yes. For personal and advertising offenses that take place in cyberspace, the coverage territory is worldwide.

Pollutants

26. Read definition 15, **pollutants.**

This definition gives you two new terms to consider: **pollutant** and **waste.** For the purposes of this form, waste is considered to be a pollutant. Other things that are considered pollutants are also spelled out in this paragraph.

While waste is considered to be a pollutant, it also has specific meaning in the CGL form. Which one of the following is waste?

A. Certain materials that will be treated and converted to fuel

B. Gases that escape into the atmosphere during a chemical manufacturing process

Answer: A is correct.

Your Product

27. At this point, we are going to ask you again to temporarily bypass several definitions and go to definition 21, **your product**. We will discuss the meanings of both your product and definition 22, **your work**, now because these are critical to your understanding of another definition.

    Read definition 21, **your product**, before continuing.

    To separate the elements of this definition, study this flow chart.

Does It qualify as "Your Product"?

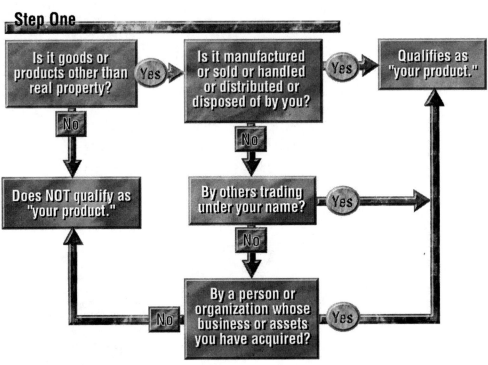

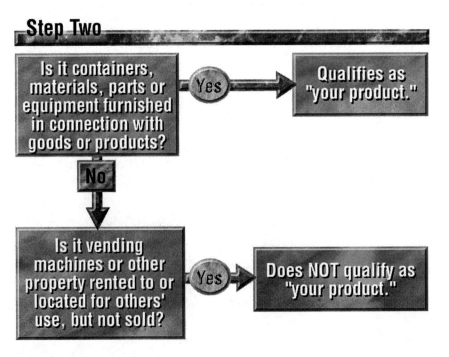

Part of the definition of "your product" describes warranties and representations.

"Your Product" Includes:

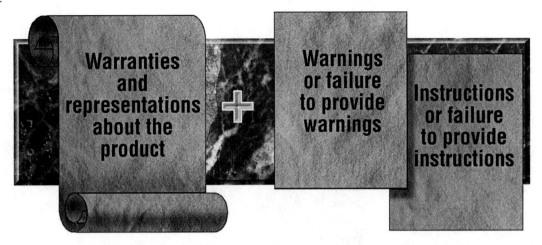

Power Oil Company manufactures petroleum products and also distributes and sells them in PoCo filling stations.

A. In addition to the products themselves, would "your product" include the can in which motor oil was sold?   ( ) Yes   ( ) No

B. Does it include the filling station premises where the products are stored for sale?   ( ) Yes   ( ) No

C. Does it include the gasoline transport trucks used to deliver bulk shipments to the PoCo stations?   ( ) Yes   ( ) No

Answer: A. Yes. Containers are included in the definition of "your product"; B. No. Real estate is not included; C. No. A truck is a vehicle, which is specifically excluded even though it is being used as a container.

28. Although this definition includes warranties and representations, it does not mean that product warranty insurance is provided. To fall within the definition, there must be bodily injury or property damage, other than to the product, resulting from the warranty or representation.

Suppose Luscious Lipsticks advertises a new breakthrough, guaranteeing its lipsticks will not become soft in the tube even in the hottest temperatures. Vanessa Allen is so thrilled with these lipsticks that she purchases a dozen tubes one morning. Vanessa tosses the bag of lipsticks onto the back seat of her car, drives to the beach, and parks in an unshaded lot. After several hours in the 100 degree heat, she returns to her hot car to find the lipsticks have melted and leaked on her white velour upholstery. She files a suit against Luscious Lipsticks, and the company is found liable for the damage.

A. Because Luscious Lipsticks warranted that the lipsticks would not become soft and Vanessa relied on that warranty, does this situation fit the definition of "your product"?   ( ) Yes   ( ) No

B. Does *damage* to the lipsticks themselves fit the definition?
( ) Yes   ( ) No

Answer: A. Yes; B. No

Your Work

29. Now read the definition of **your work**. Study this flow chart, and then answer the questions following.

Does It Qualify as "Your Work"?

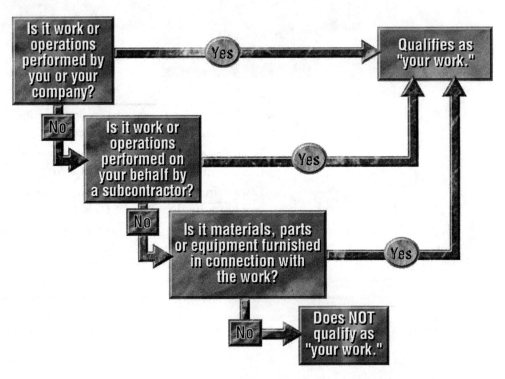

A. Dooley Plumbing has contracted with J&L Builders to do the plumbing work on a new office building. Because of completion deadlines for three other jobs Dooley is working on, Dooley subcontracts part of the J&L job to a local subcontractor. Does the subcontractor's work qualify as "your work"?   ( ) Yes   ( ) No

B. Which of the following items would be included in the definition of "your work"?

1. Steel I-beams used for building construction

2. Rivets used to fasten the beams

3. A hoist to raise materials to upper levels

C. Are such intangibles as the fitness, quality, durability, or performance of the insured's work included as part of this definition?
( ) Yes   ( ) No

Answer: A. Yes. Work on your behalf may include a subcontractor's work; B. 1, 2, and 3 are correct; C. Yes

Products-Completed Operations Hazard

30. Now that you understand "your product" and "your work," turn to the definition of the **products-completed operations hazard**. Read only Items 16.a.(1) and the first sentence of 16.a.(2).

    The following table summarizes this information. Study it, and then answer the question.

The Products-Completed Operations Hazard

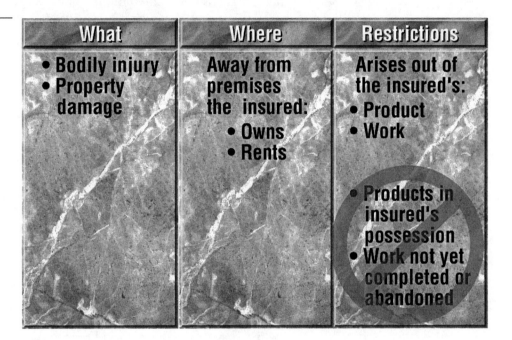

Which of the following are within the products-completed operations hazard?

A. Jeri Packard uses a home hair coloring preparation said to give silky golden tresses. Instead, her hair falls out.

B. While visiting the Rainbow Spray Paint Factory on a field trip with his kindergarten class, George Leland was invited to try out the new Rainbow spray paint product. The container leaked red paint on George's leather jacket.

C. A sales representative from the Gleaming Polish Company arrived at Nita Vermont's house to demonstrate samples of a new auto polish. During the demonstration, the paint came off Nita's new car and she developed a severe rash from its contact with her skin.

Answer: A is correct. B is not correct because the damage did not occur away from the premises. C is not correct because the product was still in the possession of the insured.

31. Now carefully read the remainder of 16.a.(2) and the paragraph at the end of this item.

You've learned that the definition of "your work" includes parts, material, or equipment furnished in connection with the job or work that's being done. Next, you must consider what a completed operation is. The term *operation* simply refers to the work an organization does. An entire project does not necessarily have to be finished in order to have a completed operation. Certain jobs may be comprised of other operations that are completed in sequence, rather than simultaneously. The overriding consideration is: **During what action or event does the loss occur?**

Briefly, the reason we are concerned with the conditions under which the loss occurs is that some risks are covered under one type of insurance and other risks by a different type of coverage. If the loss occurs because of an action or event covered by an insurance company other than the specific insurer in question, that specific insurer is not the one responsible for indemnifying for the loss.

EXAMPLE   Truebuilt Construction loads company equipment on a truck, transports it to a work site, unloads it, uses it to perform a contracted job, loads it back on the truck, and returns it to the storage yard. Truebuilt has performed several operations and has been confronted with several different exposures to loss. Some of these exposures may be insured under different coverage parts of the same policy, or they may be insured by separate policies issued by more than one company. In this example, loading the equipment on the truck is an operation; when finished, it's a completed operation. Both exposures might be covered by a liability policy written by ABC Insurance Company. On the other hand, coverage for *transporting* the equipment might come under an automobile policy written by XYZ Insurers.

The company that will pay in the event of a loss depends on the answer to the question asked earlier: During what action or event does the loss occur? It is possible that the insured does not have insurance to cover some of the risks to which she may be exposed. In this event, the insurance company must know what action led to the loss to determine whether or not there is coverage.

Which of the following statements is correct?

A. To have a completed operation, the entire project must be finished.

B. All exposures involved in any project are always covered by the same liability policy.

C. A vital consideration in determining the insurer's responsibility to pay is the action or event during which the loss occurs.

Answer: C is correct.

32. This definition stipulates that work is completed at the earliest of the three events listed. The first possibility is that all of the work contracted for is finished.

    The second possibility occurs in relation to work at more than one job site. For a completed operation to exist, work must be completed at least *one job site*.

    And third, if part of the work is being used for its intended purpose, then that operation is considered complete.

    Which of the following are examples of completed operations?

    A. Lorax Painting Company has a contract to paint the front of a hardware store. In four hours, the work is completed according to the contract and the hardware store approves it.

    B. Mailer Construction contracts with Big Bird Restaurants to build three new restaurants. Mailer completes half of the job on the first restaurant and starts on another.

    C. A building is still being constructed when a tenant moves into the ground floor suite, which is finished. The tenant suffers an injury when a window falls out of the frame.

    D. A florist is hired to provide a large number of floral arrangements for a corporate reception. While en route to deliver the flowers, the florist's delivery truck is totaled in an accident. The arrangements are never delivered.

    Answer: A and C are correct.

33. The final paragraph of Item 16.a.(2) deals with work that may need service, maintenance, correction, repair, or replacement. If the work is otherwise completed, it is still considered a completed operation.

    For example, Assume Truebuilt Construction had contracted to construct and maintain a dam for a city reservoir. After the dam is complete and the reservoir filled with water, officials from the city notice small cracks in the dam. They call Truebuilt to make repairs the next day. Overnight, the dam bursts in the area of the cracks and damages surrounding property. Does this loss arise from completed operations?   ( ) Yes   ( ) No   Why?

    _____

    _____

    Answer: Yes. Even though repairs are required, the form stipulates the operation is complete since the work was put to its intended use.

34. 16.b describes situations that are *not* included in the products-completed operations hazard. Read this item now.

Losses arising out of the transportation of property are not considered part of the products-completed operations hazard. However, an exception is made if:

■ the loss arises out of a condition created when the insured is loading or unloading a vehicle; and

■ the vehicle is not owned or operated by the insured.

Note that this exception does not apply to the *act* of loading or unloading, but to a *condition created by* loading or unloading.

The insured rents a truck and hires a driver to transport a load of chemical products. When the insured loads the truck, he does not properly strap down the product boxes. In transit, several boxes break loose from the load and strike a car traveling behind the truck, causing bodily injury to the car's driver and property damage to her car. Is this situation included in the products-completed operations hazard?   ( ) Yes   ( ) No   Explain your answer.

_____

_____

Answer: Yes. The loss arose out of a condition created when the insured was loading a vehicle that he did not own or operate.

35. Item b.(2) indicates that the products-completed operations hazard does not include situations regarding tools, uninstalled equipment or abandoned or unused materials.

Waterspots Plumbing contracts with General Construction to install the finished plumbing materials on the premises of a new car dealership. The day before the plumbing job is to begin, Waterspots' foreperson takes the materials to be installed to the site and locks them in a supply room that General Construction has provided for this purpose. Later that afternoon, the owner of the car dealership enters the supply room, trips over the materials, and severely injures his leg.

This injury (did/did not) _____ arise from the products-completed operations hazard because _____

_____

_____ .

Answer: did not, because injury due to the existence of uninstalled equipment is specifically excluded from this definition

36. Item b.(3) refers to the classification of certain business exposures. The business classification listed in the declarations or policy schedule may note that products-completed operations are subject to the general aggregate policy limit, instead of the separate products-completed operations aggregate policy limit that would usually apply. In this case, these risks or operations

are not included within the definition of the products-completed operations hazard in the CGL. (You will learn more about the CGL's policy limits in a later unit.)

The insured's business classification in the declarations states that products-completed operations are subject to the general aggregate limit. The products-completed operations definition (does/does not) _____ apply to this insured.

Answer: does not

Property Damage

37. Now let's consider definition 17, **property damage**. Read only paragraphs a. and b. before continuing.

     Note that the definition refers to **tangible** property, so intangible property is *not* included. However, **loss of use** of tangible property that is not physically injured is considered to be property damage. Where there is a loss of use of tangible property that is not physically injured, the losses are likely to be economic, occurring because the injured party could not use the property, and thus lost the money the property could have generated.

EXAMPLE

A mishap at the Ace Chemical Company causes a serious explosion that scatters massive amounts of debris on access roads to Ace Chemical Company and two nearby businesses. The roads are closed for two days while the debris is cleaned up. This shutdown causes economic loss to the two nearby businesses, since they cannot conduct business during this time.

Which of the following may be considered property damage?

A. Construction materials owned by Readyright Construction Corporation fall off a trailer and completely block the entrance to Sesterhenn's Department Store on the new store's opening day.

B. Readyright has just begun to repair an elevated water tower when the cables on Readyright's properly operated crane break, and the beam falls on a neighboring florist's greenhouse.

C. Mrs. Huey Van Patton, a very wealthy customer of Upscale Department Store, is offended by an Upscale salesperson's demeanor. She tells Upscale's owner that the store has lost her as a customer forever.

Answer: A and B are correct. In C, loss of good will and potential profits are not considered property damage because they are intangible.

38. The last two paragraphs of the definition of property damage define another term, **electronic data**. Read this last part of the definition.

According to the definition, is electronic data *tangible* property?
( ) Yes   ( ) No

Which of the following might be considered property damage?

1. The insured's computer was stolen.

2. Data stored on the hard drive of the insured's computer was lost when the computer was stolen.

3. The insured had to lease a computer for a month before he was able to purchase one to replace the one that was stolen.

4. The insured had to pay an employee overtime wages to re-key the electronic company data that was lost.

Answer: A. No; B. 1 and 3 are correct.

Suit

39. Read the next definition, **suit**.

The basic dictionary meaning of a suit is **an action or process in a court for the recovery of a right or claim**. The CGL coverage form expands upon that basic definition to include:

- a civil proceeding in which damage because of BI, PD, or personal and advertising injury is alleged;

- arbitration proceedings; and

- any other alternative dispute resolution proceeding.

Arbitration proceedings and alternative proceedings are included because they may provide a way to resolve insurance disputes outside of a court of law.

In addition, there must be an allegation of injury or damage *for which the policy provides coverage*. Notice also that the insured must submit to proceedings with the insurer's consent.

Which of the following are examples of a suit as defined in the CGL?

A. Smith breaks into Jed's Convenience Mart while it is closed to steal food. After Smith has broken in, he is attacked by two guard dogs and bitten on both legs. Smith sues Jed's for the injuries he sustained.

B. Tyler sues Sawyer Shoes, the insured, for injuries she sustains in an accident at the premises of that shoe store. Sawyer then files a claim with its insurer, Secure Insurance Company. When the claim is denied, Tyler files suit directly against Secure. The suit is eventually settled through arbitration among Tyler, her attorney, and Secure Insurance Company, instead of in court.

C. Saunders writes a nasty letter to the president of Modern Men's Clothing Store complaining about rude treatment on the part of a salesperson. Saunders states in the letter that he not only refuses to buy clothing from the store, but also suffered mental anguish as a result of the salesperson's rudeness.

Answer: A and B are correct. C is not correct because no covered damages have been alleged, and Saunders wrote a letter instead of filing a suit.

This completes your study of the definitions section of the CGL. By referring to this section as you work through the remainder of the coverage forms, you'll develop an even clearer understanding of what the definitions mean in context.

In the next unit, you'll begin your study of the first coverage in the commercial general liability occurrence form.

UNIT

5

The Occurrence Form
Section I: Coverage A

INTRODUCTION

1. In the next several units, we will thoroughly analyze the coverages in the commercial general liability coverage forms, first as provided by the occurrence form and then by the claims-made form.

   Both forms provide essentially the same broad general liability coverage and are nearly identical in policy format. There are three major coverages.

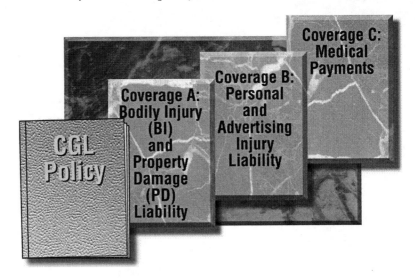

These three coverages are written into the coverage forms, but Coverages B and C may be excluded by endorsement if desired.

Section I of the coverage form refers to all three coverages plus another part, **Supplementary Payments** for Coverages A and B.

Each of the three coverages has a different insuring agreement and exclusions section, and we will look at each separately. Each coverage is also specifically defined, but a brief description of each follows.

Under Coverage A, **bodily injury and property damage liability** mean exactly that—liability for injuring another person or damaging another person's property.

Under Coverage B, **personal and advertising injury liability** refers to such injuries as libel, slander, copyright infringement, wrongful arrest, and violation of the right of privacy, among others.

Under Coverage C, **medical expenses** may be paid under certain circumstances, such as when first aid is administered when a customer at the insured business is injured.

Assume an insured has the CGL, and all policy conditions are met. Indicate whether each situation following would be covered under Coverage A, B, or C.

A. An individual claims the insured has made libelous statements that have damaged the individual's career. _____

B. An insured is held responsible for damaging a client's shipment of products. _____

C. When a visitor at the insured's warehouse is injured, the fire department is called to provide emergency treatment, for which the fire department levies a fee. _____

Answer: B. A; A. B; C. C

2. In this unit, we will look at Section I, Coverage A of the CGL. We'll start with the **occurrence** form, CG 00 01. Locate this form in your Forms and Endorsements, and read through the first four paragraphs following the form title and preceding the Section I heading.

These introductory paragraphs clarify some terms and refer you elsewhere to learn the meaning of others. You have already studied the definitions section, and we will be reminding you of various definitions as these terms are used in the form. You will learn the specific meaning of *insured* when we discuss Section II of the form.

According to what you read in these opening paragraphs:

A. Who is referred to in the policy as **"you"** and **"your"**? _____
    _____ and _____
    _____

B. Who is referred to as **"we," "us,"** and **"our"**? _____
    _____

Answer: A. The named insured shown in the declarations and any other person or organization qualifying as a named insured; B. The insurance company

3. This section refers not just to *any* insured, but specifically to the **"Named Insured shown in the Declarations and any other person or organization qualifying as a Named Insured."** This designation helps differentiate between the person or organization actually named on the declarations page as the insured and others who may be considered insureds under Section II, which we will discuss in a later unit.

    The words "qualifying as a Named Insured" are included to allow for any organization or business the insured might acquire after the policy is already in force and that would qualify as a named insured.

    Suppose the name "Franklin L. Burford" is the only name that appears on the CGL declarations page. Franklin's junior partner is his brother, Corey J. Burford, whose name does not appear on the declarations. Who is a named insured?

    A. Franklin L. Burford
    B. Corey J. Burford
    C. Both Franklin and Corey Burford

Answer: A is correct because only Franklin's name is shown on the declarations.

COVERAGE A: BODILY INJURY AND PROPERTY DAMAGE LIABILITY

Insuring Agreement

4. In the **insuring agreement**, the insurer sets out what it agrees to do for the insured under **Coverage A** of the policy. Read Item 1.a through the end of the paragraph following sub-Item 1.a.(2).

   The insurer agrees to pay sums the insured is **legally obligated** to pay as damages because of bodily injury or property damage. The insured's legal obligation may arise from a variety of situations, such as negligence or breach of contract, but note that there must be a legal obligation.

   Suppose a customer entering the XYZ Store drops his briefcase, trips on it, and breaks his toe through no fault of the store owner. The owner, however, wants to compensate the customer to promote good will. According to the insuring agreement, would XYZ's CGL policy pay for the injury? ( ) Yes ( ) No   Explain your answer. _____

   Answer: No. The policy pays only if there is a legal obligation on the part of the insured, which is not the case in this example.

5. The insuring agreement says the policy will pay for **bodily injury or property damage**, terms you studied in an earlier unit. Damages claimed that fall outside the definitions of BI and PD are not covered under Coverage A.

   For example, suppose a stock clerk in Shop-Quick Market drops a carton of eggs on the floor and fails to clean them up promptly. A customer slips on the eggs and skates crazily across the floor before regaining his balance. While not injured, the customer is very embarrassed. Would Coverage A cover a claim for damages for embarrassment? ( ) Yes ( ) No   Why?

   Answer: No. The customer did not suffer BI or PD.

6. This part of the insuring agreement is further modified by the words "**to which this insurance applies**." This means there is no coverage if the BI or PD is otherwise excluded. We will soon discuss these exclusions in detail.

   In general, BI and PD for which the insured is legally liable are covered, according to the insuring agreement,

   A. under all circumstances.

   B. provided no part of the claim for damages is for embarrassment.

   C. unless otherwise excluded by the policy.

Answer: C is correct.

7. Earlier, we noted that the policy will only pay claims that are covered by the policy. Likewise, the insurer will only defend the insured against lawsuits alleging BI or PD that is covered by the policy.

   One of the insured's employees suffers a serious work-related injury and files suit against the insured. This type of loss is excluded by the CGL. Would the insurance company defend this suit?   ( ) Yes   ( ) No

   Answer: No

8. The insurer is permitted to investigate and make settlements **at its own discretion**.

   Suppose an insured is convinced a suit filed by another person is false and the insurer should not pay. However, the insurer chooses to negotiate a settlement with the person who has filed suit and settles out of court. May the insurer do this without the insured's agreement?   ( ) Yes   ( ) No
   Explain your answer. _____
   _____

   Answer: Yes. This action is at the insurer's discretion, with or without the insured's agreement.

9. Items 1.a.(1) and (2) set additional limits on when and how claims might be paid. First, limitations imposed upon the available coverage amounts are described in Section III of the policy, which we will discuss later.

   In addition, there is a point beyond which the company is no longer obligated to defend the insured. If necessary, reread Item (2).

   Suppose an insured has up to $200,000 available for Coverage A liability. She has been found liable during the first nine months of her policy for this entire amount, which has been paid by the insurer. A month later, the insured is sued for another $10,000. Will the company defend this suit?
   ( ) Yes   ( ) No   Why? _____
   _____

   Answer: No. After the limits have been used, the duty to defend ends.

10. Notice also that Item (2) refers to having used up the limits for payments under Coverage A *or* B *or* C. The reason for this is that the three coverages are subject to a **general aggregate limit** applying to all three. If the general

aggregate has been exhausted by, for example, Coverages A and B, a subsequent claim under Coverage C would be denied defense by the company, even if no other Coverage C costs had been paid.

We will discuss exactly how the coverage limits apply and fit within the general aggregate limit later. For now, you know that

A. the general aggregate limit applies separately to each coverage, and the company's duty to defend continues until the limit has been exhausted for each of Coverages A, B, and C.

B. when the general aggregate limit has been used up by any or all coverages, the company's duty to defend ends.

C. except for Coverage C, no further defense is required of the company after the general aggregate limits have been exhausted.

Answer: B is correct.

11. The insuring agreement goes on to stipulate that there is no other obligation to provide coverage unless coverage falls under the supplementary payments section, another area we will cover later.

The remainder of the insuring agreement sets out additional conditions under which the coverage applies. Read Item 1.b.(1) now.

According to the item you just read, BI or PD must be caused by an **occurrence in the coverage territory.** You have learned the definitions of **coverage territory** and **occurrence.** Remember that a key word defining an occurrence is *accident*— the event must be unexpected and not intended by the insured.

Suppose a shop owner has been warned repeatedly by fire inspectors that exposed frayed wires in a stock room are dangerous and could result in a fire, but the shop owner fails to remedy the situation. One day, a fire breaks out, spreading quickly to the showroom. One customer, badly injured as a direct result of the fire, sues and is awarded a judgment against the shop owner. Assume this occurs in the coverage territory as defined. According to the insuring agreement, would the policy pay for this situation? ( )Yes ( )No Explain._____
_____
_____
_____
_____

Answer: Technically, no. Although this appears to be an accident, and was surely not what the insured intended, it could hardly be classified as unexpected considering the warnings from the fire department. Be aware, however, that many court cases have involved interpretations of what constitutes an accident, and judicial interpretation is subject to variation.

Occurrence Trigger

12. Now read Item 1.b.(2) of the insuring agreement, which includes the phrase that indicates what will trigger coverage under this policy. Called the **occurrence trigger**, it says that the bodily injury or property damage must occur during the policy period. The policy in effect when the BI or PD occurs then pays the claim, even if the claim is not made until after the policy expires. Here's an example of how this works, using a situation where an individual is injured by using the insured's product.

The Occurrence Trigger

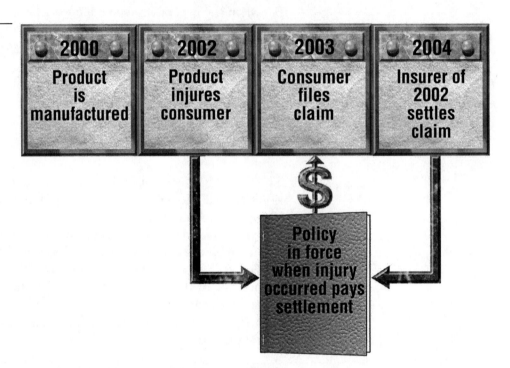

In the previous situation, assume the insured has changed insurers several times, and the following insurance companies provided CGL coverage over the years of this event:

■ 2000: Insurer is ABC Insurance Company

■ 2002: Insurer is HIJ Insurance Company

■ 2003: Insurer is OPQ Insurance Company

■ 2004: Insurer is XYZ Insurance Company

A. Which insurer's policy is in effect when the product injures the consumer? _____

B. Which insurer's policy is in effect when the consumer files the claim? _____
_____

C. Which insurer's policy is in effect when the claim is settled? _____
_____

D. According to the occurrence trigger, which insurer's policy applies to this claim? _____ Why? _____
_____

Answer: A. HIJ Insurance Company; B. OPQ Insurance Company; C. XYZ Insurance Company; D. HIJ Insurance Company, because the injury occurred during the policy period of its policy.

13. The next several paragraphs of the insuring agreement, which appear only in the occurrence coverage form (not in the claims-made coverage form), deal with **known injury or damage**. Read Paragraphs 1.b.(3), 1.c, and 1.d.

    You will recall from your earlier studies that an occurrence may be continuous in nature, but must take place during the policy period in order for coverage to apply. This portion of the policy clarifies the intent of the coverage. The CGL occurrence form does *not* cover losses of a continuous or ongoing nature that were, before the policy period, known to the insured or employees authorized to report losses.

    When the insured purchases a CGL policy from XYZ Insurance Company, it does not inform the insurer that a customer has threatened to sue the company for injuries she claims were caused by one of the company's products. Two months after the policy goes into effect, the customer makes good on her threat and files a lawsuit. Would the CGL provide a defense for this claim?   ( ) Yes   ( ) No

    Answer: A. No, because the insured knew about this loss before the policy period

14. The CGL does not limit the possibility for recovery of certain damages to the policy period because some damages could continue beyond the policy period. Read Item 1.e before continuing.

    Care, loss of services, or death from BI that occurred during the policy period could result *at any time* and still be covered.

    Suppose the insured is held liable for an accident at his place of business that occurred shortly before his policy expired. As a result of this accident, an individual involved requires six months of round-the-clock nursing care. In addition, the individual's spouse sues for damages for loss of services. Assume all other conditions of the policy have been met. Because the policy has now expired, would these damages be covered?   ( ) Yes   ( ) No Explain. _____

    _____

    Answer: Yes. Care, loss of services, or death resulting from BI may be covered at any time if the BI occurred during the policy period.

COVERAGE A EXCLUSIONS

Expected or Intended Injury

15. In any insurance coverage form, **exclusions** specifically state what the policy does *not* cover. Item 2 under Coverage A lists the exclusions for this coverage. Read the first exclusion, **Expected or Intended Injury**.

    You have learned that covered BI or PD must be an accident—not intended or expected by the insured. While this exclusion clearly makes that point, it also gives the insured permission to do what is necessary to protect property or persons without losing coverage. This is described as using **reasonable force**.

    Notice that the use of reasonable force is exempted only for *bodily injury*, while property damage is not mentioned. Any property damage that might result from such force would not be covered.

    Suppose the owner of an electronics store returns to the premises after hours to discover a burglar loading electronics equipment onto a truck. When the burglar refuses to stop, the owner pulls him off the truck, causing the burglar to suffer a dislocated shoulder. The burglar later sues the owner for the costs associated with his bodily injury.

    A. The store owner's CGL (will/will not) _____ provide him with a defense because _____
    _____.

    B. If the insured had also damaged the burglar's truck and the burglar sued for those damages, is there coverage?   ( ) Yes   ( ) No   Why?
    _____
    _____

    Answer: A. will, because the owner caused the bodily injury while using reasonable force to protect the property being stolen; B. No. The use of reasonable force is exempted for bodily injury but not property damage.

Contractual Liability

16. Read the **Contractual Liability** exclusion.

    According to this exclusion, contractual liability is generally not covered. However, exceptions are made when:

    ■ the insured would be held liable for the loss even if no contract or agreement existed; or

    ■ the contract meets the policy's definition of an insured contract AND the BI or PD occurs after the contract or agreement is executed.

    The first part of the exception refers to situations where the insured would be liable even if no contract or agreement existed. You have learned that tort liability may be imposed by law regardless of whether an individual voluntarily assumes such liability. Negligence is an example of this concept.

The insured, White Glove Janitorial Service, has a contract with Martin & Martin Insurance Agency to perform cleaning services. The contract states that White Glove will be held liable for any damage caused by its employees. One day, a White Glove employee accidentally spills cleaning solution on one of the agency's computers and ruins it. White Glove is found liable for the loss. The contractual liability exclusion (will/will not) _____ apply to this loss because _____ _____.

Answer: will not, because White Glove would have been liable for the loss even if it had not assumed liability under the contract

17. Liability assumed under a contract that meets the policy's definition of an insured contract is also covered if the BI or PD occurs after the contract or agreement is executed.

    Rise & Fall Elevator Service, the insured, signed a contract agreeing to keep the elevators in the Hamilton Office Building properly maintained. After the contract was executed, several customers were injured trying to escape the elevator when it got stuck between floors. Rise & Fall is found liable for the accident. Does the contractual liability exclusion apply? ( ) Yes   ( ) No   Why? _____

    Answer: No. The contract fits the policy's definition of an insured contract, and the BI occurred after the contract was executed.

18. As part of an insured contract, the insured may also assume liability for any defense costs incurred by or for a third party. These costs are considered covered damages if they are incurred when the insurer defends the third party against a loss that is insured by the policy.
    Because these costs are classified as covered damages, they will reduce the policy's limit of liability. In a later unit, you will learn that the insurer will sometimes pay these costs *in addition to* the policy's limit of liability.

    Defense costs incurred by or for a third party are considered covered damages when they are
    A. assumed by the insured under an insured contract
    B. incurred when the insurer defends the third party against a covered loss
    C. incurred when the insurer defends the third party against any loss, even one that is excluded by the policy

    Answer: A and B are correct.

Liquor Liability

19. Read the **Liquor Liability** exclusion.

Let's first consider the final paragraph of this exclusion, indicating the exclusion applies only to insureds **in the business of:**

■ manufacturing;

■ distributing;

■ selling;

■ serving; or

■ furnishing alcoholic beverages.

The words *in the business of* are significant, implying that providing liquor as an incidental part of a business does not trigger the exclusion. The intent is to exclude those specifically described because their chance of being held liable is greater. Later, you will learn about an endorsement used to exclude all liquor liability.

Which of the following are excluded from coverage?

A. The insured is J. C. Rand of the Rand Pottery Manufacturing Company, who hosts a cocktail party for Rand sales representatives and their spouses. One sales representative who becomes intoxicated at the party drives away and is involved in an auto accident where another party is injured.

B. A bartender continues to serve an obviously inebriated customer at the Stop and Sip Saloon. When the inebriated customer falls down a flight of stairs at the tavern and breaks his ankle, he sues the insured, the Stop and Sip owner.

C. At the Kramer Publishing Company holiday party held at the Marvel Hotel, the insured company has an open bar for the pleasure of employees and their guests. One employee drinks too much and begins throwing stemware through the windows of the hotel. The hotel sues Kramer, the insured.

Answer: B is correct. The others are not correct because neither the manufacturer nor the publisher are in the alcoholic beverage business.

20. Now that we know to whom this exclusion applies, let's consider exactly what is excluded. The excluded BI or PD liability may arise from any of the circumstances described in Items c.(1), (2), and (3), summarized here.

Situations Involving Liquor Liability

- Causing anyone's intoxication
- Contributing to anyone's intoxication
- Furnishing liquor to anyone under the legal drinking age
- Furnishing liquor to anyone under the influence of alcohol
- Violating statutes, ordinances, or regulations concerning sales, gifts, distribution, or use of alcoholic beverages

While these situations are fairly self-explanatory, let's briefly consider the significance of statutes, ordinances, and regulations and their relationship to liquor liability.

Under common law, a person injured by someone who had become intoxicated at a tavern or bar had no cause of action against the bartender or tavern owner. To impose liability, many states passed **dramshop**, or **liquor control laws**. These laws basically provide anyone injured by an intoxicated person with a cause of action against the tavern operator and, in some states, the owner or lessor of the premises. This CGL exclusion makes it clear that the policy will not respond for insureds that are subject to such laws.

Read each of the following situations and answer the questions in view of the liquor liability exclusion.

A. The JJ Tavern, owned by Jay James, is the insured. Although the tavern does not meet its state's legal requirements for serving alcoholic beverages, Jay serves a customer anyway. The customer is involved in an accident causing bodily injury to a pedestrian, and Jay is found liable. Will the CGL cover Jay's liability?   ( ) Yes   ( ) No

B. Torrey visits 10 different bars in one evening between 6:00 and 11:00, drinking several alcoholic beverages at each bar. On the way home, Torrey causes an accident resulting in both BI and PD. If each bar is covered by a CGL policy, which would be obligated to pay damages?

  1. Each bar but the first one
  2. Each bar but the last one
  3. All of the bars' insurers
  4. None of the bars' insurers

C. Flaherty is the owner of a tavern. The following events occur at the tavern, each followed by an accident for which Flaherty is found liable. Which are excluded under the CGL?

  1. Flaherty sells beer to his young neighbor who is celebrating his 18th birthday. The state's legal drinking age is 21.
  2. Flaherty serves one drink to a middle-aged man who is already obviously intoxicated.
  3. Flaherty serves beer to a high school freshman who shows a false identification card.

Answer: A. No; B. 4 is correct. The exclusion applies since bars are in the business of selling alcoholic beverages; C. All would be excluded because Flaherty is in the liquor business.

Workers' Compensation and Similar Laws

21. Read the **workers' compensation and similar laws** exclusion before continuing.

This exclusion applies to other employment-related laws as well. The insured's obligation referred to here applies whether or not the insured actually has met the legal requirement. Therefore, if an insured legally must provide certain employment-related coverages but does not, liability still exists. However, this type of liability is excluded from coverage under the CGL because there are other types of insurance specifically designed for this purpose. A CGL insurer will not assume these legal obligations of the insured.

An employee of the insured employer injured on the job is eligible for workers' compensation benefits. If the insured submits the employee's claim to the insurer providing the CGL, that insurer (would/would not) _____ pay the claim.

Answer: would not

Employers Liability

22. This exclusion also concerns the **employee-employer relationship**. Read the Employers Liability exclusion, and then refer back to the definition of *employee* in the definitions section of the policy.

Which of the following would be excluded, assuming the insured employer is found liable?

A. A leased worker's finger is broken while he is trying to correct a paper jam in a copy machine.

B. A temporary factory worker trips in a hole in the company's parking lot and sprains an ankle.

C. An employee falls on wet stairs at the insured's place of business and breaks her hip.

D. A client of the insured is signing a contract in the insured's office when the insured spills a pot of hot coffee, scalding the client's hands.

Answer: A and C are excluded. The injured persons in B and D are not employees, per the definition, so the exclusion does not apply.

23. Item e.(2) refers to **consequential damages** that may result to an employee's relatives because of injury to the employee. While this exclusion may appear to be extreme, it exists to prevent double recovery because such claims are normally covered through the employers liability insurance available in tandem with workers' compensation coverage.

Suppose a research scientist in a pharmaceuticals laboratory contracts a deadly virus during an experiment. The scientist's entire family is exposed and contracts the virus from the scientist. All die except one of the scientist's daughters, who lives in another state. The daughter sues the insured, the pharmaceuticals company, for loss of the companionship of her family. Will the CGL insurer defend this claim?   ( ) Yes   ( ) No

Answer: No

24. So far, we have considered only the employee's relationship to the employer on the job. The next section of the employers liability exclusion indicates that the exclusion applies in regard to any other capacity as well.

Often referred to as the **dual capacity doctrine**, this means that an employer might be held liable not only under workers' compensation laws, but also in areas not directly related to employment.

Here's an example. An employee of Cool Cola Company might buy and drink Cool Cola from a machine in the company's employee lunchroom. Suppose that during a company-paid break, the employee purchases a cola from the machine, and it explodes as soon as the employee picks it up. Flying metal from the container lodges in the employee's eye.

Under the dual capacity doctrine, the employee could collect workers' compensation benefits and then also sue the employer for a defective product as a member of the general buying public. Even though the injury occurred on the job, the defective can of cola might just as readily have been in a public soft drink machine off the premises, so the injury could have occurred aside from the employment. The employee might then attempt to recover from the employer's CGL.

The purpose of the employers liability policy in conjunction with workers' compensation insurance is to cover dual capacity situations such as the one just described; hence, the exclusion in the CGL.

Which of these situations are excluded?

A. An employee of Wizard Motors, the insured, is required to engage the ignition of new autos as they come off the assembly line. While the employee is doing so, a fire breaks out under the hood, and as a result of a defective fire wall, the employee is burned. Because the car would have been made available for sale to the public, the employee sues Wizard Motors, which in turn submits a claim to its CGL insurer.

B. Jason's employer makes machines that automatically throw tennis balls for practice. On his day off, Jason practices at the tennis club where he is a member. It happens that the club uses his employer's machines. One of the machines malfunctions, and Jason is badly battered by wildly flying tennis balls. He sues his employer.

Answer: A is correct. B is not correct because Jason's activities when he was injured were not directly related to his employment.

25. The final paragraph of the employers liability exclusion is an exception. Suppose an insured's contract with a janitorial service meets the definition of an insured contract under which the insured assumes liability for the safety of anyone on the insured's premises when the janitorial service employees are on the premises performing work called for by the contract. While the janitorial workers are waxing the insured's floor, an off-duty employee of the insured stops by the premises, slips on the wet floor, falls, and suffers a back injury. In this case, the insured's CGL policy (will/will not) _____ pay any claim because _____

_____.

Answer: will, because the insured has assumed liability under an insured contract

Pollution

BI and PD Excluded

26. Read the entire **pollution** exclusion. We'll look at the exclusion in small sections.

    Coverage for bodily injury and property damage liability resulting from pollutants is almost wholly excluded from the CGL, with minor exceptions. Insureds who have a significant pollution exposure may obtain pollution coverage through other sources. As a general rule, the pollution exclusion effectively prevents relying on the CGL to cover pollution liability. We will, however, point out the areas where very limited coverage is available.

    The exclusion is divided into two parts:

- ■ **bodily injury and property damage** arising out of actual pollution as described in the form; and

- ■ **clean-up costs** associated with pollutants.

    Let's consider the first situation, bodily injury and property damage, and the first paragraph of the exclusion, f.(1). This paragraph effectively excludes all the potential ways in which pollutants might enter the environment. Also notice the words *actual, alleged, or threatened*, eliminating any question about potential pollution and actual pollution.

    According to this paragraph, what are the six ways pollutants might cause BI or PD?

    A. _____

    B. _____

    C. _____

    D. _____

    E. _____

    F. _____

    Answer: (In any order) A. Discharge; B. Dispersal; C. Seepage; D. Migration; E. Release; F. Escape

27. Item f.(1)(a) excludes pollution that originates from any:

    ■ premises;

    ■ site; or

    ■ location

    that *is currently* or *was at any time*:

    ■ owned by any insured;

    ■ occupied by any insured;

    ■ rented by any insured; or

    ■ loaned to any insured.

    Notice this does not apply just to the *named* insured, but to *any* insured. To make certain the exclusion is complete, this item appears to encompass any place any insured has used at any time.

    Which of the following situations preclude pollution liability coverage?

    A. The insured, Inglewood Corporation, occupies a rented building on the property of QCD Company. The insured is sued for damages resulting from pollutants emitted from the building owned by QCD, but occupied by Inglewood.

    B. The insured is held liable for pollution damage to others originating from premises the insured owns and occupies.

    C. Siskoski, the insured, lives rent-free in a property owned by a relative. During Siskoski's occupancy, she is sued for pollution damage although the pollutants were emitted not from her operations, but from other operations on the relative's property.

    D. All of these situations preclude pollution liability coverage.

    Answer: D is correct.

28. Now we'll consider three exceptions to the pollution exclusion. Review the first exception, Item f.(1)(a)(i).

    This exception clarifies that any bodily injury resulting from smoke, fumes, vapor, or soot that is produced by or originates from a building's **heating, air conditioning, dehumidifying, or water heating equipment** should not be considered pollution, and resulting damages are covered under the CGL.

    A crack in the heat exchanger of the insured's commercial furnace emits carbon monoxide fumes and causes several people to become ill. Under CGL Coverage A, this situation (is/is not) _____ covered.

    Answer: is

29. Now review the second exception, Item f.(1)(a)(ii).

    This exception preserves the policy's pollution coverage for BI and PD under one specific, but common, situation:

    ■ A contractor, the insured, is performing work at the location of an owner or lessee.

    ■ That owner or lessee is added as an additional insured to the contractor's CGL.

    ■ The location has never been owned or occupied by any insured other than the current owner or lessee.

    Walls and More, an insured contractor, is remodeling the office configuration at the Cure All Pharmaceuticals building. One of the contractor's workers accidentally backs a forklift into a chemical storage tank, releasing pollutants.

    A. In the preceding example, if Cure All is an additional insured on the contractor's CGL, might this incident be covered?   ( ) Yes   ( ) No

    B. Suppose that Cure All is the second additional insured on the contractor's CGL to occupy the building. Would there be coverage in that case?   ( ) Yes   ( ) No

    Answer: A. Yes; B. No

30. Look over the third exception, f.(1)(a)(iii). Also, if necessary, review the definition of hostile fire.

    This exception gives back BI and PD coverage for damage arising out of heat, smoke, or fumes from a **hostile fire**.

    An accident in the insured's warehouse causes the building and its contents to catch fire, producing toxic smoke. Pedestrians become ill from inhaling the smoke. If these individuals make BI claims against the warehouse owner, would the pollution exclusion apply?   ( ) Yes   ( ) No   Explain. _____

    _____

    Answer: No. The exclusion does not apply because the smoke is produced by a hostile fire.

31. Not only does the pollution exclusion preclude coverage for any place any insured has used or owned, but also any place used by or for *anyone* as a **waste disposal or treatment site**. Review Item f.(1)(b) and then answer the following question.

    The insured sends certain wastes off his premises for storage and, sometimes, disposal. When an accident occurs at the place where the insured's waste materials are sent, passersby are injured. They later sue the disposal company as well as the insured, whose waste materials were involved in the injuries. The insured's premises were not involved in this accident. Coverage for these damages (is/is not) _____ excluded.

Answer: is

32. Item f.(1)(c) deals with exclusions when waste is handled in various ways.

    Suppose certain waste materials are being stored for the insured off premises, awaiting reclamation by the ZBD Company. While on ZBD's premises, the waste seeps into the ground and into a nearby water system. Any BI or PD resulting from this situation (is/is not) _____ covered by the CGL policy.

Answer: is not

33. The final part of the BI and PD section of the exclusion, Item f.(1)(d), specifies yet another situation that is excluded. But this section also implies that *some* pollution liability coverage *is* provided.

    Review the first paragraph of f.(1)(d). Notice that this section applies to places where operations are being performed by:

    ■ any insured;

    ■ any contractors while working directly or indirectly on any insured's behalf; or

    ■ any subcontractors while working directly or indirectly on any insured's behalf.

    Note that this exclusion refers to pollutants that insureds or contractors **bring onto the site**— not to pollutants that were already there.

    While working at the site of new commercial construction, the insured construction company hires a subcontractor for back hoeing and bulldozing. The subcontractor's equipment accidentally damages a sewage disposal pipe, allowing raw sewage to escape. A series of subsequent related events results in bodily injury to several people at a neighboring location. The insured is sued. Is coverage available to the insured in this situation?
    ( ) Yes   ( ) No   Explain. _____
    _____

Answer: Yes. The sewage that was the source of pollution causing bodily injury was not brought to the site by any of the parties involved.

34. Also notice the implication that only *current operations* are excluded by virtue of the present tense wording: "working" and "are performing." Because the exclusion applies to current operations, the CGL coverage form apparently provides coverage for the products-completed operations exposure as long as no other exclusion applies. For example, even though there might be some coverage for products-completed operations, if such a loss occurred at a waste disposal or processing site, it would still be excluded by Provisions f.(1)(b) and (c).

    As you know, the products-completed operations exposure arises *after* the insured has completed work or released a product. The work or product must then be at some location other than the insured's premises.

    Suppose an insured's product is a chemical used in making printer's ink. An accident at the ink manufacturer releases chemical pollutants into the air, and bodily injury occurs to neighbors of the ink manufacturer. The insured is included in a lawsuit filed by the injured people. Is there coverage under the CGL for the chemical-producing insured?   ( ) Yes   ( ) No   Why? _____

    Answer: Yes. This represents the products-completed operations exposure, which appears not to be part of the exclusion.

35. Items f.(1)(d)(i), (ii), and (iii) describe three exceptions to the pollution exclusion. Review these now.

    Notice that Item (d)(iii) makes an exception for BI or PD resulting from a hostile fire. We covered this situation earlier, so we won't go over it again here.

    The first exception, Item (d)(i), pertains to the exclusion for pollutants brought to a job site by the insured or a contractor. The exception makes clear that the pollution exclusion does not apply to the *accidental* escape of fuel, lubricants, or other operating fluids from mobile equipment when these materials escape from the vehicle parts designed to hold them. However, any BI or PD that results from the *intentional* release or discharge of pollutants is still excluded.

    The insured is hired to perform bulldozing work at a commercial construction site. While on the job, the bulldozer's gas tank is accidentally damaged, causing gasoline to spill all over the site. Some building materials owned by another contractor are damaged as a result of the spill, and that contractor files suit against the insured. Is this situation covered by the CGL? ( ) Yes   ( ) No   Explain. _____

    Answer: Yes. The exclusion for pollutants brought to a job site by an insured does not apply to the accidental escape of fuel, lubricants, or other operating fluids from mobile equipment when these materials escape from the vehicle parts designed to hold them.

36. The next exception, Item f.(1)(d)(ii), provides coverage for bodily injury or property damage resulting from the release of gases, fumes, or vapors from materials brought onto a job site in connection with operations being performed by the insured or a contractor. For example, BI or PD is covered when it arises from the fumes of paint, cleaning and chemical supplies, glue for carpet and tile repairs, and the like.

    At first glance, this exception may appear to contradict the first paragraph of Item f.(1)(d), which excludes pollution coverage for pollutants brought onto the site. This exception, however, differentiates between pollutants—such as paint—and the fumes that are given off by the paint. The insured, for example, brings the pollutant paint onto the site, but the insured doesn't bring the fumes.

    Industrial Carpets, the insured, was installing carpeting at the Best Office building. Fumes from the carpet glue made several people sick, and they sued for damages. Does the CGL cover this situation? ( ) Yes   ( ) No   Explain.

    Answer: Yes. The CGL makes an exception for fumes released from materials brought onto the site.

37. Review Item f.(1)(e). This paragraph excludes coverage for BI and PD at any location where the insured or someone on behalf of the insured is performing operations related to environmental clean up. The topic of clean up is touched on here, but covered more fully in the next section of the pollution exclusion.

    An insured manufacturer dumps waste into a nearby lake. Because of environmental regulations, the insured must regularly test the level of contamination in the water. While testing the water level, a contractor hired by the insured suffered serious skin irritation from contact with the contaminated lake water. If the contractor sues, would the CGL provide coverage? ( ) Yes   ( ) No

    Answer: No

Clean-Up Costs Excluded

38. The second section of the pollution exclusion, f.(2), deals with what are commonly known as **clean-up costs**. You will notice that this term is not actually used in the CGL form, but is in common usage and does appear as a defined term in separate forms and endorsements that *do* cover pollution clean-up costs.

Essentially, clean-up costs are costs incurred to remove or neutralize pollutants. These costs are excluded in two cases:

- The first case is when the insured is ordered by a nongovernmental entity, such as a bank before the sale of property, to test, monitor, clean up, or perform related operations.

- The second case is when the insured is mandated by the government by statutory or regulatory requirements or by other government suits or claims to clean up or to pay for any losses, costs, or expenses that arise from clean up.

Which of the following are excluded?

A. A federal government agency wins a lawsuit against the insured, requiring the insured to remove and dispose of contaminants that leaked into the earth from the insured's operations.

B. A citizens' action group demands that the insured test for and report on pollutants the group believes the insured's manufacturing plant is emitting into the atmosphere.

Answer: Both A and B are correct.

39. The last paragraph of the pollution exclusion may appear to be an exception, but actually is mostly just a clarification of the coverage.

Whether or not the insured is ordered to clean up pollutants, the CGL will provide coverage if a third party sues the insured for property damage, as long as the damage arises from an unexcluded pollution incident. In other words, property damage arising from incidents not excluded from section f.(1) of the pollution exclusion are covered.

However, if the government orders the clean up of pollutants, as specified in Item f.(2)(b), the CGL will not provide coverage.

A. Suppose that a claimant's property is damaged by a pollution incident that is covered by the insured's CGL. Could the CGL cover these property damages?   ( ) Yes   ( ) No

B. A government agency hires a contractor to neutralize pollutants in the lake near the insured manufacturer's business. The agency sues the insured for the costs of this clean up. Would the CGL cover these expenses?   ( ) Yes   ( ) No

Answer: A. Yes; B. No

Aircraft, Auto or, Watercraft

40. Let's move on to the **Aircraft, Auto, or Watercraft** exclusion. Read only the first two paragraphs before continuing.

This Item excludes BI and PD that result from owning, maintaining, using, or entrusting to someone else any aircraft, autos or watercraft. This includes aircraft, autos, or watercraft owned or operated by an insured or rented or loaned to an insured. The exclusion applies even in cases of an insured's negligence or negligent supervision.

Precise definitions are very important to understanding this exclusion, so refer to them if you need to, paying special attention to **auto** and **loading or unloading**.

The meaning of **insured** has special implications as well. We will be discussing who exactly are insureds in greater detail later, but for the purpose of this section, you should know that an insured's employees acting in their employment roles are considered insureds.

Consider this situation. The named insured is J. S. Digwell, whose company owns a small Beechcraft flown by T. Carlsen to transport Digwell clients from local airports and to and from Digwell's corporate offices high in the mountains. During a flight, Carlsen fails to latch the cargo door properly. The client's bags fall out of the plane and through the roof of a house in a residential area below. As Carlsen realizes what is happening, he becomes so unnerved that he clips a tall pine with a plane wing, causing the plane to crash into a small warehouse. Carlsen and the client are injured, the plane is severely damaged, and the warehouse is destroyed. The client, the homeowner, and the warehouse owner all sue Digwell.

A. Which of the following items will Digwell's CGL cover?

1. The bodily injury claims only

2. The property damage claims only

3. Only the property damage to the client's luggage and equipment because this fits into the definition of loading or unloading

4. All the bodily injury or property damage listed because the plane was operated by someone other than the insured

5. None of the above because all damages arose out of the use of an aircraft by an insured as defined in the policy

B. Suppose that in one suit, the client accuses Digwell of negligence for hiring a careless pilot. In fact, Carlsen had a previous flying incident that was his fault, but Digwell didn't check Carlsen's flying record before hiring him. Might the CGL policy cover Digwell's liability in this case?   ( ) Yes   ( ) No

Answer: A. 5 is correct. Choice 3 might have misled you if you did not note that in this exclusion "loading or unloading" (including handling property while it is in an aircraft) is considered to be "use"; B. No. The CGL policy doesn't provide any liability coverage for aircraft, regardless of whether or not the insured was negligent.

Exceptions

41. Read the remainder of the Aircraft, Auto, or Watercraft exclusion to determine the types of situations to which this exclusion does *not* apply.

    This exclusion does *not* apply if watercraft is **ashore on premises the insured owns or rents**.

    One of Greene's functions as co-owner of his insured business is to entertain clients on the company's pontoon boat. While he is at a public beach preparing to put the boat into the water, the boat slips and smashes a bystander's foot. Greene is confident that if he is held liable, the CGL will cover this loss because the watercraft is still ashore. Is Greene correct? ( ) Yes   ( ) No   Why? _____

    _____

    Answer: No. Although the craft is ashore, it is not on the insured's premises as required by the policy.

42. Also exempt from the exclusion is any **nonowned watercraft** that is:

    ■ less than 26 feet long; and

    ■ not being used to carry people or property for a fee.

    Which of the following situations *are* covered by the insured's CGL?

    A. James, the insured, owns a bait and tackle business at a public marina. He borrows another business's 16-foot motorboat to run an errand across the lake. While docking, he rams into a pier. The pier owner sues James, who is held liable.

    B. Pat Rutledge, owner of Rutledge Corporation, has a cabin and a 12-foot motorboat on Lake Restful, where she entertains clients. With a client in the boat, Pat passes too closely to another boat, which capsizes. The boat cannot be recovered, and Pat is held liable.

    C. As part of his sailboat sales business, Nels advertises by giving rides across the local lake for a $2 fee. He does this during his city's annual summer water festival. This year, his usual boat is being repaired, so Nels rents one to use for this same purpose. Unfortunately, he misjudges the distance while docking and damages another boat. He is held liable for the damages.

    Answer: A is correct. In B, Pat owns the boat, so it is excluded. In C, Nels is carrying passengers for a fee, so the exclusion applies.

43. The next exception, Item (3), indicates that the exclusion does not apply to **parking an auto** under certain circumstances:

   ■ The parking occurs **on or next to premises the insured owns or rents,** *provided*

   ■ the auto is **not owned by, rented, or loaned to any insured.**

   One effect of this exception is to permit liability coverage for valet parking.

   Which of the following situations are **not** covered?

   A. Ms. Morgenstern, the insured, owns a restaurant with valet parking. An attendant bringing a customer's car to the entrance backs the car into an adjoining businessowner's property and damages a wall.

   B. When Ms. Morgenstern arrives at the restaurant, she asks the attendant to park her car. The attendant cuts a corner too sharply and damages the adjoining businessowner's fence.

   C. While parking a customer's car, the attendant strikes and injures another customer walking across the parking lot.

   D. When the parking attendant arrives for work, he tries to park his own car close to a parked motorcycle. The attendant's car knocks down and runs over the motorcycle.

   Answer: B and D are correct. B is not covered because it is the insured's car that causes the damage. D is not covered because the employee is considered an insured in the situation, and he is parking his own car.

44. Item (4) makes an exception for liability assumed under an insured contract involving ownership, maintenance, or use of aircraft or watercraft.
   Notice this exception applies only to aircraft and watercraft. Automobiles are not included because autos must be covered under a business auto policy, not the CGL.

   To promote a lakeside project, a real estate developer hires a helicopter and pilot to give potential buyers free helicopter tours over the project. The agreement is that the real estate developer, who is the insured, will hold the helicopter owner harmless for any liability arising during the rides. If an accident occurs for which the insured developer is held liable, which of the following is correct?

   A. Coverage under the CGL is excluded because the damage arose from aircraft rented to an insured.

   B. Coverage would apply because the developer does not own the aircraft.

   C. Assuming the agreement meets the definition of an insured contract, the CGL would apply under this exception to the exclusion.

   Answer: C is correct.

45. The final exception to the aircraft, auto, or watercraft exclusion, Item (5), makes an exception for BI and PD arising out of the **operation of certain equipment**. This is equipment discussed earlier as part of the definitions of auto and mobile equipment.

Because this equipment was designated to the auto definition, and so would normally be excluded, this part of the exclusion gives back the coverage. Therefore, if an insured were operating an air compressor permanently mounted to a truck bed and injury occurred to a third person, the CGL policy would

A. cover the loss because of this exception to the aircraft, auto, or watercraft exclusion

B. not cover the loss because the equipment meets the policy definition of an auto because it is permanently attached to a truck

Answer: A is correct.

Mobile Equipment

46. The **Mobile Equipment** exclusion addresses certain types of bodily injury and property damage related to mobile equipment. Read this exclusion.
    As a general rule, liability arising out of the use of mobile equipment is covered under the CGL, but the coverage does not apply in the two situations described here.

The exclusion for **transportation of mobile equipment,** Item (1), applies when:

■ the transporting occurs by an auto as defined in the policy; and

■ the auto is owned or operated by or rented or loaned to an insured.

With these two qualifiers in mind, indicate which of the following situations are excluded.

A. A generator owned by the insured is being pulled across a work area by a bulldozer, which is also owned by the insured. The generator breaks loose and injures a bystander, who sues the insured.

B. A forklift the insured owns is being transferred by one of the insured's trucks to another insured location. While trying to make a sharp turn, the truck driver crashes into a parked car. The car owner sues the insured.

C. The insured hires a trucking company to transport a bulldozer the insured owns to another city. During the trip, the trucker falls asleep at the wheel, the truck overturns, and the bulldozer rolls off the truck. The bulldozer smashes property belonging to an individual who lives on the transport route. The property owner sues both the trucking company and the insured.

Answer: B is excluded because the insured owns the auto moving the equipment. In A, the generator is not being transported by an auto as defined in the policy, so it is covered. In C, the transportation is provided by an auto that is not owned or operated by or rented or loaned to the insured.

47. In Item (2), coverage is excluded when mobile equipment is used in connection with certain specified **hazardous activities**. Notice the exclusion applies when these activities are *prearranged*.

    A. Paul, the insured, owns a farm machinery store. Every year he sponsors and participates in a tractor pull contest where participants try to pull the largest loads with their farm tractors. While practicing in his parking lot for the event, Paul loses control of the tractor and damages a number of parked cars. This loss (is/is not) _____ covered by Paul's CGL.

    B. Now let's suppose that Paul is simply trying out a new farm tractor at the same time a potential customer is also test driving one of Paul's tractors. During a playful moment, Paul and his customer decide to race their tractors the length of Paul's parking lot. Once again, Paul loses control of his tractor and damages some parked cars. Does the exclusion preclude coverage in this case? ( ) Yes   ( ) No   Why? _____

    _____

    _____

    Answer: A. is not; B. No. Although mobile equipment is involved, the race was not prearranged, so coverage is not excluded.

War

48. Read the **War** exclusion. The three broad categories in this exclusion encompass most warlike acts, including responses to those acts.

    The insured is an archaeological firm that has negotiated digging rights in a Mideastern country. Much to the chagrin of a small religious sect, the digs are located near a burial ground the sect considers sacred. While the government with whom the insured negotiated is aware of this, the insured is not. Shortly after work begins at the site, angry members of the sect declare a holy war on both the insured's expedition and the government. The government sues the insured for the ensuing injury and damage.

    Would the insured's CGL cover this liability?   ( ) Yes   ( ) No

    Answer: No.

Damage to Property

49. Read only Items (1) through (6) of the **Damage to Property** exclusion. We will cover the paragraphs at the end of the exclusion later in our discussion.

    Item j.(1) excludes **property damage to any property the insured owns, rents, or occupies.** The primary purpose of this first part of the property damage exclusion is to stress that the CGL will not cover anything that should be covered by other types of insurance. In this case, the insured's property should be protected by property insurance, not liability insurance. There is only one exception, which appears at the end of the exclusion section, and we will discuss it when we reach that point.

    As you might expect, costs for normal maintenance, repairs, and enhancements to property are excluded. Even when repairs are for the purpose of preventing injuries, the CGL does not provide coverage.

    Which of the following are excluded?

    A. Equipment the insured leases on a yearly basis for use in her business

    B. Temporarily unoccupied real estate the insured owns in the name of his business

    C. Equipment and tools left inadvertently and without the insured's knowledge on the insured's premises by a renovator following work at the insured's place of business

    D. A building the insured occupies, but which is not listed on the policy as an insured premises

    E. The cost to repair a broken step leading up to the front door of the insured's business in order to prevent customers from falling and getting hurt

    Answer: A, B, D, and E are excluded.

50. Item j.(2) concerns what is often referred to as **alienated premises,** a term that includes selling, giving away, or abandoning the premises. The exclusion applies to property damage that arises out of any part of this type of premises.

    Two key points in this exclusion are that:

    ■ property damage, but not bodily injury, is excluded and

    ■ damage to property other than the alienated premises is *not* excluded.

    The insured is Ms. Fox, who recently sold a building to the Crowe Company. When the Crowe Company moves in, a series of unfortunate events occur, and Ms. Fox is held liable for the resulting damages. Read about each of these events in the following items, and check any excluded by Ms. Fox's CGL.

A. A Crowe employee trips on a section of carpet that is not properly fastened to the floor. The employee breaks his arm in the fall.

B. Defective wiring in the building becomes apparent when the circuit breaker for the air conditioning system is activated. A fire breaks out, damaging the west side of the building.

C. During this same fire, the Crowe Company's new photocopier is destroyed.

D. A faulty hot water heater on the premises produces scalding water from the tap. Crowe's young son, who is on the premises on moving day, turns on the tap and is badly burned.

Answer: B is correct. A and D involve bodily injury, which is not excluded. C involves damage to property other than the alienated premises, which is also not excluded.

51. An exception to the Item j.(2) exclusion appears in the second paragraph following Item (6). Read that paragraph now.

    This exception permits coverage for building contractors who build on speculation. Such a building meets the definition of "your work" for a contractor who is a named insured. A further requirement is that the builder has never occupied, rented, or held the property for rental. This gives speculative builders the same coverage available for builders who do the work without ever having owned the property. This is completed operations coverage, which is treated in a separate exclusion.

    The alienated premises exclusion does not apply to a contractor's property built on speculation provided the premises were never

    A. sold

    B. damaged as a result of a problem arising out of the premises

    C. occupied, rented, or held for rental by the insured

    D. covered by a property insurance contract

    Answer: C is correct.

52. Item j.(3), relating to **property loaned to the insured,** appears to be aimed at covering all possible bases. Property loaned to the insured could conceivably fall under either Item (1) or Item (4), but the policywriters have seen fit not to leave interpretation to chance. As it is worded, the exclusion applies to

    A. real estate property only

    B. personal property only

    C. any type of property, whether personal property or real property

    Answer: C is correct.

53. Item j.(4) is sometimes referred to as the **care, custody, and control** exclusion. It applies only to personal property, not to real property.

    Quite a bit of judicial interpretation has taken place concerning the meaning of care, custody, and control, and the final word may not be in yet. However, general definitions have evolved and are reliable for the time being.

    ■ **Care** generally refers to the degree of concern people of ordinary prudence would demonstrate with regard to the relative importance of the subject or object.

    ■ **Custody** refers to the immediate care and keeping of something; *immediate* implies a situation that is temporary and current rather than permanent and absolute.

    ■ **Control** means having power or authority over something.

    You don't have to memorize these definitions because they may be subject to varying interpretations, but a general understanding of them will help you understand the purpose of the exclusion.

    The major purpose of the CGL is protection against third-party claims rather than the insured's claims. Therefore, property that is in the insured's care, custody, or control, whether or not it is the insured's own property, falls outside the scope of coverage because the insured would be expected to treat such property with the same degree of care as his own property.

    The terms imply that the insured knows the property is, in fact, in his care, custody, or control. Therefore, property that might be left on the insured's premises by accident or without the insured's knowledge (would/would not) _____ be subject to this exclusion.

    Answer: would not

54. Using this information about the care, custody, and control exclusion, decide which of the following situations would be excluded from CGL coverage.

    A. Ms. Ling, an antique dealer, is the insured. A friend of hers decides to sell his antique firearms collection on consignment from her place of business. Ms. Ling inadvertently leaves her shop unlocked one night, and the firearms are stolen. She is held liable for her friend's loss.

    B. The insured, Pavel Corporation, closes down completely for two weeks during the month of July. During the shutdown, employees of a neighboring business park their cars in Pavel's parking lot because it gives them easier access to the freeway than their own lot. When a fire of mysterious origin burns through the wall at Pavel's, several cars belonging to the neighboring employees are destroyed. Pavel is held liable.

    C. Reed, the insured, is a building contractor. One of the subcontractors on a certain job has asked to use space in Reed's building to store new cabinetry the subcontractor will be installing in a house Reed is building. Reed gives permission, and the cabinets are stored on Reed's premises. One of Reed's employees spills a container of acid used to clean concrete over the cabinets, ruining them. Reed is liable for the damages.

Answer: A and C are correct. B is not excluded because the cars were not in the insured's care, custody, or control.

55. Items j.(1), (3), and (4) are subject to an exception. Read the first paragraph after Item j.(6).

The exception provides coverage for damage to property and its contents for premises rented to the insured, such as a hotel room or party house, for seven consecutive days or less. The exception gives back coverage for damage (other than fire damage) to the rented premises and its contents. We will discuss fire damage to rented property later in this unit.

Suppose that Clyde Klutz, the insured, rented a motel room during a three-day business trip. While eating breakfast ordered from room service, Klutz knocked over his tray and permanently stained the carpeting with food and drinks. Would Klutz's insurance company pay for damages to the carpeting?   ( ) Yes   ( ) No

Answer: Yes

56. Item j.(5) refers specifically to **real property**, rather than personal property. If property damage occurs when the insured or a subcontractor is working on real property and the work is responsible for the damage, coverage is excluded *only* for the part that is being worked on. Damage to other parts of the real property resulting from this occurrence can be covered.

Suppose the insured has been engaged to fix a central vacuum system, which would be considered real property because it is a permanent part of the house. The insured accidentally causes a fire to start within the vacuum system. Part of the system itself is damaged, as well as surrounding walls. The insured's CGL would cover damage to (the system/the walls/both the system and the walls) _____because _____
_____
_____.

Answer: the walls (because) they are not the particular part being worked on. Coverage is excluded for the vacuum system, which is the part being worked on.

57. Item j.(6) refers to what is commonly known as **faulty workmanship** and applies to both real and personal property. Read the final exception paragraph, which applies to (6).

    Exactly what phase the insured's work was in when the damage occurred is important because the exclusion does not apply to property damage that is included in the products-completed operations hazard. However, this does not necessarily mean completed operations are covered because there is still another exclusion that further addresses this hazard. You will see it shortly.

    Suppose the insured was hired to repair the old gaslights in a Victorian house. Unfortunately, the insured is not as knowledgeable about this job as he should be, and when he turns on the gaslights to see whether they are working, they all break. The loss of these antique lights is significant and the customer sues. The insured is found liable. Will the insured's CGL pay for the cost of replacing or restoring the broken gaslights?   ( ) Yes   ( ) No   Why? _____

    _____

    _____

    Answer: No. This is specifically excluded because the insured incorrectly did the work that caused the damage.

58. The damage to property exclusion has one more exception, which applies to Items j.(3), (4), (5), and (6). Read the *third* paragraph following Item (6).

    The Tortoise Rail Company parks some of its railroad cars on the sidetrack at a local factory, the Bezee Corporation, while the cars are being loaded. Bezee assumes liability while the cars are there. A fire breaks out in the chemical solvent being loaded, and two of the railroad cars are destroyed. Would there be coverage under Bezee Corporation's CGL?   ( ) Yes   ( ) No   Why?

    _____

    Answer: Yes. This exception says the exclusion does not apply to a sidetrack agreement.

Damage to Your Product

59. Read the **Damage to Your Product** exclusion.

    This exclusion applies to damage to the insured's product that results because there is a defect in all or any part of the product.

    Suppose the insured manufactures power drills, including the motors that run them. While a purchaser is using one of these drills, the drill shorts out because of a faulty motor. Not only is the drill burned out, but the purchaser receives third-degree burns on his hands and arms. He sues the insured, and the insured is held liable.

A. The insured's CGL policy (will/will not) _____ cover liability for the individual's burns because _____
_____ .

B. The insured's CGL policy (will/will not) _____ cover liability for the damaged drill because _____
_____ .

Answer: A. will, because BI arising from the product is not excluded; B. will not, because PD to the product that arises from the product is excluded

Damage to Your Work

60. Read the **Damage to Your Work** exclusion.

    This exclusion applies to **damage to the insured's work**, as defined in the policy, arising from it or any part of it, *and* limited to work that falls within the products-completed operations hazard. You already learned about the damage to property exclusion, which covers work in progress that is not yet completed.

    Considering only the first paragraph of this exclusion, assume the insured is a plumber, hired to handle all of the plumbing for a new residence. The job is completed, and shortly afterward, a pipe breaks because the plumber incorrectly installed a coupling. Not only is the pipe damaged, but there is also damage to the floors, walls and carpeting from the water that escaped.

    Which of the following damaged items will *not* be covered by the plumber's CGL?

    A. Damage to the pipe
    B. Water damage to the floors
    C. Water damage to the walls
    D. Water damage to the carpeting

    Answer: A is correct. This exclusion applies only to the insured's work that falls within the products-completed operations hazard.

61. The second paragraph of the Damage to Your Work exclusion, along with a change in circumstances, can alter how the CGL coverage applies. Remember that the definition of *your work* specifically includes work performed on the insured's behalf, possibly by a subcontractor. However, this paragraph says that in some cases, a subcontractor's work will *not* place the insured at a disadvantage under the CGL.

    Let's see how this might work in relation to the plumber in an earlier example. Assume that the plumber, who is the insured, is held liable for the subcontractor's work in the situation described in the following paragraph.

The plumber is acting in the capacity of a general plumbing contractor, but actually performs only the finish plumbing work—sinks, toilets, bathtubs, and shower stalls. Another plumber, who is not employed by the insured, is the subcontractor who installs the pipes, water lines, and taps.

A. If the same unfortunate event occurs with the broken pipe as described earlier, is there coverage for the cost of the damaged pipe?
( ) Yes   ( ) No   Why? _____

_____

B. Continuing with the same plumbing scenario, suppose this broken pipe, installed by a subcontractor, also resulted in damage to wood cabinets in the bathroom that were installed by the insured, the general plumbing contractor. The CGL (would/would not) _____
_____ cover damage to the cabinets because _____
_____.

C. Let's consider another scenario. This time, the insured, the general plumbing contractor, installs the pipes, water lines, and taps. The subcontractor, on the other hand, installs the finish plumbing, including the cabinets. The same damage occurs. In this situation the CGL will cover damages to the (pipes/cabinets) _____
but not to the (pipes/cabinets) _____ because

_____

_____.

D. Finally, if any of the previously described situations happen while the work is in progress, rather than after the work has been completed, which of the following is true?

1. The damage to your work exclusion applies.

2. The damage to property exclusion applies.

3. No exclusion applies.

Answer: A. Yes. The damage arose from part of the subcontractor's work, so the exclusion does not apply; B. would, because the damage arose out of the subcontractor's work, not the insured's work; C. (will cover) cabinets (but will not cover) pipes (because) damage to the insured's work arising out of his work is excluded, while damage to the subcontractor's work arising out of the insured's work is not excluded; D. 2 is correct.

Damage to Impaired Property or Property not Physically Injured

62. The **Damage to Impaired Property or Property Not Physically Injured** exclusion is sometimes referred to as the **failure to perform** exclusion. Read this exclusion carefully before continuing.

While impaired property essentially refers to the loss of use of tangible property, this exclusion encompasses other property damage as well, including damage to property that is not physically harmed.

The latter part of the exclusion appears to be aimed at diluting the effect of court decisions regarding diminution of value of property that is not otherwise harmed. Court decisions about diminution of value have had the effect of providing unintended coverage for what might be called the risk of doing business. Briefly, such decisions held that if a bad job, such as poor brick veneering, diminished the value of the building, even in the absence of any other physical injury to the building, the cost of replacing the veneer was covered under the liability policy.

This exclusion treats such a situation where the property has not actually been physically injured by (excluding/including) _____ it, so that a diminution in value judgment (does/does not) _____ trigger coverage under the CGL.

Answer: excluding, does not

63. For both impaired property and property that has not been physically injured, damages excluded arise from one of two general conditions. The first involves a **defect, deficiency, inadequacy, or dangerous condition**. Any of these circumstances must exist in relation to the insured's product or work for the exclusion to apply. If the problem is in something other than the insured's product or work, this exclusion does not apply.

Suppose the insured's product is a pump used in conjunction with another piece of machinery that separates liquids of different chemical makeup in a research laboratory. When attached to this machinery, the pump is designed to pump out only certain liquids. When one of these pumps is put to use at Quest Laboratories, a defect causes it to pump out *all* liquids, rather than just the selected one. Days of use of the machinery are lost as a result of this defect because the process cannot be completed without a properly operating pump. The laboratory sues the insured, and the insured is found liable for the loss of revenue and the expenses incurred before the defect was discovered. The insured's CGL (will/will not) _____ cover this loss because _____
_____.

Answer: will not, because the loss occurred to impaired property as a result of a defect in the insured's work, which is excluded.

64. The second situation that can trigger this exclusion is a **delay or failure to perform a contract**— either by the insured or someone acting on behalf of the insured.

The grand opening of the local symphony's new home, Harrington Hall, is scheduled for December 31 in upper Wisconsin. The symphony group is counting on attendance at this event to provide a major portion of its fundraising for the following season. Unfortunately, Natural Gas of the

North, the company responsible for connecting the natural gas heating lines to Harrington Hall, has misplaced the work order and is unaware that its contract agrees to have the Hall heated comfortably for an 8:00 pm performance. When the temperature dips to minus 25 degrees Fahrenheit, the performance must be canceled. The symphony sues Natural Gas of the North for the lost revenues. Will Natural Gas's CGL cover this loss if the company is found liable?   ( ) Yes   ( ) No   Why?_____

Answer: No. Failure to perform as agreed in a contract resulting in damage is excluded.

Recall of Products, Work, or Impaired Property

65. This exclusion is sometimes referred to as the **sistership exclusion**. Before you read it, here is a brief background about the term *sistership*.

    In the aircraft industry, if a plane crashes because of a defect, all similar planes—called sisterships—might be recalled to assure that they do not have the same type of defect. These recalls, while costly, do not represent the type of loss anticipated by liability policies. Because similar recall costs could occur in many industries, an exclusion was added to liability policies in the mid-1960s to exclude this type of coverage, and the term *sistership liability* was born, even though the products might be something other than air "ships."

    Now read the **Recall of Products, Work, or Impaired Property** exclusion.

    This exclusion categorically excludes coverage for losses, costs, or expenses resulting from sistership situations, regardless of who is responsible for the recall, withdrawal, or other contingencies mentioned in the exclusion.

    Suppose United American Motorcar Company produces the new JZ500 sports car, which soon gains a reputation for having a faulty firewall. All JZ500s are withdrawn from the market, incurring tremendous expense to the company, which is the insured, as well as to many retail dealers and producers of other parts for the car. Under which of the following circumstances is coverage for these losses excluded by the CGL?

    A. If the federal government ordered the withdrawal

    B. If the company voluntarily withdrew the cars

    C. If the withdrawn cars are found to be faulty

    D. If the withdrawn cars are not found to be faulty

    E. All of these losses are excluded by the CGL.

Answer: E is correct.

Personal and Advertising Injury

66. Read the **Personal and Advertising Injury** exclusion. You may also want to review the definition of personal and advertising injury before you continue.

    Bodily injury that is a consequence of personal and advertising injury is *not* covered by Coverage A. This type of bodily injury can be covered only under Coverage B, which you will study in a later unit.

    The owner of Sparkling Jewels, the insured, accused Lefty Sykes of pocketing a diamond ring from the insured's jewelry store. When the police arrested him, Lefty bumped his head on the squad car and needed stitches. After Lefty was found innocent and released, he sued the jeweler for false arrest.

    Would the expenses for Lefty's stitches be covered under Coverage A?
    ( ) Yes   ( ) No   Explain. _____

    _____

    Answer: No. Coverage A excludes bodily injury that arises from personal and advertising injury, such as false arrest.

Electronic Data

67. The final Coverage A exclusion applies to **electronic data**. Read this exclusion now.

    The insured, an Internet service provider, releases a program update that, unbeknownst to the insured, contains a virus that destroys all data on computers on which the update is installed. Several customers who installed the update sue the insured. Would the insured's CGL cover the damages arising out of this suit?   ( ) Yes   ( ) No

    Answer: No

Fire Damage Exception

68. The final paragraph of the Coverage A exclusions provides an exception that permits limited fire legal liability coverage. Read this final paragraph, and then answer the following questions.

    A. Which exclusions are excepted?_____

    B. Only two types of premises have this fire damage coverage. What are they?

        1. _____

        2. _____

    Answer: A. Exclusions c through n; B. (In either order) 1. Premises rented to the insured; 2. Premises temporarily occupied by the insured with the owner's permission.

69. This exception does *not* apply to Exclusion a, expected or intended injury or Exclusion b, contractual liability, but a brief discussion is in order because the contractual liability exclusion can cause confusion in relation to this paragraph.

    You will recall that an insured is charged with some types of liability even in the absence of a contract assuming liability. One type is that which arises from a fire resulting from the insured's *negligence*. Therefore, if an insured were negligent with premises rented to her or temporarily occupied by her with the owner's permission, liability would exist with or without a contract.

    On the other hand, in the absence of any contract assuming liability, and in the absence of a situation where the insured would have been liable anyway, the CGL does *not* protect against fire damage.

    The insured is renting a building. Assuming all other policy requirements are met, if a fire for which the insured is legally liable occurs on the rented premises, would the contractual liability exclusion apply?
    ( ) Yes   ( ) No   Explain your answer. _____

    _____

    Answer: No. The contractual liability exclusion does not apply to liability that the insured would have had in the absence of a contract or agreement, such as negligence.

    Now that you've analyzed Coverage A of the CGL, you're ready to go on to the next unit, where you'll study Coverages B and C and the Supplementary Payments section.

6

The Occurrence Form Section I: Coverages B, C, and Supplementary Payments

COVERAGE B: PERSONAL AND ADVERTISING INJURY LIABILITY

Insuring Agreement

1. The second of the three types of coverages provided by the CGL is Coverage B: Personal and Advertising Injury Liability. Locate this section in your sample policy and read Item 1.a of the insuring agreement, including the subparagraphs and the final paragraph under (2).

   Because this section of the Coverage B insuring agreement is essentially the same as the insuring agreement for Coverage A, we will not review the same material. The major difference in the insuring agreements is that, instead of bodily injury and property damage coverage, the insuring agreement for coverage B provides coverage for _____ injury.

   Answer: personal and advertising

2. Take a minute to refresh your memory about the definitions of **personal and advertising injury** and **advertisement** before continuing.

   Although bodily injury is primarily covered in Coverage A of the CGL, one specific type of bodily injury is covered under Coverage B. According to the definition of personal and advertising injury, any consequential bodily injury that results from personal and advertising injury is covered under Coverage B: Personal and Advertising Injury Liability, rather than under Coverage A: Bodily Injury and Property Damage Liability.

   Suppose that someone suffers a broken arm while being falsely arrested and sues the insured for damages.

   A. In this example, would damages for the claimant's broken arm likely be covered under the insured's CGL?   ( ) Yes   ( ) No

   B. Under which section of the CGL would this bodily injury be covered?
      1. Coverage A: Bodily Injury and Property Damage Liability
      2. Coverage B: Personal and Advertising Injury Liability
      3. Coverage C: Medical Payments

   Answer: A. Yes; B. 2 is correct. The broken arm is a consequential bodily injury that falls under Coverage B.

3. Read Item 1.b.

   Item 1.b details the coverage trigger for personal and advertising injury. We learn that the offense must arise from the conduct of the insured's business.

Which of the following represent personal and advertising injury offenses arising out of the conduct of the insured's business?

A. Gary, who lives next door to the insured's residence, sues Trevor, the insured. Gary claims Trevor told all their neighbors lies that slandered him. Trevor is found liable.

B. The insured rents housing properties at various locations in her city. When a tenant misses a rent payment, the insured has him evicted two days later, even though a contract exists that prevents eviction so quickly. The insured is found liable in a suit for wrongful eviction.

C. The insured takes out a full-page advertisement stating that her health food store is superior to that of her competitor whom, she claims without giving evidence, sells contaminated and dangerous items. The competitor sues, and the insured is found guilty of libel.

Answer: B and C are correct. A is not correct because the offense does not arise out of the insured's business.

4. Item 1.b also indicates that, for coverage to apply, an offense must have been committed subject to two important conditions. What are they?

A. _____

B. _____

Answer: (In either order) A. The offense must have been committed in the coverage territory; B. The offense must have been committed during the policy period.

Coverage B Exclusions

5. Read the first exclusion that applies to personal and advertising injury, Item 2.a, **Knowing Violation of Rights of Another**, as well as Item 2.d, **Criminal Acts**.

In the insuring agreement and in the definition of personal and advertising injury, you may have noticed that the CGL uses the term **offense** rather than the term **occurrence**, which is typical in other sections of the form. The term *offense* is used here because personal and advertising actions are *intentional* offenses rather than occurrences, which are accidents. For example, eviction, publishing advertisements, and having someone arrested are all intentional actions.

Even though the CGL allows coverage for personal and advertising intended actions, it does not allow coverage for injuries resulting from actions that violate the rights of another. Nor does the CGL cover intentional criminal acts by the insured or directed by the insured.

Consider an insured, Sylvan Batista, whose business is leasing residential buildings he owns. Batista operates in a state that has a law against eviction accompanied by breach of the peace, such as physical violence. This law carries up to a $10,000 fine for a violation. Batista knows about the leasing laws in his state. One of Batista's tenants is six weeks behind in his rent, and Batista goes to the tenant's apartment to discuss the situation. The tenant refuses to pay because Batista has not fixed a long-standing plumbing problem. Tempers flare during the discussion, and Batista punches the tenant in the eye. While the tenant is seeking medical attention at a nearby emergency facility, Batista evicts him, moving the tenant's personal property out of the building. The tenant sues for wrongful eviction.

The landlord's CGL (will/will not) _____ cover this liability because _____

_____.

Answer: will not, because the insured both violated the tenant's rights and intentionally committed a criminal act

6. Read Item 2.b, **Material Published with Knowledge of Falsity**.

Both **oral** and **written publication** of any material that causes injury are excluded if the insured knows the information is false and does it or orders it done anyway.

Suppose the insured, Calorie Kitchens, produces what it claims is a revolutionary new, low calorie, healthful line of desserts. The insured relies on a testing service's report that consumers prefer the insured's product three to one over the insured's best-known competitor. Calorie Kitchens advertises that information in the media, along with purported consumer comments that in comparison, the competitor's products were unappealing. Unfortunately, the testing service was unscrupulous, and in fact, taste tests showed consumers liked the competitor's product better. During the advertising blitz, the competitor lost significant revenue as a result of the insured's advertising and sues the insured. Calorie Kitchens is found liable for the damages.

A. The insured's CGL (will/will not) _____ apply because _____

_____

_____.

B. If Calorie Kitchens had known the information was false and allowed the advertising to be used anyway, coverage for the injury (would/ would not) _____ be excluded.

Answer: A. will, because the insured was not aware that the information advertised was not true; B. would

7. Read Item 2.c, **Material Published Prior to Policy Period**.

Considering this exclusion, and continuing with the situation previously described, suppose Calorie Kitchen's CGL has an effective date of April 1.

The claim for injury is made the following June 15. The advertisement was first used the previous February 10. Is coverage excluded in this case? ( ) Yes   ( ) No   Why? _____

_____

Answer: Yes. First publication occurred before the beginning of the policy period.

8. Read Item 2.e, **Contractual Liability**.

This part of the exclusion deals with **contractual liability** assumed by the insured, a subject also discussed in the exclusions under Coverage A.

What is the only exception to the exclusion of coverage of personal and advertising injury for which the insured has assumed liability in a contract or agreement? _____

_____

Answer: Such damages are covered only if the insured would be held liable for the damages even if the contract or agreement did not exist.

9. Read Exclusion 2.f, **Breach of Contract**.

Personal and advertising injury that arises from **breach of contract** is not covered in most instances.

Suppose the insured, Francesca Pirelli, is a furniture retailer who is advertising a sale to rid herself of older inventory. Pirelli has a contract with High-Style Furnishings that says she will not sell their line at lower than their suggested retail price without HighStyle's permission. When she includes some HighStyle furniture in an advertisement at 40% off, the HighStyle company sues her for breach of contract. Will Pirelli's CGL defend this claim?   ( ) Yes   ( ) No   Why? _____

_____

Answer: No. Breach of contract is generally excluded.

10. Although breach of contract is generally excluded, Item 2.f indicates that using another's advertising idea under an **implied contract** *is* covered. Let's change some of the elements of the previous example to see how this might work.

Suppose that in its own advertising, HighStyle Furnishings calls its products the *Crème de la Crème* of furnishings and uses a related symbol as a trademark. Before they are allowed to represent HighStyle, retailers must agree that any advertising be approved by HighStyle to avoid lowering HighStyle's standards and to avoid conflicts with HighStyle's own advertising.

Pirelli takes it upon herself to design an advertisement in which she claims her furniture store can save shoppers hundreds of dollars by skimming off the *Crème de la Crème*. HighStyle is very offended and takes Pirelli to court claiming they have an implied contractual agreement not to use HighStyle's trademark in a disparaging manner. Pirelli's CGL insurer (will/will not) _____ defend this claim because _____

_____

_____.

Answer: will, because it involves the use of advertising ideas under an implied contract.

11. Read Items 2.g, **Quality or Performance of Goods—Failure to Conform to Statements**, and 2.h, **Wrong Description of Prices**.
    Excluded from personal and advertising injury coverage are:

    ■ failure of any insured's goods, products, or services to be what the insured advertised them to be and

    ■ a wrong price included in the insured's advertisement.

    A. An insured car dealer advertises that a particular auto gets 45 miles per gallon of gasoline. A buyer sues the dealer when the car fails to get that kind of mileage. The CGL (will/will not) _____ defend such a claim.

    B. The same car dealer places an advertisement offering a brake job for $50. Because of a printer's error, the brake job is advertised for $5. When the dealer refuses to honor the $5 price, a customer sues. Will the CGL defend that claim?   ( ) Yes   ( ) No

    Answer: A. will not; B. No

12. The next exclusion is the first of four that consider Internet exposures. Read Exclusion 2.i, **Infringement of Copyright, Patent, Trademark, or Trade Secret**.
    Excluded from coverage are personal and advertising injuries that are the result of infringement of the intellectual property rights of copyrights, patents, trademarks, and trade secrets. This exclusion, however, does not apply to the infringement of copyright, trade dress or slogan in the insured's own advertisement.

For which of the following might an insured find coverage under the CGL form?

A. The insured was sued for posting a copyrighted article on his company's Website without permission.

B. The insured's television advertisement used a slogan and product colors that were similar to a competitor's advertisement. The competitor sued the insured for infringement of slogan and trade dress.

C. A month before a competitor's release of a new product, the insured released a very similar product. The competitor sued the insured for allegedly stealing trade secrets.

Answer: B is correct. The exclusion of copyright, trade dress, or slogan infringement does not apply to the insured's own advertisement.

13. Read Item 2.j, **Insureds in Media and Internet Type Businesses.**
    Personal and advertising injury liability coverage is not designed for the media because its chance of loss is much greater than that of other business risks. Advertising agencies, publishers, broadcasters, and telecasters must look to special insurance protection for this particular liability exposure.

    This exclusion applies to

    A. television and radio stations.

    B. newspapers, magazines, and other periodicals.

    C. anyone who prepares advertising for others.

    D. any business that advertises through the media.

    E. Internet Service Providers (ISPs).

    F. companies that provide Internet search services.

    G. businesses that design Website content for others.

    Answer: A, B, C, E, F, and G are correct. An insured that advertises is covered for personal and advertising injury as long as her company isn't a media or Internet-type business.

14. Some personal and advertising coverage, however, is available for people in a media or Internet-type business. Look over the first three items in the definition of personal and advertising injury. As Item 2.j indicates, coverage is available to insureds in these businesses for some of the items in the definition.

    For which of the following personal and advertising injuries might an insured broadcaster be covered under the CGL?

    A. Copyright infringement

    B. False arrest

    C. Wrongful eviction

    D. Slander

    E. Malicious prosecution

Answer: B, C, and E are correct.

15. Review the last paragraph of Exclusion 2.j, which clarifies what is *not*, by itself, considered to be the business of advertising, broadcasting, publishing, or telecasting.

    Which of these activities, when they are peripheral to an insured's business, might be covered?

    A. Placing a link from the insured's Website to another company's site, with that company's permission
    B. Putting a blue frame around the featured product of the month on the insured's company Website
    C. Posting a banner advertisement across the bottom of the insured's Website
    D. Displaying the insured's advertisement in a space purchased on another company's Website

    Answer: All of these activities might be covered when the insured is not in a media or Internet-type business.

16. Now read Exclusion k, **Electronic Chatrooms or Bulletin Boards.**

    Suppose that an insured hosts an electronic bulletin board. Is the insured's liability as a publisher covered?   ( ) Yes   ( ) No

    Answer: No

17. The last exclusion related to the Internet is Item l, **Unauthorized Use of Another's Name or Product.** Read that item, and then answer the following question.

    Suppose that the insured has created a brand new company Website. Anxious to attract potential customers, the insured registers the site's domain name as *insure4less*, knowing full well that the domain name of a successful competitor is *insureforless*. When the company that sponsors *insureforless* sues the insured, might the insured's CGL respond?   ( ) Yes   ( ) No

    Answer: No. Personal and advertising injury that arises from intentional tactics such as this, meant to divert another company's customers, is excluded.

18. Exclusions 2.m and 2.n address pollution losses. Read these exclusions before continuing.

    Logically, one is likely to associate pollution with Coverage A: Bodily Injury and Property Damage Liability. Although infrequent, there have been some cases where insureds were able to recover pollution liability losses under earlier versions of the CGL's Coverage B because the policy's definition of personal and advertising injury refers to wrongful entry into another's premises.

    Newer editions of the CGL now contain a pollution exclusion in Coverage B to prevent insureds from obtaining personal or advertising injury coverage for pollution liability. Also included is an exclusion for clean-up costs, Item 2.n, which is basically the same as the exclusion found in Coverage A.

    The CGL's pollution exclusion applies to

    A. Coverage A only.

    B. Coverage B only.

    C. both Coverage A and Coverage B.

    Answer: C is correct.

19. The final Coverage B exclusion excludes personal and advertising injury losses arising out of war. Read exclusion o. **War** before continuing.

    An individual claiming to belong to a terrorist organization sends an anonymous letter threatening to blow up the insured's building. After receiving the threat, the company's security personnel locks down the building and detains an individual who tries to enter the building because they believe his actions are suspicious. After questioning, it is determined that the individual is not a member of a terrorist organization but is, instead, an employee's spouse who had arrived to take her to lunch. He later sues the insured for false detainment. Would this loss be covered under Coverage B of the insured's CGL?   ( ) Yes   ( ) No

    Answer: No

COVERAGE C: MEDICAL PAYMENTS

Covered Medical Expenses

20. The third and final type of coverage provided by the commercial general liability coverage forms is for **medical payments.** Payment for medical expenses is available *without regard to who is at fault*. If other policy requirements are met, the CGL will cover these expenses even if the insured would not have been held liable.

Medical expenses include these items:

Medical Expenses

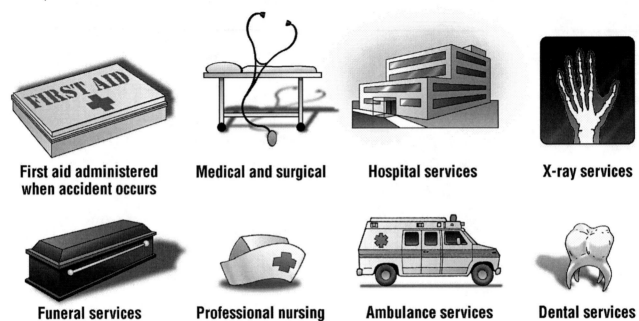

First aid administered when accident occurs

Medical and surgical

Hospital services

X-ray services

Funeral services

Professional nursing

Ambulance services

Dental services

Assuming all other requirements are met, which of the following would the CGL cover under Coverage C?

A. An ambulance called to the insured's premises to take an injured person to an emergency room

B. Replacement of an injured person's dentures when they are broken in an accident on the insured's premises

C. First aid products the insured, a medical supplies retailer, sends to the site of a downstate flood

D. Charges by a nearby hospital for emergency outpatient services to an insured's injured customer

Answer: A, B, and D are correct. Choice C is not correct because the first aid was not administered at the time of the accident.

Insuring Agreement

21. Read all of the Coverage C insuring agreement, Items 1.a and 1.b, in your sample policy.

    In general, medical payments coverage is intended to pay for medical expenses incurred by members of the public who suffer bodily injury that is otherwise covered in the CGL. The insuring agreement indicates that to be covered, the injury must arise from an accident that occurs:

■ on premises the insured owns or rents;

■ adjacent to premises the insured owns or rents; or

■ because of the insured's operations.

Note that there is no requirement that the injury occur because of the insured's operations on or adjacent to the premises. Rather, a covered situation could arise where an individual was injured on the premises, but not because of the insured's operations. Conversely, an accident might occur because of the insured's operations, but not on or adjacent to the premises. Both situations would be protected under Coverage C.

The insured owns a retail store. Which of the following events would be covered by Coverage C?

A. A shopper in the insured's store is injured when a fleeing bank robber decides to use the insured's store as a shortcut escape route. The robber shoves the shopper into a display that falls and injures the shopper.

B. Continuing with the situation described in A, another shopper rips her jacket on the fallen display while attempting to help the injured person.

C. A shopper who has not yet entered the insured's store falls on the sidewalk in front of the store, injuring his arm on the sidewalk.

D. The insured is a participant in a retail fair taking place in an open-air pavilion several miles from the insured's premises. While looking over some of the insured's goods at the fair, a shopper trips and is injured when she falls into the insured's merchandise.

Answer: A, C, and D are covered. B is not covered because no bodily injury is involved.

22. Other conditions that must be met for Coverage C to apply appear after Item 1.a.(3), preceded by the words "provided that." Refer to this section as needed to answer the following questions.

A. The accident must occur (where?) _____ and (when?) _____.

B. Expenses associated with the injury must be incurred *and* reported ___ _____ _____.

C. If the insurance company so desires, the insured person must agree to be examined by physicians. These examinations will be paid for by _____ and the physicians will be selected by _____.

Answer: A. in the coverage territory, during the policy period; B. within one year of the date the accident occurs; C. the insurer, the insurer

Coverage C Exclusions

23. Certain persons and certain acts do not qualify for medical payments coverage. Following is a summary of the conditions that preclude coverage.

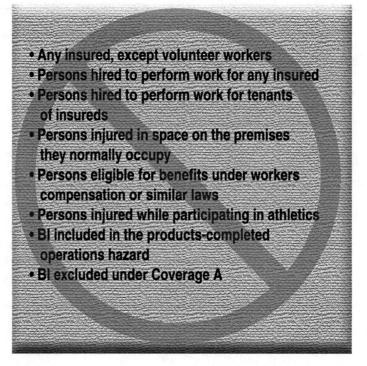

• Any insured, except volunteer workers
• Persons hired to perform work for any insured
• Persons hired to perform work for tenants of insureds
• Persons injured in space on the premises they normally occupy
• Persons eligible for benefits under workers compensation or similar laws
• Persons injured while participating in athletics
• BI included in the products-completed operations hazard
• BI excluded under Coverage A

Based on the illustration, decide which of the following are *not* eligible for medical payments coverage under Coverage C.

A. A shopper is injured in the insured's retail store when a box falls on him from an overhead shelf.

B. The insured sponsors a foot race on the land surrounding his retail store. A participant is injured during the race.

C. An individual hired by the insured to paint her business office falls off a ladder and is injured.

D. One of the insured's employees is injured while on the job.

Answer: B, C, and D are excluded from coverage.

Any Insured

24. Let's look at some specific applications of the Coverage C exclusions. Read all of the Coverage C exclusions, and refer to them as needed as you complete this section.

You know that any insured is ineligible for medical payments coverage. While you have not yet learned the complete list of people who can be considered insureds under the CGL, we have mentioned that employees qualify. Partners and spouses are also considered insureds. This means that the exclusion does not apply only to the *named insured.*

You studied the definition of volunteer workers. They also are considered insureds while performing duties related to the insured's business. Volunteer workers, however, as you see in Item 2.a, are an exception to this medical payments exclusion.

A. Margaret Parsons is the named insured. Her husband, Eldridge, who is not employed by Margaret's business, is helping Margaret stock shelves one weekend. If Eldridge suffers a bodily injury requiring first aid while on Margaret's premises, will the medical payments coverage be available for this injury?   ( ) Yes   ( ) No

B. The insured asked volunteers from the Reading Is Fun organization to set up a book fair at the insured's publishing offices. While unloading the books, one volunteer dropped a carton on her foot and had to be taken to the hospital for x-rays. Will the medical payments coverage be available for these expenses?   ( ) Yes   ( ) No

Answer: A. No. Spouses are considered insureds and therefore, are excluded from medical payments coverage; B. Yes. Volunteers are covered for bodily injury while they are performing duties directed by the insured.

Hired Person

25. Per Item 2.b, there is no coverage for someone who has been hired to work for or on behalf of the insured or a tenant.

Suppose the insured is Bigtime Holding Corporation, which leases space in its building to the Cosmic Corals Company. Cosmic Corals hires a decorating contractor to make some changes in its office. One of the decorator's workers is injured in Cosmic Corals' suites during the redecoration and requires first aid. Will Bigtime Holding Corporation's CGL cover these expenses?   ( ) Yes   ( ) No   Why?_____

_____

Answer: No. The injured person was hired to do work for a tenant of the insured.

Injury on Normally Occupied Premises

26. People who normally occupy any part of premises the insured owns or rents are ineligible, according to Item 2.c.

Suppose the injured person in the previous exercise was *not* an employee of the decorator, but was the president of Cosmic Corals. In this situation, medical payments coverage (is/is not) _____ available because _____

_____

_____.

Answer: is not, because the injured person normally occupies the premises owned by the insured

Workers' Compensation and Similar Laws

27. Exclusion 2.d is similar to the one we discussed under Coverage A for injuries normally covered by workers' compensation insurance.

    In an earlier exercise, we used an example of a decorator's employee who was injured while doing work for the insured's tenant.

    A. If this employee is required to be covered by workers' compensation by the decorator's business, the insured's CGL (would/would not) _____ provide medical payments.

    B. Suppose the decorator was supposed to provide workers' compensation benefits, but did not. In this case will the insured's CGL cover the injury?   ( ) Yes   ( ) No   Explain your answer.

    _____

    _____

    _____

    _____

Answer: A. would not; B. No. Coverage is barred in two ways. First, this exclusion applies if benefits must be provided, not just if they are provided. Second, Exclusion 2.b would also preclude coverage.

Athletics Activities

28. Exclusion 2.e **Athletics Activities** excludes coverage for any person injured while practicing, instructing, or participating in any physical exercises, games, sports, or athletic contests.

    Who of the following would be excluded from medical payments coverage?

    A. Members of a Little League baseball team sponsored by the insured's business

    B. A professional basketball player whose team was hired by the insured to play for a charity event

    C. An Olympic swimmer competing in a pool provided by the insured's facility

    D. All of these would be excluded from medical payments coverage.

Answer: D is correct.

Other Exclusions

29. The remaining Coverage C exclusions include elements that were discussed in the context of Coverage A.

    Exclusion 2.f eliminates coverage for any medical expenses associated with the **products-completed operations hazard**. These costs would be included in Coverage A, subject to its exclusions.

    Exclusion 2.g excludes anything that is listed under the **Coverage A exclusions**.

    Coverage for medical expenses associated with the products-completed operations hazard (is/is not) _____ available under Coverage C.

    Answer: is not

SUPPLEMENTARY PAYMENTS: COVERAGES A AND B

30. Under some conditions, the CGL will pay additional amounts known as **supplementary payments.** These are paid *in addition to* the amounts paid for liability claims under Coverages A and B and do not reduce the limits of insurance available for these coverages.

Supplementary Payments

- Expenses the insurer incurs
- Cost of bail bonds up to $250 for violations arising from vehicles to which BI coverage applies
- Cost of bonds to release attachments
- Expenses the insured incurs at the insurer's request
- Up to $250 a day for the insured's lost earnings because of time off from work to assist in investigation or defense
- Costs taxed against the insured
- Prejudgment interest the insured is required to pay
- Interest that accrues after a judgment and before it is paid, offered or deposited in court
- Defense costs for an indemnitee

Which of the following would be paid as supplementary payments?

A. At the insurer's request, the insured lost three days' wages totaling $300 while working with the insurance company attorneys to prepare a defense.

B. The insurance company pays travel expenses for a witness it wants at a trial involving the insured.

C. At his own initiative, the insured takes a plane from Philadelphia to Louisville to talk with a witness about testifying on the insured's behalf at an upcoming liability trial.

D. When one of the insured's vehicles to which BI coverage applies is involved in an accident causing injury to a third party, the insured is required to post a $100 bail bond.

Answer: A, B, and D are correct. C is not correct because the expenses were not incurred at the insurer's request.

31. The Supplementary Payments section of the CGL appears after the Coverage C exclusions. Read only Items 1.a, b, and c.

    Item 1.b lists very stringent requirements for bail bonds. One must be cautious here because only certain vehicles have bodily injury liability coverage under the CGL. For example, if the valet parking attendant for the insured causes an accident while parking a customer's car and is arrested, requiring a bail bond, the CGL will cover the cost.

    The insured is arrested when he causes an accident while driving his company-owned car. He is required to pay a bail bond for his arrest. Would the CGL cover this bail bond?   ( ) Yes   ( ) No   Why? _____
    _____
    _____

    Answer: No. Autos owned by and operated by the insured are excluded.

32. Item 1.c addresses the possibility that an insured's property might be **attached**, or legally taken from the insured, pending the outcome of a suit. The CGL will pay the cost of the bonds to release any attachments, within limits. If a bond exceeds the policy limits of liability, its cost will not be covered.

    Assume that an insured's policy limits total $500,000. The insured must post a $1 million bond to release attachments on her property. Will the cost of the bond be paid by the CGL Supplementary Payments provision? ( ) Yes   ( ) No   Why? _____

    Answer: No. The cost of the bond is more than the policy limits.

Defense Costs

33. The next four items address amounts commonly known as **defense costs**—money spent to defend a claim or suit, plus settlements and judgments. Read Items 1.d and e of the Supplementary Payments section.

    Which of the following expenses would be *fully* paid under the Supplementary Payments provision?

    A. The insured spends $60 on gasoline while transporting witnesses the insurance company asked her to bring to the trial of the liability suit against her.

    B. The insured loses $300 a day in wages for four days. The four days were spent, at the insurance company's request, working with its lawyers and witnesses to prepare a defense.

    C. At his own initiative, the insured flies from Portland, Oregon, to Miami Beach to talk with a witness about testifying on his behalf at an upcoming liability trial.

    D. Costs totaling $9,000 are taxed against the insured as a result of a suit the insurer is defending.

    Answer: A and D are fully covered. B is partially covered, to the limit of $250 per day. C is not covered because the insurer did not ask the insured to make the trip.

34. Read Items 1.f and g of the Supplementary Payments section.

    The essence of these two items is that any interest due on a judgment will be paid, with two exceptions. The first exception involves **prejudgment interest.** Prejudgment interest is an amount—usually a percentage of the final judgment in a claimant's favor—that the claimant requests in addition to the judgment itself.

    The premise behind prejudgment interest is that the claimant could have had use of the money from the date of loss to the date of the award if the claim had been settled earlier. As a result, the claimant should be awarded interest for the period when the money was not available. Prejudgment interest might or might not be awarded when it is requested, but it is *never* awarded if the claimant does not ask for it.

    If awarded, the interest is covered here, with one exception. The exception occurs when the insurer offers to settle a suit for the policy limit out of court and the claimant refuses. In this case, if prejudgment interest is awarded at trial, the insurer pays interest only up to the date the settlement was offered.

    Petrowski sues the insured for a loss that occurred on January 12. On April 3, the insurer offers to settle with Petrowski for the policy limits. Petrowski refuses. On November 11, a court finds in Petrowski's favor and awards prejudgment interest as well. The CGL will pay prejudgment interest for

    A. the period from January 12 to April 3.

    B. the period from April 3 to November 11.

    C. the period from January 12 to November 11.

Answer: A is correct.

35. Generally, the insurance company is responsible for all interest due on the entire judgment, even though the judgment exceeds the policy's limits of liability. But a second exception applies.

Suppose a judgment of $900,000 exceeds the policy's $750,000 limit of liability. The insurer will pay interest on the entire $900,000 up to the time when the insurer actually pays, offers to pay, or deposits with the court the $750,000 policy limit. It will not, however, pay any interest on the remaining $150,000, regardless of how much time passes before the claimant receives that amount from the insured.

A suit defended by the insured's CGL insurer results in a $1 million judgment. The policy limit is $500,000. Interest payable to the claimant accrues from July 9, the date the award is made, until July 30, the date the insurer pays the full policy limits.

A. The insurance company will pay interest on ($1 million/$500,000/neither amount) _____.

B. The insured does not pay the claimant the remaining $500,000 until August 20. For the period between July 30 and August 20, the insurance company will pay interest on ($1 million/$500,000/neither amount) _____.

Answer: A. $1 million; B. neither amount

36. In a previous unit, you learned that a third party's defense costs assumed by the insured under an insured contract are covered damages if they are incurred when the insurer defends the third party against a loss that is insured by the policy. Because these costs are classified as covered damages, they will reduce the policy's limit of liability. The final section of the Supplementary Payments section provides that, if certain conditions are met, the insurer will:

■ pay the defense costs for an **indemnitee** (a party who is not an insured but who is under contract to provide goods or services to an insured) **in addition to** the policy's limit of liability; and

■ provide a defense for the indemnitee.

Read the first paragraph of Item 2. in the Supplementary Payments section.

The following conditions must be met before the insurer will provide a defense for the indemnitee.

■ Both the insured and the indemnitee are named in the same lawsuit.

■ The insured has assumed the indemnitee's liability for bodily injury or property damage AND liability for the indemnitee's defense in the same insured contract.

- The liability assumed by the insured is covered by the policy.

- There is no conflict of interest between the insured and the indemnitee.

- Both the indemnitee and the insured ask the insurer to defend the indemnitee in the suit and agree that the same attorney may be used to defend both parties.

The insurer will provide a defense for an indemnitee if certain conditions are met. Which one of the following is NOT one of those conditions?

A. The insured and the indemnitee may not be represented by the same attorney.

B. The insured and the indemnitee must be named in the same suit.

C. The insured has assumed the indemnitee's liability for bodily injury or property damage AND liability for the indemnitee's defense in the same insured contract.

D. There is no conflict of interest between the insured and the indemnitee.

E. The liability assumed by the insured is covered by the policy.

Answer: A is correct. The insured and the indemnitee must agree to be represented by the same attorney.

37. Read the remainder of the Supplementary Payments section.

In addition to the conditions we have already discussed, the indemnitee must also agree in writing to cooperate with the insurer in defending the suit and provide the insurer with any records and documents related to the suit. If there is other insurance available, the indemnitee must contact those insurers and help coordinate the other coverage with that provided by the CGL.

A CGL insurer has agreed to defend an indemnitee in a lawsuit. The indemnitee has other insurance coverage that applies to the suit. The indemnitee must

A. agree not to use the other coverage to pay any part of the claim.

B. contact the other insurer and help coordinate that coverage with the coverage provided by the CGL.

Answer: B is correct.

This concludes your review of Coverages B and C and the Supplementary Payments section. In the next unit, you will learn who are considered insureds under the policy.

UNIT

7

The Occurrence Form Section II: Who Is an Insured

INTRODUCTION

1. We have previously discussed specifically who is a named insured, as well as the fact that employees are, in some cases, considered insureds. Now we will look closely at exactly who may be considered insureds and under what conditions, as indicated in the CGL coverage form Section II: Who Is an Insured. Locate Section II in your sample CGL occurrence form.

   We will follow a slightly different format for your study in this unit. The information about insureds is listed in two tables. Table 1 covers Item 1 of Section II; Table 2 covers Items 2 and 3. You will study Table 1 briefly and then refer to it to answer a series of questions. You may also refer to your sample form at any time.

   After you have completed the questions covering Table 1, you will go on to Table 2 and follow the same procedure.

   Study Table 1 before continuing.

Who Is an Insured

Table 1
Section II, Item 1

Designation in Declarations	Who Are Insureds	Restrictions
■ Individual	■ You ■ Your spouse	Only in connection with sole proprietorships
■ Partnership or joint venture	■ You ■ Your members and their spouses ■ Your partners and their spouses	Members, partners, and their spouses are insureds only in connection with conducting the business
■ Limited liability company*	■ You ■ Members ■ Managers	Members are insureds only in connection with conducting the business Managers are insureds only in connection with their duties as managers
■ Organization other than partnership, joint venture or limited liability company	■ You ■ Executive officers and directors ■ Stockholders	Executive officers and directors are insureds only in connection with conducting the business Stockholders are insureds only in connection with liability as stockholders
■ Trust	■ You ■ Trustees	Trustees are insureds only in connection with their duties as trustees

*A company structured like a corporation, but with additional tax and liability advantages for its members

WHO IS INSURED

Individuals

2. Janine Polk is the CGL's named insured as sole proprietor of Polk Catering. Her spouse, Lyle, is a carpenter.

   A. If Lyle is helping Janine in her catering business, he (is/is not) _____ an insured.

   B. If Lyle is found liable for injury arising from his business as a carpenter, he (is/is not) _____ an insured under Janine's CGL.

   Answer: A. is; B. is not

3. Which of the following are true when the named insured is designated in the declarations as an individual?

   A. The named insured's spouse might also be an insured.

   B. The named insured must be at least a part owner of the business involved.

   C. The named insured and spouse are insureds only in activities related to the business of the named insured as a sole proprietor.

   D. Any activities for which a named insured might be held liable qualify the individual as an insured, but only business activities qualify the individual's spouse as an insured.

   Answer: A and C are correct.

Partnerships and Joint Ventures

4. Sisters Magda and Eva are partners in a menswear retail store called ME. ME is designated in the declarations as the named insured. Magda's and Eva's husbands are not owners of the business, but both are present and assisting at an open house on the ME premises at which champagne is served during normal working hours. One customer leaves after drinking a glass of champagne and immediately causes an auto accident in which one person dies. Relatives of the deceased sue ME, Magda, Eva, and their husbands. Name the insureds in this situation, and explain why they are insureds._____

   _____

   _____

   Answer: Magda, Eva, and both husbands are insureds because the situation arose while conducting the business partnership of Magda and Eva.

5. Suppose L. Nuygen and B. Lee are involved in a joint venture. Both are named insureds in the declarations. Nuygen has a dog at his residence, and he occasionally takes the dog on business trips. At home one day, Nuygen's dog bites a neighbor, who sues Nuygen. If he is held liable, will Nuygen be an insured for this action under the CGL he and Lee own?   ( ) Yes   ( ) No

   Why? _____

   _____

   Answer: No. The incident had nothing to do with the conduct of business under the joint venture.

Limited Liability Companies

6. The named insured is Horizons, a limited liability company. Mark, a manager for Horizons, has a party at his home one night. One of the party guests drinks too much alcohol and vandalizes property belonging to Mark's neighbor. The neighbor sues Mark for the damages. In this situation, would Mark be considered an insured under Horizons's CGL?   ( ) Yes   ( ) No

   Why? _____

   _____

   Answer: No. Managers of limited liability companies are insureds only in connection with their duties as managers.

Other Organizations

7. Phil Morrison and Ben Hedges do business as a corporation called Smoke-No-More, Inc. The name of the corporation is listed on the declarations page as the named insured. Which of the following statements are true?

   A. Any employee of the firm is an insured acting in any capacity within the organization.

   B. Morrison and Hedges are insureds as owners of the corporation.

   C. Executive officers and directors are insureds provided they are acting in the scope of their duties as officers and directors.

   D. Stockholders are insureds acting in any capacity within the organization.

   Answer: B and C are correct.

8. The insured is a trust company that manages employee pension plans for other companies.

Who must be listed in the declarations of the CGL policy?

A. The trust company only

B. The names of the trustees only

C. Neither the trust company nor the names of the trustees

D. Both the trust company and the names of the trustees

Answer: A is correct. If the trust company is listed, then the trustees are automatically insureds with respect to their duties as trustees.

9. Review Table 2 before continuing.

Table 2
Section II, Items 2 and 3

Who Are Insureds	Restrictions
■ Employees who are not executive officers or managers, and volunteer workers	■ Only within the scope of their employment by the insured or while performing duties related to the conduct of the insured's business ■ Not for bodily injury or personal and advertising injury to named insureds, co-employees, partners, members, or other volunteer workers while in the course of their employment or while performing duties related to the conduct of the insured's business ■ Not to co-employees' or volunteer workers' spouses, children, parents, brothers, or sisters as a result of bodily injury or personal and advertising injury ■ Not for obligations to share or repay damages to someone else who pays because of bodily injury or personal and advertising injury ■ Not for bodily injury or personal and advertising injury associated with professional health care services ■ Not for property damage to property that named insureds, employees, volunteer workers, partners, or members own, occupy, use, rent, have in their care, custody or control, or exercise physical control over for any purpose
■ Persons (other than employees or volunteer workers) or organizations acting as the named insured's real estate manager	■ Only while acting in that capacity
■ Persons or organizations with proper temporary custody of a deceased named insured's property	■ Only in connection with liability arising from the maintenance or use of the property ■ Only until a legal representative is appointed
■ Legal representative of a deceased named insured	■ Only in connection with duties as the legal representative
■ Newly acquired or formed organizations	■ Must not be a partnership, joint venture or limited liability company ■ Named insured must own or have a majority interest ■ Organization has no other similar insurance available ■ Coverage extends only to earlier of 90 days or end of policy period ■ No Coverage A for bodily injury or property damage occurring before acquisition or formation ■ No Coverage B for personal and advertising injury if offense occurred before acquisition or formation

Note: No status as an insured exists for current or past partnerships, joint ventures or limited liability companies not shown as a named insured in the Declarations.

Employees, Volunteer Workers, and Others

10. The insured is Advance Advertising Agency, owned solely by Lanie Lamont. Brad Bevel and Zelda Zimmerman are two Advance employees, working in a highly competitive atmosphere. Brad becomes incensed when he believes Zelda slandered him to a potential client whose account they both hoped to acquire for Advance. Brad sues Zelda, Lanie, and Advance.

   A. Is Zelda considered an insured in this situation?   ( ) Yes   ( ) No
      Why? _____
      _____

   B. If Lanie had suffered the personal injury instead of Brad, is Zelda an insured?   ( ) Yes   ( ) No   Why? _____
      _____
      _____

   C. Suppose Brad angrily leaves the Advance building to call on another client, and while in the parking lot, backs his car rapidly into Zelda's parked car. Zelda, claiming that Lanie has failed to exercise an employer's duty of reasonable control over employee Brad, sues both Lanie and Brad. Who is an insured in this case?

      1. Brad

      2. Lanie

      3. Both Brad and Lanie

      4. Neither Brad nor Lanie

   Answer: A. No. Because Brad and Zelda are co-employees involved in personal injury during the course of employment, neither is an insured; B. No. The same exclusion applies when the named insured has been injured by an employee; C. 2 is correct.

11. Drugs Rx Laboratories, the insured, does pharmaceutical research. The laboratory employs two research technicians. In addition, after classes and while on breaks from college, an unpaid student intern cleans glassware and helps with research.

   A. While working in the lab, is the student intern considered an insured? ( ) Yes   ( ) No

   B. One day, when the intern was in classes, the technicians were arguing about who would clean the glassware. One of them impulsively locked the other in the small cleaning room for three hours. Are the technicians insureds for this detention offense?   ( ) Yes   ( ) No

   C. Even though he was running a fever and coughing, one technician came to work with bronchitis. The other technician became ill several days later, and his wife and son also took ill. Might the technicians be considered insureds in relation to the bodily injury suffered by the second technician's family members?   ( ) Yes   ( ) No

   Answer: A. Yes; B. No; C. No

12. The named insured is a large operation doing business as Maxima, Inc. Maxima employs a full-time physician on its staff. A visitor to Maxima has his arm between the elevator doors when they close. Because the visitor is in pain, Maxima employees escort him to the company physician, who diagnoses the injury as a bruise. She wraps the arm in an elastic bandage and sends the visitor on his way. That evening, the visitor goes to a local emergency room, where his injury is diagnosed as a fracture. Following complications from the injury, the visitor sues both Maxima and its full-time physician.

   A. Is Maxima's physician an insured in this case? ( ) Yes ( ) No
   Why? _____
   _____

   B. Is Maxima, Inc., an insured in this case? ( ) Yes ( ) No
   Why?_____
   _____

   Answer: A. No. She is excluded as an insured because the injury arose from her providing professional health care services; B. Yes. Nothing excludes the named insured in this situation.

13. In the following situations, Riley is an employee of the company holding the CGL. In which of these situations is Riley an insured?

   A. Riley's car is parked in the company parking lot when a sign falls from the employer's building and crushes the hood.

   B. Riley is the only worker in a laboratory that is a separate small building near the employer's main offices and on the same premises. The building is damaged by a small explosion caused when Riley inadvertently combines the wrong chemicals.

   C. During the explosion mentioned in B. above, another employee's car parked near the lab is damaged.

   D. While Riley is picking up supplies to be used in the laboratory, he trips and spills acid on a stranger, who then suffers burns on his leg.

   Answer: D is the only correct answer. Choice A is not correct because it involves damage to an employee's property. B involves damage to property occupied by an employee. C involves another employee's property.

14. The named insured is Scenic View Apartments. Susan Andres is the real estate manager for Scenic View. If Susan is paid a fee by Scenic View when she performs some service related to the business's real estate, is she an insured? ( ) Yes ( ) No   Explain your answer. _____
   _____

   Answer: Yes. She is acting in the capacity of a real estate manager.

15. The named insured is Catterson Associates, owned and operated by Michael Catterson. When he dies, his sister Julia has temporary custody of the business property.

   A. If Julia is sued in connection with Catterson business during this period, the CGL (does/does not) _____ consider her to be an insured.

   B. What time limitation is placed on Julia's being considered an insured?

   _____

   C. Now let's suppose that during the period she has temporary custody of Michael's property, Julia is also the named insured on a separate CGL covering her car wash business. If one of Julia's car wash customers should sue her and win, might that customer also be able to collect from the Catterson CGL for which Julia is now an insured?
   ( ) Yes   ( ) No   Why? _____

   _____

   _____

   D. Once a legal representative has been appointed, Julia (would/would not) _____ continue to be an insured under Catterson's policy.

   Answer: A. does; B. Only until a legal representative has been appointed; C. No. Julia is an insured under Catterson's CGL only for liability arising from Catterson's property; D. would not

Newly Acquired or Formed Organizations

16. An insured has just acquired a business and has not yet had an opportunity to notify the insurance company. Depending on the type of business described, decide whether the insured has coverage under the CGL for this new acquisition.

   A. A newly formed sole proprietorship (is/is not) _____ covered.

   B. A corporation over which the named insured has majority control (is/is not) _____ covered.

   C. A partnership, joint venture, or limited liability company (is/is not) _____ covered.

   Answer: A. is; B. is; C. is not

17. Suppose an insured acquires a business where the former owner maintained a CGL in the business's name. This insurance policy period has three days remaining before expiration when the named insured acquires the business. Is this newly acquired organization a named insured under the new owner's CGL during those three days? ( ) Yes ( ) No   Explain your answer.

   _____

   _____

   _____

   Answer: No. Other similar insurance is available.

18. The named insured forms a new business on May 1.

   A. If the current CGL had an expiration date of September 25, when would the new business cease being a named insured under the policy?

   _____

   B. The current CGL expires on July 25. The new business is a named insured until
   1. May 1.
   2. July 25.
   3. July 31.

   Answer: A. July 31, 90 days after the new business is formed; B. 2 is correct because July 25 is the earlier of the two dates.

19. Read each of the following situations, and check any that represent a newly acquired or formed organization that is considered to be an insured under the existing CGL. In each situation, assume the insurer has been notified of the acquisition of the new company and that no other insurance is available.

   A. Chung Moon is the sole owner of a retail camera shop covered by a CGL that will expire on October 11. Moon's shop is located next to City Sales, a retail television and radio store, whose owner decides to sell the store and retire. Moon purchases City Sales on August 31. On September 5, Moon climbs a ladder to place a new sign outside the door of City Sales. He drops a box of tools onto a customer who is entering the newly acquired shop. The customer files a claim for the resulting injury.

   B. Kathleen O'Shea is the owner of O'Shea Enterprises, Inc., which is covered by a CGL expiring June 10. On June 1, O'Shea acquires the McCarthy Corporation. On June 5, a private individual sues the McCarthy Corporation for bodily injury that occurred on May 15.

   C. Vince Potenza is the sole proprietor of Capezio Cafe, covered by a CGL with an expiration date of April 9. Potenza forms a partnership with Al Vittorio, and they open the Capezio Bakery next door to the cafe on March 4. On March 19, a competitor sues the Capezio Bakery for libel.

Answer: A is correct. B is not correct because the injury occurred before O'Shea acquired the business. C is not correct because a newly formed partnership or joint venture is excluded.

20. Arlo Webster owns a hardware store that he operates as a sole proprietorship. He has a CGL with himself as the named insured to cover the operations of this business. Arlo is also a partner in a supermarket.

    A. If bodily injury arises out of conducting the business of the supermarket, the CGL (would/would not) _____ apply to this injury.

    B. How could Arlo assure that the supermarket partnership would be covered in liability situations? _____

    _____

    _____

Answer: A. would not; B. He could have the supermarket partnership designated as an insured in the declarations.

In the next unit, you will learn how the limits of insurance are applied in the CGL.

UNIT

8

The Occurrence Form Section III: Limits of Insurance

INTRODUCTION

1. The insuring agreements for Coverages A and B indicate that:

    ■ damages the insurer will pay are limited by Section III of the form; and

    ■ the insurer's right and duty to defend end when the applicable limits of liability have been exhausted.

    In this unit, you will see exactly how the limits of insurance are applied.

    This application is based on how the limits are structured along two general liability insurance sublines:

    ■ premises-operations; and

    ■ products-completed operations.

    The limits of insurance for the CGL forms are divided along these sublines, with a **separate aggregate amount** available for each.

    When you studied the CGL definitions section, you learned that **products-completed operations** refer to injury and damage that arise from the insured's product and the insured's work occurring away from the insured's premises. Manufacturers have a significant exposure for **products** liability, and contractors have a similar exposure for **completed operations** liability. On the other hand, some businesses have a very insignificant, if any, products-completed operations exposure. For example, health clubs, pool halls, and costume rental shops have very little exposure. Their major exposures fall into the other subline, premises-operations.

    Premises-operations liability arises from the use of the insured's premises and the day-to-day operation of the insured's business. Some operations could occur away from the premises, but typically these are exposures with a fairly insignificant risk, so they need not be covered separately as products-completed operations.

    For example, costume rental shops deal with a product of sorts, but the liability exposure from that product is so minor it can be covered under the general premises-operations limits. While it is possible that a customer injured off the premises while wearing the rented costume might attempt to hold the shop responsible, this is a very slight completed-operations exposure. The commercial lines rules for writing this type of risk indicate when the premises-operations rates include this very incidental type of products-completed operations hazard, so no separate products-completed operations aggregate limit of insurance is required.

    On the other hand, a manufacturer of bicycles would need coverage under both sublines because there is a substantial liability exposure for both the premises and the completed bicycle product.

Suppose a manufacturer of lawn maintenance equipment, such as clippers, trimmers, and lawn mowers, wants liability coverage.

A. Does this type of business have a products-completed operations loss exposure because of the products it manufactures?   ( ) Yes   ( ) No

B. Does this business have the typical exposure to loss from maintaining a business premises on which operations are performed?
( ) Yes   ( ) No

C. In order to fully protect itself against potential liability losses, this manufacturer should have

1. products-completed operations coverage only because the aggregate amount of this coverage would probably be sufficient for all losses

2. premises-operations coverage only because this is where the greatest exposure lies

3. products-completed operations coverage and premises-operations coverage, each with a separate aggregate limit

Answer: A. Yes; B. Yes; C. 3 is correct.

Aggregates and Sublimits

2. The **aggregate amount** of insurance is the total amount that will be paid for all covered damages. When the aggregate is exhausted, the insurer pays no further damages. But the aggregate is not the only limit. Some *coverages* also have separate **sublimits** that fall within the aggregate and reduce it. This illustration shows how this works.

Basic Liability Limits

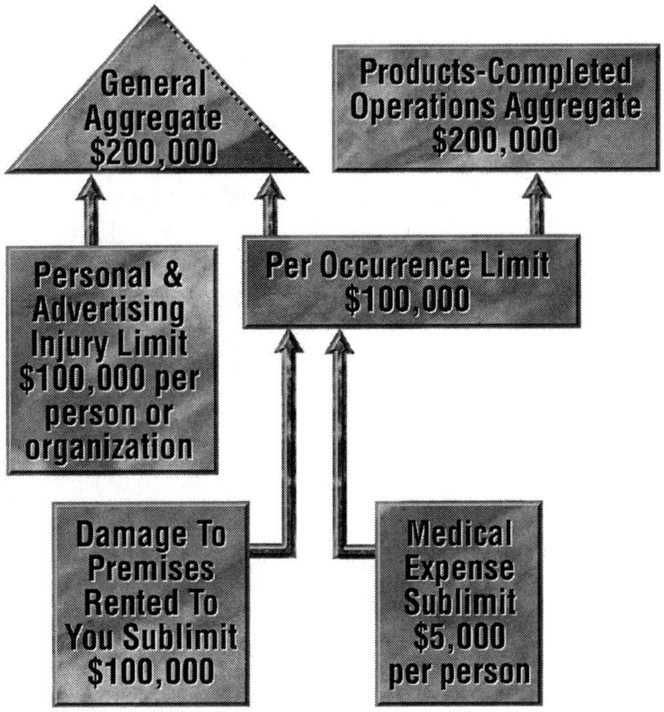

General Aggregate $200,000

Products-Completed Operations Aggregate $200,000

Personal & Advertising Injury Limit $100,000 per person or organization

Per Occurrence Limit $100,000

Damage To Premises Rented To You Sublimit $100,000

Medical Expense Sublimit $5,000 per person

The aggregates are shown at the top of the illustration. On the left, the **general aggregate** is the total amount available in one policy year for all coverages *except* those in the products-completed operations hazard.

On the right is the separate aggregate amount applicable for **products-completed operations** losses. This also represents the total amount that will be paid for this type of loss during one policy year.

The dollar amounts shown in the illustration are the **basic policy limits,** which can be increased at the insured's option with the insurer's consent.

Ask your supervisor or trainer what your company's basic liability limits are for CGL coverage.

What are the basic CGL limits for the

A. general aggregate? $_____

B. products-completed operations aggregate? $_____

Answer: A. $200,000; B. $200,000

PRODUCTS-COMPLETED OPERATIONS AGGREGATE

3. Because the workings of the **products-completed operations aggregate** are a little less complex than the general aggregate, let's first consider how it works. Locate Section III—Limits of Insurance in your sample CGL policy and read Items 1 and 3 Skip Item 2 for now.

    Item 1 indicates that the limits shown in the declarations *are* the limits, no matter how many insureds, claims, suits, people, or organizations are involved.

    A. If a policy's products-completed operations aggregate limit is $200,000, and two suits for $200,000 are each brought and awarded against the insured, the most the policy will pay is ($200,000/$400,000)

    _____.

    B. Suppose two people are named insureds on the same CGL, which has a products-completed operations aggregate of $200,000. Two separate $200,000 judgments are awarded against the two insureds. For these two claims, the insurer will pay a total of ($200,000/$400,000)

    _____.

Answer: A. $200,000; B. $200,000

4. Item 3 focuses *specifically* on the products-completed operations aggregate as the maximum payable under Coverage A for both bodily injury and property damage included in the products-completed operations hazard.

   Suppose, under the products-completed operations area, bodily injury damages of $200,000 are claimed, plus property damages of $100,000. Under the basic aggregate, the maximum the insurer will pay of this $300,000 loss is $_____.

   Answer: $200,000

Per Occurrence Limit for Products-Completed Operations

5. In addition to the basic aggregate limit for products-completed operations, there is also a sublimit on the amount that will be paid for each occurrence. On the illustration, this is the **per occurrence limit** of $100,000, the basic limit of liability. The arrow on the illustration indicates that this falls under and is further limited by the products-completed operations aggregate limit.

   Read Item 5 in Section III.

   Suppose an occurrence under the products-completed operations hazard results in bodily injury damages of $140,000 under Coverage A. Because this amount is well within the products-completed operations *aggregate*, it appears to be fully covered. However, because of the *per occurrence limit*, this might not be so. Let's say this insured has the basic aggregate of $200,000 and basic per occurrence limits of $100,000 when the $140,000 loss occurs. How much of the $140,000 loss will the CGL cover? $_____

Answer: $100,000—all that will be paid for a single occurrence when a policy has the basic limits.

6. In the previous example, the per occurrence limit was used up by a single loss. In addition, the products-completed operations *aggregate* limit is also reduced by the same amount.

    The series of illustrations following, numbered 1 through 5, demonstrate how the per occurrence limit works during the policy period and how it affects the aggregate. Study the illustrations carefully, and then answer the questions following.

How the Per Occurrence Limit Operates and Reduces the Products-Completed Operations Aggregate

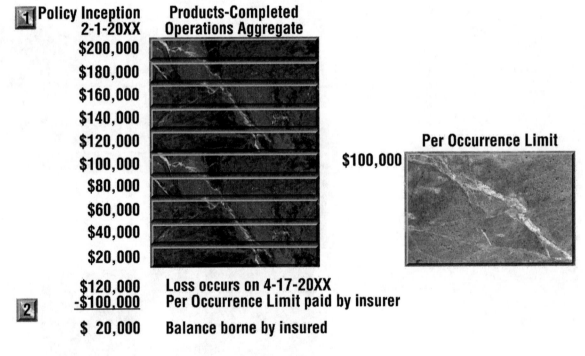

1 Policy Inception 2-1-20XX

Products-Completed Operations Aggregate

$200,000
$180,000
$160,000
$140,000
$120,000
$100,000
$80,000
$60,000
$40,000
$20,000

Per Occurrence Limit

$100,000

$120,000	Loss occurs on 4-17-20XX
2 -$100,000	Per Occurrence Limit paid by insurer
$ 20,000	Balance borne by insured

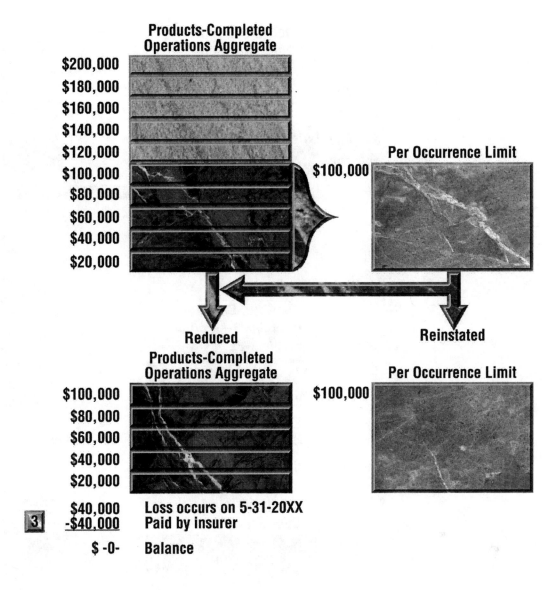

Products-Completed Operations Aggregate

$200,000	
$180,000	
$160,000	
$140,000	
$120,000	
$100,000	
$80,000	
$60,000	
$40,000	
$20,000	

$100,000

Per Occurrence Limit

Reduced
Products-Completed
Operations Aggregate

$100,000	
$80,000	
$60,000	
$40,000	
$20,000	

Reinstated

Per Occurrence Limit

$100,000

3 $40,000   Loss occurs on 5-31-20XX
-$40,000   Paid by insurer

$ -0-   Balance

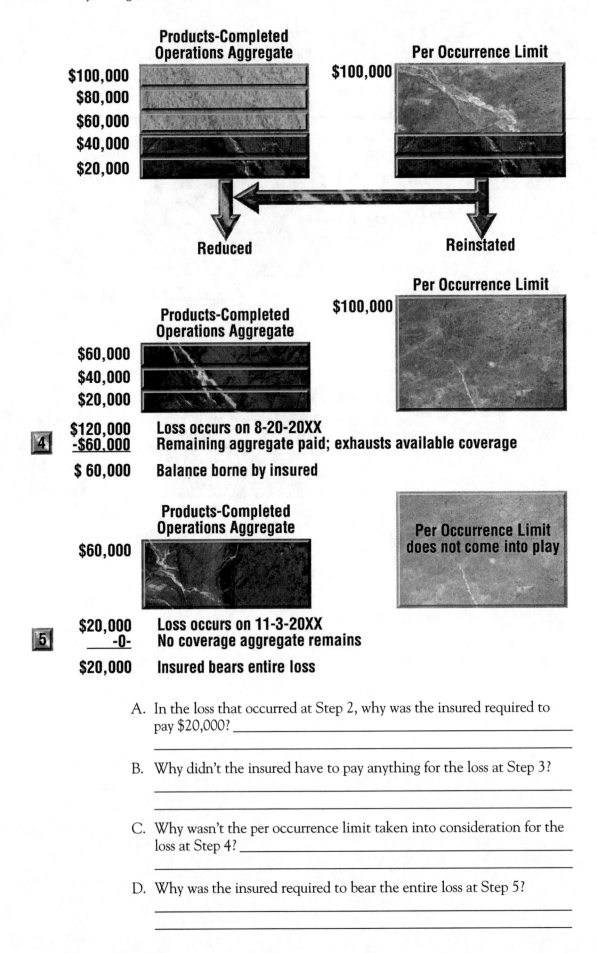

Products-Completed Operations Aggregate

$100,000
$80,000
$60,000
$40,000
$20,000

Per Occurrence Limit

$100,000

Reduced

Reinstated

Products-Completed Operations Aggregate

$60,000
$40,000
$20,000

Per Occurrence Limit

$100,000

4 $120,000   **Loss occurs on 8-20-20XX**
      -$60,000   **Remaining aggregate paid; exhausts available coverage**
      $ 60,000   **Balance borne by insured**

Products-Completed Operations Aggregate

$60,000

Per Occurrence Limit does not come into play

5 $20,000   **Loss occurs on 11-3-20XX**
          -0-   **No coverage aggregate remains**
      $20,000   **Insured bears entire loss**

A. In the loss that occurred at Step 2, why was the insured required to pay $20,000? _____

_____

B. Why didn't the insured have to pay anything for the loss at Step 3?

_____

_____

C. Why wasn't the per occurrence limit taken into consideration for the loss at Step 4? _____

_____

D. Why was the insured required to bear the entire loss at Step 5?

_____

_____

Answer: A. $20,000 was the amount of loss that exceeded the per occurrence limit; B. This loss was within the per occurrence limit; C. At this point, the aggregate was reduced below the per occurrence limit, and the aggregate was the most that could be paid; D. The aggregate limits were completely exhausted, so the insurer was no longer required to pay.

7. The limits we have just discussed are the only dollar limits that apply to the products-completed operations hazard.
   A. The total amount available for the products-completed operations hazard for the policy year is called the (aggregate/per occurrence) _____ limit.

   B. The second limit, which indicates how much will be paid for losses in any one event, is the (aggregate/per occurrence) _____ limit, which (does/does not) _____ reduce the other limit.

   Answer: A. aggregate; B. per occurrence, does

GENERAL AGGREGATE

8. The **general aggregate** applies to everything except products-completed operations for Coverages A, B, and C. Read Item 2 in Section III, which describes how the general aggregate limit applies.

   Assume an insured has the basic general aggregate limit of $200,000. During the policy year, losses have been paid on three different occurrences as follows:

   ■ Occurrence 1: $80,000 under Coverage A premises-operations

   ■ Occurrence 2: $40,000 under Coverage A premises-operations

   ■ Occurrence 3: $80,000 under Coverage B

   Before the end of the policy year, the insured has another loss of $3,000 in medical payments under Coverage C.

   Which one of the following correctly describes how this fourth loss will be paid, and why?
   A. The full $3,000 will be paid because it falls within both the per occurrence and the general aggregate limits, and no previous Coverage C losses were paid.
   B. The full $3,000 will be paid because it falls within the per occurrence limits, which are available even when the general aggregate has been exhausted.
   C. None of the $3,000 will be paid because the general aggregate, which has been exhausted, applies for all coverages combined for the policy year.

Answer: C is correct.

Per Occurrence Limit Under the General Aggregate

9. The **per occurrence limit** under the general aggregate applies the same way as the products-completed operations per occurrence limit for Coverage A BI and PD *and* Coverage C medical payments. Coverage B is treated separately, and we will look at it later.

   For now, let's consider only Coverages A and C. Suppose an insured's general aggregate limit is $200,000, and the per occurrence limit is $100,000. In one occurrence, losses are assessed for:

   - $40,000 for bodily injury;

   - $80,000 for property damage; and

   - $5,000 for medical payments.

   The general aggregate amount has *not* been reduced by losses before these. Which one of the following best describes how these losses will be paid?

   A. The total of all losses combined will be paid because this sum does not exceed the general aggregate limit of $200,000.

   B. The total for each loss will be paid, not because of the general aggregate limit availability, but because none individually exceeds the per occurrence limit.

   C. Only $100,000, the per occurrence limit, will be paid because the sum of Coverages A and C must be combined under the per occurrence limit.

   Answer: C is correct.

10. The general aggregate limit is also the *overall* limit.

    Therefore, in the previous question, if the general aggregate of $200,000 had previously been reduced by other losses to $60,000, what is the maximum amount the insurer would pay for the loss described in the previous question? $_____

    Answer: $60,000, all that remains available of the general aggregate.

Medical Expense Sublimit

11. Under the general aggregate, the per occurrence limit is not the only limit that applies to Coverage C. The illustration shows there is also a sublimit on the amount of medical payments. Read Item 7 in Section III.

The **medical expense sublimit** applies to **each person** who might require medical treatment for any one occurrence.

A. What is the basic sublimit for medical payments indicated in the illustration? $ _____ (per person/per occurrence) _____.

B. Suppose an accident for which the insured is found liable results in immediate medical expenses for three people of $1,000, $500, and $7,000. Assuming a $5,000 limit and no previous losses, how much will the CGL pay for the medical expenses of each of these people?

1. For the person incurring $1,000 in expenses: $ _____

2. For the person incurring $500 in expenses: $ _____

3. For the person incurring $7,000 in expenses: $ _____

Answer: A. $5,000, per person; B. 1. $1,000; 2. $500; 3. $5,000—the per person maximum for any one occurrence.

12. The medical expense sublimit is subject to both the per occurrence limit and the general aggregate limit. It also reduces these limits as well as reduces the amounts available for Coverage A losses, as indicated in Item 5.

Suppose an insured has a general aggregate limit of $200,000, which has been reduced by previous losses to $120,000. The basic $5,000 medical expense sublimit applies. In one occurrence, the following losses are incurred:

- $6,000 medical expenses for one individual;

- $3,000 medical expenses for one individual;

- $2,000 medical expenses for one individual; and

- $100,000 in premises-operations property damage and bodily injury liability, awarded sometime after the medical expenses were incurred.

A. What is the total amount of medical expenses the CGL will cover?
$_____ Explain. _____
_____
_____

B. After the medical expenses are paid, how much will be paid for the property damage and bodily injury award? $ _____
Explain. _____
_____

C. After this loss is paid, how much remains of the general aggregate?
$ _____

D. Suppose before the policy period ends, the insured still has another claim under Coverage C. Six different people incur medical expenses of $4,000 each. Will this claim be covered entirely?   ( ) Yes   ( ) No
Why? _____
_____

Answer: A. $10,000. This includes the maximum of $5,000 per person paid for the $6,000 loss, plus $3,000 and $2,000 paid for the other two individuals. B. $90,000. With a $100,000 per occurrence limit and $10,000 already paid for medical expenses, this is the remainder available. C. $20,000 ($200,000 previously reduced to $120,000; reduced to $110,000 by the $10,000 medical expenses payment; reduced to $20,000 by the $90,000 BI/PD award); D. No. Only $20,000 remains of the general aggregate.

Damage to Premises Rented to You Sublimit

13. Still another sublimit is subject to the per occurrence and the general aggregate limits—the **damage to premises rented to you legal liability sublimit**. Read Item 6 under Section III.

Suppose that an insured has the basic CGL limits that have not been reduced by previous losses. If the insured is found liable for property damage to rented premises covered by the CGL, and that loss totals $120,000, the most the policy will pay is $100,000—first, because that is the damage to premises rented to you sublimit for property damage, and second, because that is the per occurrence limit.

Now, let's suppose that in addition to the $100,000 property damage liability loss, the same occurrence resulted in a total payment of $2,000 in medical expenses for several people. These medical expenses were paid *before* the $120,000 property damage award was made.

A. Now the total that would be paid for the property damage is
$ _____ because _____
_____
_____
_____.

B. Continuing with this same situation, assume instead that the general
aggregate limit has been reduced by previous losses, so it stands at
$80,000 when the property damage and medical losses occur. The
$2,000 has been paid by the company for medical expenses before
the $98,000 property damages are awarded. Now how much will
the CGL pay for the property damage? $ _____ because
_____
_____
_____
_____.

Answer: A. $98,000, because the $2,000 in medical payments had reduced
the available per occurrence amount to $98,000; B. $78,000, because that
is all that remains due to the reduced aggregate minus the $2,000 medical
payments.

14. The damage to premises rented to you sublimit also applies to fire damage if
the insured is found liable for one fire loss to a premises covered by the CGL
that he rents or temporarily occupies with the permission of the owner.
Remember that the damage to premises rented to you sublimit applies with
other Coverage A losses in reducing both the per occurrence limit and the
general aggregate limit.

So, if the per occurrence limit is $100,000, and the insured's losses for one
occurrence are $40,000 for fire damage legal liability, $5,000 for medical
payments, and $100,000 for Coverage A losses, the CGL (will/will not)
_____ pay the entire loss because _____
_____
_____.

Answer: will not, because the total of all three types of losses exceeds the
per occurrence limit to which all are subject.

Personal and Advertising Injury Limit

15. One final limit, subject to the general aggregate limit but not to the separate per occurrence limit, applies to **Coverage B Personal and Advertising
Injury**. Refer to the illustration to see how this fits into the aggregate, and
then read Item 4 of Section III before continuing.

The illustration shows the basic personal and advertising injury limits
are $100,000 **per person or organization**. This limit is *not* subject to a per
occurrence limit. Rather, it applies per person or organization. As a result,
the same person or organization could not, for example, collect a $100,000

judgment early in the policy year and a second judgment later in the policy year. Once the full limits are awarded to any person or organization, no other claims by that person or organization could be honored during the policy year, even if money remained available in the general aggregate limit.

On the other hand, there is nothing in the form to prevent the same person or organization from collecting a total of $100,000 in smaller *separate* awards during the same policy year, assuming that amount is available in the general aggregate.

Suppose a slander suit brought by Raymark Company is settled for $100,000. The insured has the basic policy limits. Later in the same policy year, a libel award of $20,000 is awarded to the Raymark Company against the same insured.

A. Both of these losses (will/will not) _____ be paid in full by the CGL because _____
_____
_____.

B. Still assuming the policy has the basic limits, suppose Raymark Company has received a $60,000 award for the slander suit and $40,000 for the libel suit. Would the CGL cover both of these awards? ( ) Yes   ( ) No   Why? _____
_____
_____

Answer: A. Will not, because they would exceed the per organization limit for personal and advertising injury liability; B. Yes. Together, they do not exceed the $100,000 limit per person or organization.

APPLYING LIMITS OF INSURANCE IN RELATION TO THE POLICY PERIOD

16. The final paragraph of Section III explains how the limits of insurance apply in relation to the policy period. Read this last paragraph, and then study the illustration and answer the questions.

Three-Year Policy Reinstatement of Limits

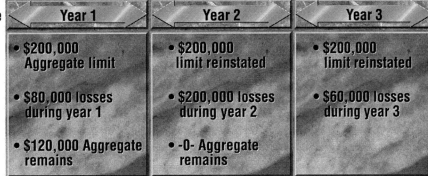

Charleston Manufacturing has a CGL with the basic limits:

- $200,000 general aggregate;

- $100,000 personal and advertising injury limit; and

- $200,000 products-completed operations aggregate.

A products-related claim has reduced the aggregate to $100,000 at the end of the first policy year on a three-year policy. In addition, a personal and advertising injury judgment of $40,000 has reduced the general aggregate. At the beginning of the second policy year, how much will be available in the

A. general aggregate? $_____

B. products-completed operations aggregate? $_____

C. personal and advertising injury limit? $_____

Answer: A. $200,000; B. $200,000; C. $100,000

17. In one situation, the full policy limits are not reinstated. For example, if an insured asks for a two-month extension of the policy, those two months would be covered as if they were part of the preceding 12-month policy period.

So, for any loss that might occur during the two-month extension, if the policy aggregate limits had been reduced, the amount available to the insured would be the (reduced/fully reinstated) _____ limits.

Answer: reduced

INCREASED LIMITS

18. Insureds are not restricted to coverage equal to the basic policy limits of the CGL. For an increased premium, the limits may be raised. Typically, an insured may purchase whatever aggregate amounts the insurer will provide. With the CGL, however, the limit for personal and advertising injury must always equal the per occurrence limit.

    In some cases, factors may be present that allow the CGL coverage to be written at a rate lower than the basic policy limits. For example, following an experience review, the insurer may determine that a business can be rated lower than the basic limits. Any rate below the basic limits is a decreased limit.

Ask your supervisor or trainer what your company's rules are for increasing or decreasing the liability limits in the CGL.

This illustration shows how limits may be increased, either automatically or optionally.

Increasing the Liability Limits

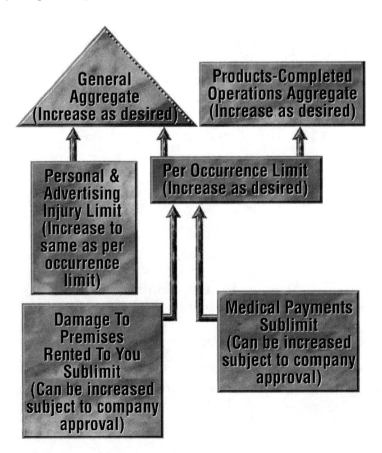

Answer the following questions based on the illustration and the information provided.

A. An insured increases the general aggregate to $300,000 and the per occurrence limit to $150,000. The limit available to this insured for Coverage B Personal and Advertising Injury, is $_____ per person or organization.

B. The sublimit for damage to premises rented to you liability coverage for the insured in A will be $_____ unless she requests a higher limit from the insurer.

C. Suppose an insured raises the per occurrence limits to $160,000. The new personal and advertising injury limit will be $_____.

D. An insured wants to raise the medical expense sublimit. Will this increase automatically follow another limit?   ( ) Yes   ( ) No
    Explain. _____
    _____

Answer: A. $150,000—it automatically increases to the same amount as the per occurrence limit; B. $100,000; C. $160,000; D. No. The insured must request the increase if desired.

There is only one section of the CGL form that you have not yet analyzed—the conditions. You will learn about conditions in the next unit.

9

The Occurrence Form Section IV: CGL Conditions

INTRODUCTION

1. You have learned about the common policy conditions that apply to all commercial insurance, including general liability. The CGL form includes additional conditions that relate specifically to general liability.

   The CGL, then, is subject to

   A. the common conditions only
   B. the CGL conditions only
   C. both the common conditions and the CGL conditions

   Answer: C is correct.

BANKRUPTCY

2. The first CGL condition concerns the insured's financial situation. Read Item 1 **bankruptcy** under Section IV of your sample CGL policy.

   Landslide Corporation is a small business that is having financial difficulties.

   A. A bodily injury damage suit is filed in a local court against Landslide on the same day the corporation files for bankruptcy. The insurer (will/will not) _____ defend the suit in light of the bankruptcy.

   B. Suppose Landslide Corporation's owner dies at the same time his business is declared insolvent. Several days later, the deceased owner's estate is sued for damages covered by the CGL. Will the insurer defend the claim under these circumstances?   ( ) Yes   ( ) No

   C. Will the policy cover the loss if the deceased insured's estate is found liable?   ( ) Yes   ( ) No

   Answer: A. will; B. Yes; C. Yes

DUTIES IN THE EVENT OF OCCURRENCE, OFFENSE, CLAIM, OR SUIT

Notification of Occurrence or Offense

3. The next condition explains certain duties the insured has to the insurance company. An insured person may become aware of an event that could

result in a liability claim. The insurer requires the insured to act responsibly in notifying the company of that possibility. Under Item 2 **duties in the event of occurrence, offense, claim, or suit,** read only Item 2.a.(1), including paragraphs (2) and (3).

This section does not limit the insured's responsibility of notifying the company of an *actual* claim. Any occurrence or offense that has the **potential to become a claim** must be brought to the insurer's attention.

A. Which of the following situations would probably be an occurrence or offense that the insurer should know about?

1. A truck driver for Express Delivery is injured on the premises of the Todd Company, the insured, when an overhead garage door in the raised position falls.

2. An employee of the Todd Company drops a valuable diamond ring down the drain in a company restroom.

3. An explosion on the Todd Company premises results in flying debris that causes property damage to the business across the street.

4. A visitor to the Todd Company chokes while drinking a can of cola purchased from a machine in the employees' dining room.

B. According to this provision, which of the following should the Todd Company, looking at the previous example, provide its insurer regarding the *truck driver's* injury?

1. Truck driver's name and home address

2. Name of the truck driver's spouse or nearest relative

3. Probable reason that the door fell

4. Name and address of Bart Boyce, Todd Company's shipping manager, who was standing nearby when the door fell

5. Name and address of an employee who arrived on the scene after the door fell

6. Date and location of the incident

7. Specific type of injury the truck driver suffered

Answer: A. 1 and 3 are correct; B. 1, 3, 4, 6, and 7 are correct.

Notification of a Claim or Suit

4. When any insured *is* sued or a liability claim is made, the insured must notify the insurer of that fact as well. Read Item 2.b, including paragraphs (1) and (2).

A. Suppose the named insured is Jason Mills. His wife, Marjorie, is sued in connection with an event that arose out of Mills's business. Jason (is/is not) _____ required to notify the insurer of this suit because _____

_____.

B. Jason Mills calls his CGL insurer the day after he receives notice that Marjorie is being sued. Has Jason met the requirements of the policy? ( ) Yes ( ) No   Why? _____

_____

C. Although Mills has telephoned the insurer, what else is he required to do as soon as practicable? _____

_____

Answer: A. is, because in this situation, Jason's wife is considered an insured under the CGL; B. Yes. The condition requires notification as soon as practicable, a requirement that was probably met in this case; C. Give the insurer written notice of the suit.

Assistance from the Insured

5. Once the insured has properly notified the insurer, other assistance may also be required of the insured. Read Item 2.c of this condition.

In which of the following situations is the insured acting within the stipulations of the provision you just read?

A. After a personal injury claim has been filed by a former employee of the insured, the insurer requests personnel records on that individual. The insured provides them.

B. The claim mentioned in A goes to court for settlement, and the insurer asks the insured to appear as a witness. The insured refuses.

C. A lawyer for a claimant contacts the insured by letter regarding one of the claimant's demands. The insured decides the letter is not important enough to send to the insurer and places it in the company files.

D. The insured is named in a suit for injuries from a product the insured sold but did not manufacture. The product was a handmade item sold on consignment in the insured's shop. When the insurer asks the insured to locate the maker of the product, the insured does so.

Answer: A and D are correct. B is not correct because the insured does not have the option to refuse cooperation in the defense. In C, the policy requires that all legal papers be submitted to the insurer.

Unauthorized Obligations

6. The insurer has the right to control expenses that might be obligated under the policy. Read the last part of this condition in your sample policy.

A. Only one type of expense may be incurred by the insured without first getting the insurance company's consent. What is it?_____

B. According to this provision, if the insured volunteers to make any payment, incur any expenses, or assume any other obligations without the insurer's consent, who will ultimately pay for these obligations?

_____

Answer: A. First aid; B. The insured

LEGAL ACTION AGAINST THE INSURER

7. The CGL places certain restrictions on the conditions under which **legal actions** may be brought against the insurer. Read all of Item 3 **Legal Action Against Us**.

   Suppose that a claim is filed and ultimately goes to an arbitrator because the insurer and the insured do not agree. An individual who believes the insured is trying to avoid paying a bodily injury claim to him attempts to have his claim included as part of the arbitration proceedings. Is this permitted according to the policy?   ( ) Yes   ( ) No

Answer: No

8. The final paragraph of Item 3 indicates two circumstances under which a person or organization may sue to recover damages. What are they?

   1. _____

   2. _____

Answer: (In either order) 1. When an agreed settlement has been reached; 2. When a final judgment against the insured has been made

9. The final paragraph also defines what is meant by an **agreed settlement**. Which of the following is an example of an agreed settlement?

   A. The insured and the claimant agree to a settlement in writing.

   B. The insured, the insurance company, and the claimant agree to a settlement in writing.

   C. The insured, the claimant, and the claimant's legal representative agree to a settlement in writing.

   D. Any of the above would represent an agreed settlement.

Answer: B is correct.

10. While the condition says the insurer may be sued to recover a final judgment, it also says the insurer will not pay for damages under two situations:

■ damages that are not covered by the policy; and

■ damages that exceed the policy limits.

A. Even with a final judgment against the insured, if the loss is not covered by the CGL, the insurer (will/will not) _____ pay.

B. If final judgment damages are more than the limits of liability of the CGL, who will pay the difference? (Insured/Insurer) _____

Answer: A. will not; B. Insured

OTHER INSURANCE

11. The availability of **other insurance coverage** can complicate the manner in which a claim is settled. The CGL sets out very definitive guidelines for the insurer's participation in losses where there is other insurance. Read through all of Item 4.

The policy refers to **primary insurance** and **excess insurance**, two fairly simple concepts that are illustrated here.

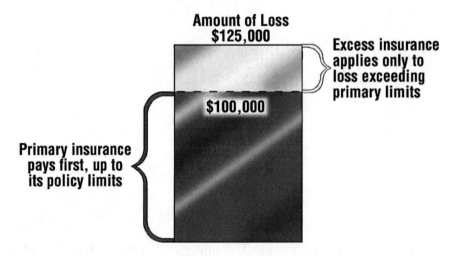

Suppose an insured has policies with ABC Insurance Company and XYZ Insurance Company. When a loss occurs, XYZ responds up to its policy limits. Because $15,000 still remains to be paid, ABC steps in and pays that amount.

A. The primary insurer is (ABC/XYZ) _____ Insurance Company.

B. The excess insurer is (ABC/XYZ) _____ Insurance Company.

Answer: A. XYZ; B. ABC

12. The opening paragraph of Item 4 indicates that the condition applies to Coverages A and B. Coverage C is not mentioned because it *always* provides primary coverage. The nature of the coverage itself is such that other insurance does not come into play.

    Therefore, if an insured has Coverage C, which one of the following would be true?

    A. Assuming the loss is otherwise within the terms of the policy, the insured's CGL will always be a primary insurer for medical payments coverage.

    B. Assuming the loss is otherwise within the terms of the policy, and the CGL provides primary insurance for Coverages A or B, the CGL will also be the primary insurer for Coverage C.

    C. Assuming the loss is otherwise within the terms of the policy, medical payments coverage will usually be considered excess under the CGL.

    Answer: A is correct.

Primary Coverage

13. Item 4.a addresses the issue of the CGL as **primary insurance**. If an insured's CGL is primary and there is no *other* primary insurance, the CGL pays as if there were no other insurance.

    Suppose an insured has a CGL with Forward Insurance Company, the primary insurer. Another policy with Overage Insurance Company provides excess coverage. The insured is found liable for a $50,000 loss, which is well within the liability limits of the Forward policy. Will Overage Insurance Company share in this loss with Forward?   ( ) Yes ( ) No   Why? _____
    _____
    _____
    _____

    Answer: No. Because there is no other primary insurance, and the loss is within the limits of the Forward policy, the excess company is not involved. Forward will cover the entire loss as the primary insurer.

Method of Sharing

14. The insurance is primary except when the section on excess insurance applies. We will cover this contingency later. First, let's see what happens when the CGL is primary and some other insurance is *also* primary. Item 4.c, **method of sharing**, explains how the insurance applies. Refer to this item as we discuss it.

The first paragraph describes a method of sharing between or among primary insurers that is known as **contribution by equal shares**. This method is used when all other insurance permits such an arrangement.

With this method, all companies divide the loss equally. If one or more companies use up their limits of liability before the loss is completely paid, then the other companies share equally in the unpaid portion up to their policy limits.

Two companies are primary insurers. Company A has limits of $100,000, and Company B's limits are $200,000. Both policies permit contribution by equal shares. A $120,000 loss occurs.

A. Company A will pay $_____.

B. Company B will pay $_____.

Answer: A. $60,000; B. $60,000

15. Assume the same two companies are primary insurers: Company A for $100,000 and Company B for $200,000. This time the loss is for $240,000.

    A. Company A pays $_____.

    B. Company B pays $_____.

    C. Explain your answers. _____
    _____
    _____

    Answer: A. $100,000; B. $140,000; C. In equal shares, Company A paid up to its limits of $100,000, and Company B paid an equal amount. Then, because the unpaid $40,000 was within its policy limits, Company B paid it as well.

16. The second paragraph of Item 4.c addresses what happens when the other insurance does *not* permit contribution by equal shares. This method, **contribution by limits**, requires each primary insurer to pay the *ratio* of its limits to the total limits of all insurance. Let's see how this works.

    Company C has limits of $200,000. Company D's limits are $400,000, for a total of $600,000. If a loss occurs, C's ratio is:

    $$\frac{\$200{,}000}{\$600{,}000} = \frac{1}{3}$$

    D's ratio is:

    $$\frac{\$400{,}000}{\$600{,}000} = \frac{2}{3}$$

Therefore, if a loss of $36,000 occurs, Company C pays ⅓ of the loss, or $12,000. Company D pays ⅔ of $36,000, or $24,000.

Assume there are two primary insurers for a liability loss. Company X has limits of $100,000, and Company Y has limits of $300,000. A $24,000 loss occurs. Determine each company's share of the loss using the contribution by limits method.

A. Company X pays $_____.

B. Company Y pays $_____.

Answer: A. $6,000, or ¼ of the loss; B. $18,000, or ¾ of the loss

Excess Coverage

17. Now, let's consider what happens when the CGL is not primary, but instead is **excess** over other primary insurance. Refer to Item 4.b.(1) if you need to during this discussion.

    Four circumstances are listed under which coverage is *always* excess over other insurance. The CGL is excess, for example, over any other insurance the insured purchases when temporarily renting property or occupying a premises with the permission of the owner. Suppose that the insured purchases liability coverage as a tenant for the rental of a party house. The intent is for the insured's CGL in that instance to be considered excess, while the liability insurance for the rental property is primary.

    Considering these four circumstances, select any situations from the following list for which the CGL is excess insurance.

    A. The insured has other insurance to cover vandalism losses to building materials at a location where the insured is the building contractor for a new warehouse operation.

    B. Other insurance applies to the insured's boat that is stored on the business premises.

    C. Other insurance is available to cover the liability for bodily injury to visitors on the insured's premises.

    D. There is other insurance to cover fire loss to a warehouse the insured rents from a local business.

    E. The insured has other insurance to cover the liability for property damage at a party house the insured has rented.

    Answer: A, B, D, and E are correct.

18. Read just the first paragraph of Item b.(2).

    > The CGL insurance is excess over any other primary insurance covering liability for damages arising out of premises or operatons or products—completed operation for which the insured has been added as an additional insured by attachment of an endorsement.

    > Suppose, for example, that a contractor installing a new roof on the insured's office building has liability coverage for damages to the premises that are a result of the contractor's operations. The contractor adds the owner of the office building as an additional insured.

    In this example, the contractor's insurance is (primary/excess) _____ and the building owner's CGL insurance is (primary/excess) _____.

    Answer: primary, excess

19. The paragraph following Item b.(2) describes the insurer's duties involving defense of a suit.

    A. According to this paragraph, if the CGL is excess and some other insurer has a duty to defend a suit, the insurance company (is/is not) _____ required to defend.

    B. The final sentence of this paragraph says the excess insurer will defend a suit under one circumstance. What is it? _____
    _____

    Answer: A. is not; B. When no other insurer defends

20. If the excess insurer does defend the suit, that insurer is entitled to the insured's rights against any primary insurance companies that refused to defend.

    Suppose an insurance company refuses to defend a suit against an insured, so the excess insurer chooses to do so. The insured is so angry at the other insurance company that she wants to institute a second suit through her own attorney to force the other insurer to pay. Is she permitted to do this? ( ) Yes ( ) No   Why? _____
    _____

    Answer: No. Because the excess insurer is defending, the insured's rights against the other insurer belong to the excess insurer.

21. The final portion of this section on excess insurance states how the insurer will determine its share of the loss. Here are the steps the insurer takes:

1. Determine the amount of insurance that is payable by other insurance.

2. Add any deductible the insured owes.

3. Add any amount the insured self-insures.

Any part of the loss exceeding the total of 1, 2, and 3 will be paid by the excess insurer or shared with other excess insurers as long as:

■ the insurers do not provide coverage that is described in b.(1) and (2) of this condition; or

■ the insurance was not specifically purchased to provide excess insurance.

Suppose Worth Insurance Company is the excess insurer for a $240,000 loss. Worth's policy limits are $100,000. The primary insurer, Class Insurance Company, has paid its limits of $200,000. The insured has paid a $10,000 deductible, and no self-insurance applies. A third insurer, Best Insurance Company, provides excess coverage on the same basis and same limits as Worth Insurance Company.

If all policies permit contribution by equal shares, how much will the excess insurers, Worth and Best, pay?

A. Each will pay $15,000—half of the remaining $30,000 of loss.

B. Worth will pay whatever amount falls within its available limits, and Best will pay the remainder if that amount falls within its available limits.

C. Each will pay $7,500—its ratio of the loss.

Answer: A is correct.

PREMIUM AUDIT

22. The fifth condition concerns premium computation and the insured's record-keeping responsibilities for computation purposes. Read Item 5. **Premium Audit**.

Which of the following statements are correct?

A. The premium shown on the policy as the advance premium is the exact amount the named insured will pay for the coverage.

B. The named insured may eventually be required to pay more than the advance premium shown on the policy.

C. It is the insurer's responsibility to record and maintain the information from which premiums will be computed.

D. The named insured could pay less than the advance premium indicated on the policy.

E. Audit and retrospective premiums are due on the due date shown on the bill.

Answer: B, D, and E are correct.

REPRESENTATIONS

23. In any insurance contract, the insurer relies on the insured to give correct information before the policy is issued. This permits the insurer to know precisely the type of risk for which it is agreeing to provide coverage. Read about **representations** the insured makes in Item 6 before continuing.

   While the information the insured supplies is not a warranty of truth, it is the basis on which the policy is issued, and **intentional misstatements** can invalidate the policy.

   A. Suppose an individual who is applying for a CGL states that he is a plumbing contractor. In fact, he is in the demolition business. He has therefore misrepresented his business in the declarations. If a liability loss involving the demolition business occurs, the insured (will always/ might not) _____ have coverage under the CGL.

   B. Remember, these are representations, not warranties. In other words, if an insured becomes confused and indicates that his business is a partnership when it is actually a joint venture, would the insurer be likely to deny coverage because of this discrepancy?   ( ) Yes   ( ) No
   Why? _____

   _____

   Answer: A. Might not; B. No. The insurer would probably not interpret a misunderstanding of terms as a misrepresentation.

SEPARATION OF INSUREDS

24. If more than one insured is named on a CGL, the policy provides that no insured will receive less protection than if only one insured were named. This does not apply to duties specifically assigned to the first named insured or to the policy's limits of insurance, which cover all insureds under the policy. Read Item 7.

   A. Suppose the first named insured is B. D. Booth. M. Oswega is also a named insured. If a suit is brought against Oswega in regard to the business, will Oswega's insurance coverage apply differently because Booth is the first named insured?   ( ) Yes   ( ) No

B. Let's assume that there are three named insureds: C. Loo, T. Yan, and K. Yang. The general aggregate limit is $200,000, and the per occurrence limit is $100,000. Each of the three insureds is sued for $40,000 by three separate third parties. The reasons for the suits are unrelated. Would the total of these losses, if awarded all at once, be completely covered?   ( ) Yes   ( ) No   Explain._____

_____

Answer: A. No; B. Yes. Each will be treated separately.

TRANSFER OF RECOVERY RIGHTS

25. Under common law, an individual has the right to take certain legal actions against others who may have done something that resulted in the first individual being held liable.

Asan example, suppose Aardvarkian Enterprises is found legally liable for $20,000 in damages resulting from the installation of materials that later were discovered to be faulty. Aardvarkian might either pay the $20,000 or, if the company has a CGL, the insurer might pay the damages. If Aardvarkian pays the damages, Aardvarkian has the right to try to recover the $20,000 from the company that sold the faulty materials. If the insurer paid the loss, then this right of recovery is transferred from Aardvarkian to the insurer. This transfer is spelled out in Condition 8. Read this condition, and then answer the following questions.

Pinkster Corporation is found legally liable for $10,000 in damages from an accident caused by a part Pinkster installed in a customer's machine.

A. If this part is found to be defective, from whom can Pinkster try to recover the $10,000?

1. The customer

2. The manufacturer of the part

3. Pinkster's insurance company

4. No one

B. Now assume instead that Pinkster had a CGL policy that paid the $10,000 liability loss. In this case, the right of recovery belongs to _____ because _____

_____.

Answer: A. 2 is correct; B. The insurer, because as a condition of payment, the right to recovery must be transferred to the insurer

NONRENEWAL

26. The final CGL condition indicates the insurer's responsibilities if it decides **not to renew** the insurance. Read Item 9 and then answer the following questions.

    If the insurer decides not to renew:

    A. How many days before the policy expires must the insurer notify the insured of nonrenewal? _____

    B. To whom must the notice be delivered? _____

    C. In what form must the nonrenewal notice be provided? _____

    Answer: A. No less than 30 days; B. The first named insured; C. In writing

    This concludes your study of the CGL occurrence form. In the next unit, you will learn about the claims-made CGL.

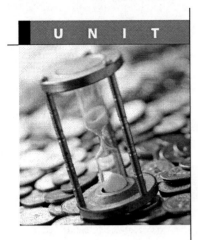

UNIT

10

The Claims-Made Form

INTRODUCTION

1. In this unit, we will analyze the claims-made version of the CGL. Keep in mind that the primary differences between the occurrence form and the claims-made form have to do with what triggers the coverage and special provisions applicable to those triggers.

    Locate the **claims-made form**, CG 00 02, in your Forms and Endorsements. The bold type under the main heading reads:

    > "Coverages A and B provide claims-made coverage. Please read the entire form carefully."

    This subheading at the top of the form helps identify which form you are dealing with. The four paragraphs following the subheading are the same as their equivalents in the occurrence form.

    In this course, we will study *only* the differences between the claims-made and occurrence versions of the CGL policy. Provisions that are the same in both forms will not be covered in this unit.

    The feature of a claims-made form that is the primary factor in determining how this form differs from the occurrence form is the feature that decides whether coverage applies, called the coverage _____.

    Answer: trigger

TRIGGER FOR COVERAGES A AND B

A Claim First Made

2. The trigger that activates both Coverage A and Coverage B in a claims-made form is **a claim that is first made** against the insured during the policy period. The injury or damage **claim** must be made during the policy period, but the occurrence or offense causing injury or damage does not necessarily have to take place during the policy term.

    The trigger for Coverage A is explained under the insuring agreement of Coverage A bodily injury and property damage liability. Locate and read paragraphs 1.b.(2) and (3). Then, go to the insuring agreement for Coverage B personal and advertising injury liability and read Items 1.b.(2) and (3). These items stipulate the trigger for Coverage B. You will see that the trigger is the same for both coverages. The only differences are in the Coverage A reference to BI and PD and the Coverage B reference to personal and advertising injury.

    If an injury occurs during the 2002 period of a claims-made policy, but no claim is made until after the coverage is renewed in 2003 by another claims-made policy, the claim will be covered only under the 2003 policy.

This assumes that the injury occurs after the retroactive date of the 2003 policy and that no exclusions apply. The retroactive date is a vital feature of the claims-made form, and we will discuss it later.

Henry Lowell has a claims-made CGL policy covering his business from January 1, 2003, to January 1, 2004. On December 10, 2003, a customer is injured in the store when a stack of plywood falls on her. The customer does not make a claim until January 23, 2004, when another claims-made policy is in effect. Disregarding any retroactive date, which of the following is correct?

A. The claim will be paid under the 2003 policy because that was the policy in effect when the bodily injury occurred.

B. The claim will be paid under the 2004 policy because that was the policy in effect when the claim was filed.

C. The claim will not be paid because the occurrence and notice of claim did not take place in the same policy period.

Answer: B is correct.

3. For a claims-made policy to respond to a loss, an actual claim for loss must be made. It is not enough for the insured to notify the company that an incident has occurred because an occurrence or offense and a claim are not the same thing.

   The conditions section of the claims-made form makes this point. Go to the conditions section of the claims-made version of the CGL and locate **2. Duties in the event of occurrence, offense, claim, or suit**. Read the short paragraph that follows Item 2.a.(3).

Which of the following would trigger coverage under a claims-made CGL policy written for XYZ Gas Refinery from January 1, 2002, to January 1, 2003?

A. The insured refinery notifies the insurance company of a gas leak that occurred at 4:00 pm on July 14, 2002.

B. A claimant writes to the insured on March 14, 2002, asking for $870. She claims the sign at the entrance to the refinery fell on her car the week before and damaged it. The insured receives the letter on March 16, 2002.

C. On March 20, 2003, a claimant writes the insured for payment for bodily injury that occurred on the insured's premises on December 22, 2002. This is the first notice of the incident the insured has received.

Answer: B is correct. A is not correct because notice of an occurrence is not notice of a claim. In C, the claim was not first made until after the policy expired.

4. An actual claim must be made to trigger coverage during the claims-made policy period. The claim may be made either to the insured or the insurer. If the insured receives a claim, certain procedures are required. Read Item 2.b. of this condition.

According to this condition, which of the following actions are required of the insured?

A. Make a record of the claim and the date it arrives

B. Promptly notify the insurance company in some way that the claim has been received

C. Notify the insurance company in writing as soon as possible

D. All of the above

Answer: C is correct.

Claim Received by Insured or Insurer

5. During this discussion, we will look mostly at Coverage A, but the provisions of Coverage B are the same except that they apply to an offense causing personal and advertising injury.

Item 1.c of the Coverage A insuring agreement states that a claim notice is valid at the earlier of these:

■ when received and recorded by any insured or by the insurance company; or

■ when the insurer makes a settlement as specified in Item 1.a.

Complete this exercise.

In the following situations, which would be considered valid claim notices under a claims-made form in effect from June 20, 2003, to June 20, 2004, for Brewster and Banes Hardware Store?

A. Tom Brewster, a partner in the business, receives a property damage claim on June 14, 2004. Tom fails to mail the notice to the insurer promptly, so it does not reach the insurance company's home office until June 23, 2004.

B. On June 9, 2004, Priscilla Dundee falls while shopping at the hardware store. Embarrassed, Priscilla hurries out of the store without telling anyone what happened. By August 30, 2004, Priscilla is suffering swelling at the knee and is having trouble walking. She decides to sue Brewster and Banes. On September 3, 2004, Howard Banes receives a summons and complaint for damages. This is his first notice.

C. On June 18, 2004, Howard Banes receives a letter from Susan Perkins claiming injury from a faulty repair to her lawn mower. Howard takes the letter to his insurance producer immediately, but the notice is not mailed to the home office until June 26, 2004.

Answer: A and C are correct.

Claims for Injury or Damage to the Same Person or Organization

6. The last two paragraphs of Item 1.c state that once a person makes a claim, any other claim for damages because of that same event will be considered to be made at the time the first claim is made. This part of the policy refers to bodily injury and property damages.

    Here's how this works. A claim first made in 2002 is covered and paid by the insured's claims-made policy. A year later, the claimant dies from the injury incurred in the preceding year. The heir to the estate files suit for loss of services. This second claim will be considered to have been made when the first claim was made and will be covered under the 2002 policy and the 2002 limits of liability. This principle applies to offenses for personal and advertising injury as well.

    Teresa Kane is one of many claimants to file a bodily injury claim against Cure-More Pharmaceuticals. She developed a long-term disability from taking a new Cure-More diabetes medicine that had adverse side effects. Her claim is handled under Cure-More's claims-made policy in effect the year her claim is made. Three years later, when the previous policy has been renewed, Kane's husband files suit against Cure-More for care and loss of services because of her increased disability. The husband's claim would be paid under

    A. the first policy that covered Kane's claim

    B. the renewal policy

    C. no policy

    Answer: A is correct.

TRIGGER FOR COVERAGE C

7. This chart summarizes the trigger for Coverages A and B under the two types of CGL forms.

Claims-Made Form	Occurrence Form
■ Trigger for Coverages A and B	■ Trigger for Coverages A and B
A claim for damages first made during the policy period	Occurrence or offense during the policy period

    The trigger for Coverage C is the same under both the occurrence and claims-made forms. Coverage C provides insurance for certain medical expenses for bodily injury caused by an **accident that takes place during**

the policy term. The policy specifies that the medical expenses must be incurred and reported within one year of the occurrence. The trigger for Coverage C, then, is an event that occurs during the policy period.

Consider an insured with a claims-made Policy #1 in 2003 and a renewal claims-made Policy #2 in 2004. The insured commits an offense of wrongful eviction with accompanying bodily injury to a tenant in 2003. Although first aid was administered at the time of the accident, the claimant does not make a claim until 2004.

The bodily injury and personal injury portions of the claim would be covered under Policy #2 because that is the policy in effect when the bodily injury claim is made. However, Policy #2 would *not* cover the first aid expenses because the Coverage C trigger applies only to events that occur during the policy period. Policy #1 would cover this part of the claim.

Now you know that the triggers for Coverages A and B are different for the occurrence and claims-made forms, but the Coverage C trigger is the same. On the following chart, fill in the coverage triggers for the two CGL forms.

Claims-Made Form	Occurrence Form
■ Trigger for Coverage A	■ Trigger for Coverage A
■ Trigger for Coverage B	■ Trigger for Coverage B
■ Trigger for Coverage C	■ Trigger for Coverage C

Answer:

Claims-Made Form	Occurrence Form
■ Trigger for Coverage A	■ Trigger for Coverage A
A claim for damages first made during the policy period	Occurrence during the policy period
■ Trigger for Coverage B	■ Trigger for Coverage B
A claim for damages first made during the policy period	Occurrence during the policy period
■ Trigger for Coverage C	■ Trigger for Coverage C
Occurrence during the policy period	Occurrence during the policy period

RETROACTIVE DATE

Purpose and Definition

8. The **retroactive date** is one of two special provisions in the claims-made form that help provide continuous coverage without gaps or overlaps between successive policies. The other is the extended reporting period, which we will discuss later.

    These provisions help ensure that only one policy will respond to a loss, preventing the stacking of limits from several occurrence type policies that has occasionally resulted from court decisions in the past. **Stacking** means the limits of insurance from many policies that were in effect at different times are stacked one upon the other and applied to a single case. This sometimes happens with latent bodily injury claims, such as exposure to asbestos, where the injury is progressive, occurring over many years during the terms of many policies. The provisions we will discuss now can help control this situation.

    Which one of the following expresses the purpose of the retroactive date provision?

    A. To ensure that the insurance company will pay as few claims as possible

    B. To control gaps and overlaps in coverage and stacking the limits of many policies

    C. To provide that all policies in effect during latent injury situations share in the cost of a claim

    Answer: B is correct.

9. The retroactive date is a date stipulated in the declarations that essentially means that the insurer will pay for claims made during the policy period, provided the incident occurred **on this date or later**. The insurer will not pay for an incident that occurred before the retroactive date even if the claim is first made during the claims-made policy period.

    A. The claims-made policy does not cover injury or damage that occurred (before/after) _____ the retroactive date.

    B. There is no coverage under the claims-made form for injury or damage that occurs after the _____
    _____.

    C. To see how the retroactive date is listed on the declarations, look at the sample CGL declarations for Jay's Jewelry Manufacturing Company in your Forms and Endorsements. The retroactive date, if any, is entered in the space just below the middle of the page. Does the CGL policy for Jay's Jewelry have a retroactive date?
    ( ) Yes   ( ) No   How do you know? _____
    _____

Answer: A. before; B. end of the policy period; C. No. The word *None* is written in this space.

Optional Uses of the Retroactive Date

10. The insured in the sample declarations has a CGL policy with no retroactive date. This is one of three options for applying the retroactive date. The three choices are:

    ■ the **same date** as the policy inception;

    ■ an **earlier date** than the policy inception; or

    ■ no retroactive date.

    Policies representing each of these three options are illustrated here. Look them over carefully, and then refer to them to answer the following questions.

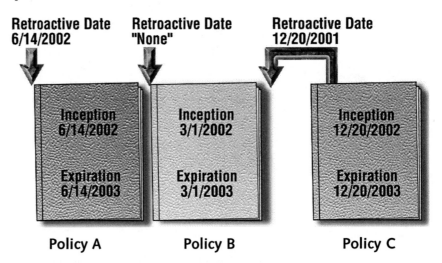

Retroactive Date 6/14/2002	**Retroactive Date "None"**	**Retroactive Date 12/20/2001**
Inception 6/14/2002	Inception 3/1/2002	Inception 12/20/2002
Expiration 6/14/2003	Expiration 3/1/2003	Expiration 12/20/2003
Policy A	**Policy B**	**Policy C**

    A. Which policy—A, B, or C—has a retroactive date *earlier* than the policy inception? Policy _____

    B. Which policy has a retroactive date that is the *same* as the policy inception? Policy _____

    C. Which policy has *no* retroactive date? Policy _____

    Answer: A. C; B. A; C. B

11. In Policies A and C in our illustration, the insurer stipulates that occurrences or offenses before the date shown will not be covered, even if a claim is first made during the policy period. Since the word *None* is entered on the declarations in Policy B, *all* prior occurrences are covered if a claim is first made during the policy period.

Refer again to the illustrations in the previous exercise to answer these questions.

A. The insured is covered by Policy C. A claim is made on February 15, 2003, for an incident that occurred on November 9, 2002. This claim (is/is not) _____ covered under Policy C because_____
_____
_____.

B. Another insured is covered by Policy A. An incident occurs on June 30, 2002, and a claim is made on July 1, 2003. The claim (is/is not) _____ covered under Policy A because_____
_____
_____.

C. Policy B covers another insured. A claim is first made on September 10, 2002, for an occurrence on December 30, 2001. This claim (is/is not) _____ covered under Policy B because _____
_____
_____.

Answer: A. is, because the incident occurred after the retroactive date and the claim was made during the policy period; B. is not, because the claim was not made during the policy period; C. is, because there is no retroactive date so all prior occurrences are covered if the claim is first made during the policy period

Same Date as Policy Inception

12. Let's look more closely at each of the three options for retroactive dates.

A claims-made policy with a retroactive date that is the same as the policy's inception date provides coverage only if both the occurrence and the claim take place during the policy period. There is no coverage for occurrences before the inception of the policy.

Let's see what happens when a claims-made form goes into effect following prior coverage under an occurrence form or a series of occurrence forms:

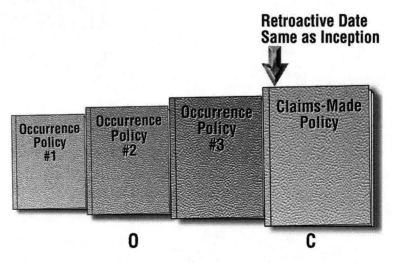

Retroactive Date Same as Inception

Occurrence Policy #1   Occurrence Policy #2   Occurrence Policy #3   Claims-Made Policy

O   C

This illustration shows an insured with a current claims-made policy that follows a succession of occurrence policies. The retroactive date is the same as the inception date of the claims-made policy.

The letter "O" under occurrence Policy #2 represents **when the occurrence** for which the insured is liable happened. The letter "C" under the claims-made policy represents **when the claim for damages is first made.**

A. Taking into account the retroactive date, would the claims-made policy in the illustration apply to a claim first made during its policy period for damages that resulted from an occurrence two years before? ( ) Yes ( ) No   Explain._____

_____

B. Would there be coverage under any policy illustrated for damages resulting from an accident that occurred two years before the claims-made policy? ( ) Yes   ( ) No   Explain._____

_____

Answer: A. No. There is no coverage for an occurrence that takes place before the retroactive date; B. Yes. There would be coverage under occurrence Policy #2 since an occurrence policy covers damage that occurs during the policy period even if the claim is made after the policy expires.

13. Now, let's consider what happens when a claims-made policy follows either as a renewal or as a replacement of another claims-made policy. In this illustration, the retroactive date of the new policy is the same as its inception date.

Under the situation illustrated, a claim is reported to the insured on June 15, 2003, for an occurrence on March 1, 2003, that resulted in property damage. Based solely on the information you have about this insured, it appears there is

A. insurance for this loss under Policy #1

B. insurance for this loss under Policy #2

C. no insurance available for this loss

D. insurance under both policies

Answer: C is correct.

14. In the previous exercise, there was no coverage under Policy #1 because the first claim was not made during the policy period. There was no coverage under Policy #2 because the loss occurred before the retroactive date. Therefore, the insured in this example is apparently left without insurance protection for this loss. Later, we will discuss safeguards to prevent this situation.

A claims-made policy with a retroactive date that is the same as the policy's inception date provides coverage

A. only if both the occurrence and the claim for damages take place during the policy period.

B. for claims first made during the policy period no matter when the occurrence takes place.

C. for bodily injury or property damage that occurs during the policy period, no matter when the claim is made.

Answer: A is correct.

Advancing the Retroactive Date

15. In the last example, the retroactive date and the inception date of the second claims-made policy were the same because the second insurer had **advanced the retroactive date**—whatever it was—that applied to the first claims-made policy. Moving the retroactive date forward left the insured without coverage for certain claims.

To avoid this situation, the rules by which claims-made CGL coverage is governed require that the insured give **written consent** to advancing the retroactive date. And, even with the insured's consent, the retroactive date may be advanced only for one or more of the following reasons.

1. A different insurance company is writing the new policy.

2. A substantive change in the insured's operations has resulted in a greater exposure to loss.

3. The insured did not provide the insurer with information the insured knew or should have known that would have been material to the insurance company's decision to accept the risk; or the insured did not provide information requested by the insurance company.

4. The insured requests that the retroactive date be advanced.

Although advancing the retroactive date can leave the insured with coverage gaps, certain safeguards are built into the claims-made form. These provisions have to do with the extended reporting period we mentioned earlier, and you will learn more about this later.

For each situation below, write in the corresponding number 1–4 that lists the reason for advancing the retroactive date. For situations where the retroactive date cannot be advanced, write N/A on the line in front of it.

_____ A. Although an insured knew a volatile chemical was used in a new manufacturing process at his plant, he did not inform the insurance company at renewal.

_____ B. The insured tells the insurance company that blasting operations formerly done at a different site will now be performed on the insured premises.

_____ C. The insured wants her present insurance company to move the retroactive date forward.

_____ D. The insured's operation has changed from baking and selling confections to merely selling them.

_____ E. When the insured's policy expires, she obtains new insurance with another company.

Answer: 3. A; 2. B; 4. C; N/A D; 1. E

Earlier Date than Policy Inception

16. The second option for establishing a retroactive date is to use a date that is earlier than the second policy's inception. This provides continuous coverage from one claims-made policy to another without coverage gaps.

    The best arrangement is for all successive claims-made policies to have the very first claims-made policy's inception date as their retroactive dates, as shown in this illustration.

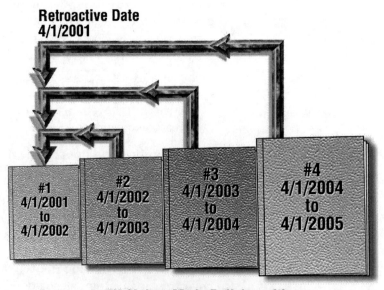

Retroactive Date 4/1/2001

#1 4/1/2001 to 4/1/2002

#2 4/1/2002 to 4/1/2003

#3 4/1/2003 to 4/1/2004

#4 4/1/2004 to 4/1/2005

All Claims-Made Policies with 4/1/2001 as Retroactive Date

Policy #1 provides coverage for damages from an occurrence during the policy period if the claim is first made during that policy period.

Policy #2 provides coverage for damages from an occurrence any time from April 1, 2001, (the retroactive date of both policies) as long as the claim is first made during Policy #2's term.

Policies #3 and #4 also provide coverage for damages from occurrences that happened on or after April 1, 2001, as long as the claims were made during their respective policy periods.

The insured under these policies receives a first claim report on January 11, 2005, for damages from an incident on June 20, 2002.

A. The incident occurred during which policy's term? _____

B. The claim was first made during which policy's term? _____

C. Does the retroactive date exclude coverage for this occurrence?
( ) Yes   ( ) No

D. If there is coverage, which policy would respond? _____

Answer: A. Policy #2; B. Policy #4; C. No; D. Policy #4

17. A retroactive date might also be earlier than the policy inception, but not as early as the date of the first claims-made policy's inception. This method might be used if a new insurer wanted to exclude occurrences in the past that could develop into claims during its policy term. The insurer could use a retroactive date later than the occurrence and before the new policy's inception.

This illustration shows a retroactive date later than an occurrence and before a new policy's inception.

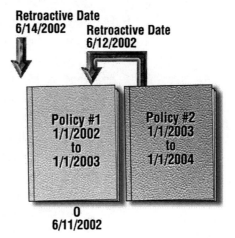

An insured covered by claims-made Policy #1 has a loss on June 11, 2002. Several claims are made and paid before the policy's expiration. The insurer of Policy #1 refuses to renew coverage. Another insurer agrees to replace the coverage with claims-made Policy #2, but sets the retroactive date at June 12, 2002, one day after the loss.

The retroactive date for Policy #2 will provide coverage

A. for all covered claims back to the inception date of Policy #1.

B. only for insured claims made during the current policy period and for events that occurred during the current policy period.

C. for all insured claims made during the current policy period and occurring back to June 12, 2002, but excluding any claims that might be brought as a result of the incident on June 11, 2002.

Answer: C is correct.

No Retroactive Date

18. The third option is to use no retroactive date. By not imposing a retroactive date, the insurance company does not exclude any prior occurrences. If a valid claim is made during the current policy term, there will be coverage no matter when the occurrence happened.

    Not imposing a retroactive date on a claims-made policy is quite unlikely for insureds whose products or work either have been available for some time or pose a high risk of latent disease or damage.

    An insurer writing a claims-made policy on a business that had been insured by occurrence policies in the past is the most likely to consider issuing a policy with no retroactive date. That is because the claims-made policy would be **excess insurance** for a loss. A claim made during the new claims-made policy, but arising from an incident that happened before the inception date, would be covered first by the occurrence policy in effect at the time of the occurrence. Any further need for coverage would then come from the claims-made policy.

    Of the following situations, which one would be most likely to be written under a claims-made policy with no retroactive date?

    A. A motorcycle manufacturer with a poor loss experience needs new coverage when the current insurer refuses to renew the existing claims-made policy.

    B. A retail clothing store owner wants to replace an occurrence policy.

    C. A previously self-insured pharmaceutical company that has just released a new vaccine wants to purchase general liability insurance.

    D. A church camp is competitively shopping for general liability insurance to replace its existing claims-made policy coming up for renewal in two months.

Answer: B is correct.

Other Insurance

19. Go to the Conditions section of the claims-made CGL and locate Item 4, **Other Insurance**. Item 4.b.(1)(a) is the only part of this provision unique to the claims-made form. Read all of Item b concerning excess insurance.

    According to this provision, the claims-made policy will be excess insurance over an occurrence policy when:

    ■ there is no retroactive date on the claims-made policy; or

    ■ the occurrence policy has a term that continues after the retroactive date on the claims-made policy.

    The Other Insurance provision in the claims-made form says that insurance under this policy is excess over any insurance provided by

    A. another claims-made policy if this policy has an earlier retroactive date.

    B. an occurrence policy if there is no retroactive date indicated on this policy.

    C. an occurrence policy with a term that continues after this policy's retroactive date.

    Answer: B and C are correct.

Premium Application

20. Rates for claims-made policies are modified by factors that increase according to how long the insured has been in the claims-made program. An insured's claims-made program is said to have **matured** after five successive years during which the insured has claims-made policies as long as each policy uses as its retroactive date the retroactive date of the **first** claims-made policy.

    The rate is lowest in the first year of a claims-made policy because the chance of loss is the lowest. For the second year, if the retroactive date is kept the same, the premium is slightly more because the insurer is now liable for reported claims over a two-year period. The premium gradually increases up to five years as long as the retroactive date of each policy stays the same as that for the first-year policy.

Study this illustration.

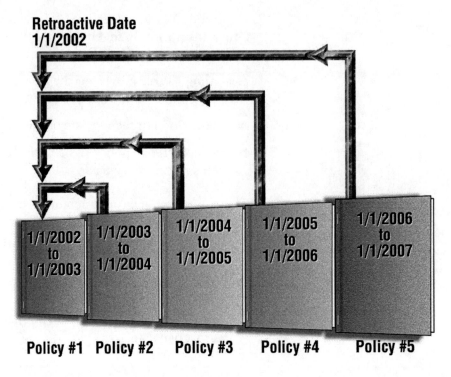

**Retroactive Date
1/1/2002**

Policy #1   Policy #2   Policy #3   Policy #4   Policy #5

Knowing that rates for a series of five claims-made policies are modified if each policy uses the retroactive date of the first claims-made policy, answer these questions about the illustration.

A. Which policy has the lowest rate? Policy _____

B. Which policy has the highest rate? Policy _____

C. The claims-made program is said to have matured after _____ years, provided what retroactive date is used? _____

Answer: A. 1; B. 5; C. 5, The retroactive date of the first claims-made policy

21. If an insurer advances the retroactive date to the inception date of its renewal or replacement policy, the new policy starts over with the first-year claims-made multiplier factor. As a result, the insurer will:

■ receive less premium; and

■ avoid paying for damages due to prior occurrences.

Study this illustration, and then answer the following questions.

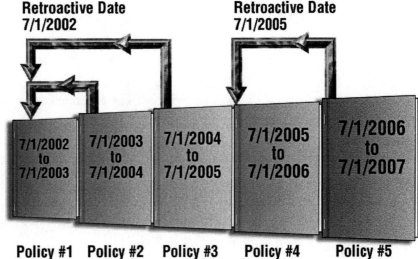

**Retroactive Date
7/1/2002**

**Retroactive Date
7/1/2005**

| Policy #1 | Policy #2 | Policy #3 | Policy #4 | Policy #5 |

A. Which two policies would have the same multiplier for figuring premium? Policy #_____ and Policy #_____.

B. Why would these two policies have the same multiplier?_____

_____

Answer: A. 1, 4; B. Policy #4 advances the retroactive date. Therefore, both Policy #1 and Policy #4 are considered the first policies in their claims-made programs.

EXTENDED REPORTING PERIODS

22. The coverage gap that results when the retroactive date on a replacement or renewal policy is advanced can be closed by a feature called the **extended reporting period (ERP)**. This is the second of the special provisions in the claims-made form that help provide continuous coverage without gaps or overlaps.

An insured can be left without coverage not only if an insurer advances the retroactive date in a series of claims-made policies, but also if claims are reported after the claims-made policy expires.

Suppose Carlson's Ski Lift receives a summons and complaint for bodily injury damages to one of its customers the week after its claims-made policy expires. The injury took place without the knowledge of the insured one month before the claim was received. Would the claim be covered under the expired policy as we have studied it so far?   ( ) Yes   ( ) No

Answer: No

23. After a claims-made policy expires, if a claim is made for injury or damage that occurred

    ■ after the retroactive date of the claims-made policy *and*

    ■ before its expiration,

    coverage may be provided by extending the period during which claims may be reported. The extended reporting period will be either:

    ■ an automatic, free, **basic extended reporting period** of 60 days or 5 years; or

    ■ on request and for an additional charge, a **supplemental extended reporting period** of unlimited duration.

    The purpose of a basic extended reporting period or a supplemental extended reporting period is to
    A. extend the policy period of a claims-made policy
    B. extend the period during which a claim may be reported for injuries occurring during the claims-made policy period
    C. avoid the necessity for annual renewals of claims-made policies
    D. do all of the above

    Answer: B is correct.

Activating Extended Reporting Periods

24. Locate Section V—Extended Reporting Periods in your sample claims-made CGL policy. This section is characteristic of the claims-made form only. Read only Item 1.

    The company will provide an extended reporting period, also known as **tail coverage**, if the current claims-made policy is:

    ■ canceled or nonrenewed;

    ■ renewed with another claims-made policy that has a retroactive date later than that of the current policy; or

    ■ replaced with an occurrence policy.

    The following paragraphs describe the consequences of these situations that result in a need for tail coverage:

    The policy is canceled or nonrenewed: The insured has no insurance because the previous claims-made policy required claims to be made during the policy period, and no policy now exists.

    The policy is renewed with another claims-made policy that has a retroactive date later than that of the current policy: Although a claim may be made during the new policy's term, if the retroactive date of the new policy is the same as the inception date of the new policy, there is no coverage for events that occurred before that date.

The policy is replaced with an occurrence policy: There is coverage only for injury during the new policy term, not for injury that occurred during the previous policy period but was reported late.

An insured with a claims-made policy is eligible for an extended reporting period if

A. coverage is canceled

B. coverage is not renewed

C. the insured replaces the claims-made policy with an occurrence policy

D. a claims-made renewal policy has a retroactive date different from the expiring policy

E. all of the above are correct

Answer: E is correct.

Extended Reporting Period Limitations

25. Read all of Item 2 of Section V—Extended Reporting Periods.

This provision does *not* extend the policy period. Only the period during which **reporting** may occur is extended. The bodily injury, property damage, or personal and advertising injury must have:

■ **occurred** before the end of the policy period; and

■ **not occurred** before the retroactive date.

Furthermore, once an ERP becomes effective, it cannot be canceled.

Consider a claims-made policy effective January 1, 2003, which is then canceled as of September 1, 2003. The retroactive date is the same as the inception date. Which of the following would be covered by an extended reporting period to this policy?

A. An accident causing property damage occurs on July 22, 2003, but is not reported to the insured until September 30, 2003.

B. An accident causing bodily injury occurs on December 6, 2002, and a summons and complaint for damages is received on September 9, 2003, as the insured's first notice.

C. A bodily injury accident occurs on September 5, 2003, and is reported on September 15, 2003.

Answer: A is correct.

ERP Limits of Insurance

26. The basic extended reporting periods neither reinstate nor increase the limits of insurance. In other words, claims reported during a basic extended reporting period must be paid from any remaining limits in the original policy.

    However, if the insured purchases the **supplemental extended reporting period endorsement**, separate insurance limits are provided. Read about two options in Section V. Item 4 addresses the basic extended reporting period limits and Item 6 the supplemental ERP. Read both items now before continuing. We will discuss Item 5 in a moment.

    Separate aggregate limits established for the supplemental ERP will be equal to the limits shown in the declarations for the general aggregate, the products-completed operations aggregate, or both, depending on what coverage the policy provided.

    Suppose an insured's policy has general aggregate limits of $1 million. There is no products-completed operations aggregate. When the insured's policy expires, she purchases the supplemental ERP to cover late claims. The insurance available to her under the supplemental ERP is

    A. the amount remaining in the original general aggregate limits after other claims have been paid during the policy period

    B. the amount remaining in the original general aggregate limits after other claims have been paid during the policy year, plus $1 million

    C. $1 million, which is equal to the original aggregate limits shown in the declarations

    Answer: C is correct.

27. Although separate aggregate limits are available for the supplemental ERP, they do not apply to every claim made during the policy period and the extended reporting period. Item 6 indicates that the separate aggregate limits apply only to claims *first* received and recorded *during* the supplemental ERP.

    An insured's claims-made policy period is from January 4, 2003, to January 4, 2004. The insured purchases the supplemental ERP, providing separate aggregate limits of insurance of $700,000. During the supplemental period—which is unlimited, remember—a claim is first made 10 years after the policy expires. During that same period, another claim is made as a follow-up to a claim made during the actual policy period. The new separate aggregate limits of the supplemental ERP are available for

    A. the claim that is first made 10 years later

    B. the follow-up claim described above

    C. both of the above

    D. neither of the above

    Answer: A is correct.

Basic Extended Reporting Periods

28. We have briefly mentioned that the basic extended reporting period of either 60 days or 5 years is available automatically and free of charge under specified conditions. Read all of Item 3 under Section V now.

    Let's first consider the **60-day basic ERP**. When a claims-made policy is terminated, a 60-day basic extended reporting period automatically becomes available. The insured does not have to apply for it, and no premium is charged. The 60-day basic ERP provides automatic coverage for any valid claim made during the 60 days after the policy expires, as long as the incident occurred between the expiring policy's retroactive date and its expiration date.

    This illustration represents a claims-made policy with a retroactive date the same as the inception date and a 60-day basic ERP. The letter "O" under the policy indicates **the time of the occurrence or offense**. The letter "C" indicates when the **claim is first made**.

Would the claim in this illustration be covered?   ( ) Yes   ( ) No   Explain.

_____

_____

Answer: Yes. The occurrence or offense took place during the policy period and the first claim was made during the 60-day basic ERP.

29. Would the claim in the next illustration be covered?   ( ) Yes   ( ) No   Explain.

_____

_____

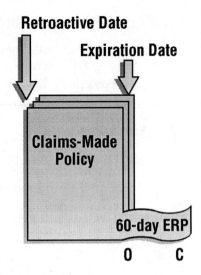

Answer: No. The event occurred after the policy expired.

30. Suppose the insured is aware of an event that took place before the claims-made policy expired, but suspects that claims may first come in *after* the 60-day basic ERP. The insured has up to 60 days following policy expiration to report the occurrence or offense to the insurer. In this case, the **5-year basic ERP** applies. Claims for damages arising from the reported occurrence can be brought any time during the five-year period, as shown in the following illustration:

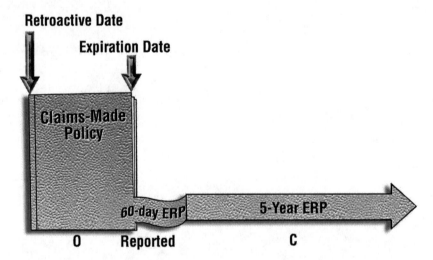

Which of the following statements about the 5-year basic ERP are correct?

A. It covers events that occurred during the 60 days after the policy expires.

B. It extends the reporting period to five years beyond policy expiration.

C. It requires the insured to notify the insurer within 60 days of policy expiration of an incident that occurred between the retroactive date and the policy expiration that could result in liability claims.

D. It applies to occurrences or offenses that happen within five years after policy expiration

Answer: B and C are correct.

Supplemental Extended Reporting Period

31. An insured who wants more than the 60-day or 5-year basic periods for reporting unknown claims may *write* to the insurer requesting that a supplemental extended reporting period endorsement be attached to the expiring policy. Additional details about this endorsement are covered in a later unit.

    Like the basic ERP, the supplemental ERP provides coverage for incidents that occurred between the retroactive date and the policy expiration. Under the supplemental ERP, however, claims may be *reported* for an **unlimited** time. This ERP is sometimes called an unlimited tail. It takes effect at the end of either the 60-day or 5-year basic period, whichever applies.

    The insurer must receive the insured's written request for the endorsement within 60 days after the end of the policy period. Once the insured pays the premium for the endorsement, it may not be canceled.

    Read about the supplemental extended reporting period endorsement in Section V, Item 5. Read up to, butnotincluding, the paragraph that begins, "We will determine...."

    Joseph Keller and Henry Jenkins, who operate K&J Amusement Park, had a claims-made CGL policy covering their amusement park and rides. The insurance company refused to renew the policy when it expired. One month before expiration, a cable supporting a gondola on the Moon Ride snapped, causing death to one passenger and severe injury to three others. The deceased's spouse files a claim with the insured during the 60-day extended reporting period. However, the owners are concerned about not having coverage for other bodily injury claims that may arise out of this accident. What would you advise Keller and Jenkins to do?

    A. Nothing. The 60-day basic ERP will be automatically extended for an unlimited period to cover any claims made after the 60 days as long as the injuries occurred before the policy expired.

    B. Either Keller or Jenkins should call the insurer and ask that the supplemental extended reporting period endorsement be added to the policy.

    C. Keller and Jenkins should write the insurer requesting the supplemental ERP endorsement and make sure the request arrives within 60 days of the policy expiration.

    D. They should purchase an occurrence form CGL policy to cover the claims that might arise from this accident.

Answer: C is correct.

Supplemental ERP Premium

32. Now read the remainder of Item 5, beginning with "We will determine…."

    If a claims-made policy is not renewed and the first named insured writes the insurer requesting an unlimited ERP, which of the following might the insurer consider as it determines the premium for the supplemental ERP?

    A. The insured has notified the company of an incident during the policy period that might result in a claim for damages.

    B. Only $10,000 remains from the original $500,000 limit of insurance.

    C. An incident that occurred before the policy expired has resulted in only one reported property damage claim. Other claims from this same incident are anticipated.

    D. There is a statute of limitations (time in which litigation may be brought after an injury occurs) in the state where an accident occurred that might result in claims against the insured.

    E. All of the above are correct.

    Answer: E is correct.

33. The maximum premium for the supplemental ERP may not be greater than 200% of the previous year's annual premium for the CGL coverage part to which the endorsement is attached. The premium for the endorsement is fully earned when the endorsement goes into effect, and neither the insured nor insurer may cancel.

    Which one of the following is correct?

    A. A catastrophic accident, which could result in a class action suit, occurs before a policy expires. As a result, the insurer will charge for the supplemental ERP whatever is needed to recover this loss.

    B. The insurer can consider the total annual premium for a commercial package policy when determining the premium for an ERP endorsement.

    C. One month after the insured pays the premium due for the supplemental ERP, the insured is able to obtain insurance from another company. The insured wants to cancel the endorsement and have the unearned premium returned.

    D. For the supplemental ERP endorsement, the insurer can charge no more than 200% of the annual premium for the expiring coverage part.

    Answer: D is correct.

Other Insurance

34. The claims-made policy indicates the roles played by both the basic and supplemental extended reporting periods when there is **other insurance** that would cover the same loss. To refresh your memory about the basic ERP, reread the final paragraph of Item 3 in Section V.

    The 60-day or 5-year ERP applies *only* if no other insurance the insured purchases to replace the claims-made form applies to the claim, or would apply if the limits had not been exhausted.

    Refer to the illustration to see an example of this other insurance provision. Assume claims-made Policy A is replaced with claims-made Policy B. Both policies have the same retroactive date.

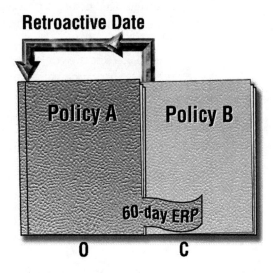

    A claim for an injury that occurred during Policy A's term is made against the insured less than 60 days after Policy B takes effect. This is illustrated by the letters "O" and "C."

    Without a new policy, the loss would be covered by the automatic basic 60-day ERP of Policy A because the claim was made within 60 days for damage that occurred during the policy period. Because there is a new policy, however, the claim will be covered under the *new* claims-made policy. There will be *no* coverage under the basic ERP of the previous policy.

    The Sullivan Company, manufacturer of unicycles, replaces one claims-made policy with another. The two policies have the same retroactive date. Twenty days after the new policy takes effect, Sullivan receives a first claim for damages due to bodily injury to a child. The claim alleges that a child riding one of Sullivan's unicycles fell off because of a faulty seat design. The accident occurred during the previous policy's term.

    A. The claim would be covered under

       1. the first policy's basic extended reporting period

       2. the new policy

       3. neither of the above—there would be no coverage for this claim

    B. If the replacement policy were written with an occurrence limit of $100,000, and the expired policy had a $10,000 limit of insurance remaining in the products-completed operations aggregate, would the basic ERP of the expired policy contribute to a $110,000 judgment against the insured?   ( ) Yes   ( ) No   Explain._____

_____

_____

_____

Answer: A. 2 is correct; B. No. There is no excess coverage under the ERP, even when recovery under a replacement policy is insufficient to cover a loss.

35. When the insured purchases the supplemental ERP, other insurance is treated differently. Reread the final paragraph of Item 5 in Section V.

When the supplemental ERP endorsement is used, the claims-made form is excess over other insurance. In addition, the endorsement is *also* excess insurance over any other policy that begins or continues after the endorsement takes effect. So, while the basic extended reporting period *never* provides excess insurance, the supplemental ERP endorsement does.

Excess insurance means the insurer providing the extended reporting period will agree to pay its share of the claim that exceeds the *sum* of:

■ the total the other insurance would pay if no excess insurance existed; and

■ the total of all deductible and self-insured amounts under that other insurance.

Look at the following illustration, which represents payment permitted by the supplemental extended reporting period endorsement after all other contributions to a claim have been made.

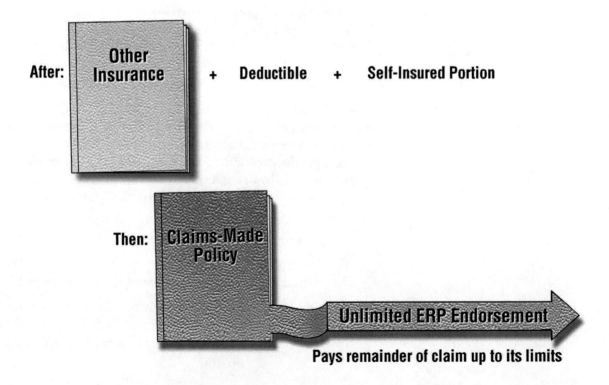

An insured's claims-made policy is canceled after a negative loss history. Unable to find replacement coverage within 60 days after cancellation, the insured purchases the supplemental ERP to protect against claims for earlier occurrences. Some time later, the insured succeeds in obtaining claims-made coverage with a retroactive date the same as that of the previous policy. After the replacement policy takes effect, a claim is made against the insured for injury that occurred during the previous policy period. The claim is covered under both the endorsement and the new claims-made policy. Which will be the primary insurance?

A. The first claims-made policy

B. The supplemental extended reporting period endorsement attached to the first policy

C. The new claims-made policy

D. None of the above

Answer: C is correct.

INSURED'S RIGHT TO INFORMATION

36. The remaining section of the claims-made form that differs from the occurrence form is found in Section IV, Conditions. The final condition concerns the insured's **right to have information** about:

■ **occurrences** of which the insurer is aware; and

■ **claims that were paid and amounts of insurance reserved** for each policy year.

This condition appears after Condition 9. **When We Do Not Renew** and begins at the top of the right-hand column on the page. Read all of this condition now.

A. If the insurance company cancels or nonrenews the policy, the information will be provided to the insured

1. within 45 days of policy expiration

2. within 60 days of policy expiration, and then only if the insured requests it

3. no later than 30 days before the date the policy is terminated

4. no later than 30 days before the termination date, but only if the insured requests the information

B. If the insured cancels the policy, under what conditions is the information made available to the insured?

1. Only if the first named insured requests the information in writing within 60 days after the policy period

2. Only if the first named insured requests the information in writing no later than 30 days before the date the policy will be canceled

C. If the insurance company unknowingly provides the insured with information that is not correct, is cancellation or nonrenewal by the insurance company prohibited?   ( ) Yes   ( ) No

D. The insured must have the insurer's permission to disclose the information to whom?_____

_____

Answer: A. 3 is correct; B. 1 is correct; C. No; D. Any claimant or claimant's representative

This completes your study of the claims-made CGL provisions. In the next unit, you will learn about some popular endorsements used with the CGL forms.

11

Common Endorsements

INTRODUCTION

1. This unit discusses a variety of endorsements used to tailor the CGL coverage part to meet the specific needs of either the insurer or the insured. Although not every available endorsement is covered here, we will discuss some of the more commonly used ones, including:

   ■ the *mandatory* Nuclear Energy Liability Exclusion endorsement (Broad Form) used for both the occurrence and claims-made coverage forms;

   ■ optional endorsements used exclusively with claims-made forms to extend the reporting period or limit coverage;

   ■ an optional endorsement restricting liability for employment practices;

   ■ optional endorsements used to fine-tune certain existing exclusions;

   ■ two optional endorsements related to pollution liability;

   ■ endorsements to limit or exclude coverage for mold-related losses;

   ■ endorsements used to comply with the federal Terrorism Risk Insurance Act of 2002 (TRIA);

   ■ optional endorsements that very specifically define excluded professional liability exposures;

   ■ optional endorsements to eliminate standard policy coverages; and

   ■ optional endorsements to broaden standard policy coverages.

   Which of the following answer choices express the purposes of the endorsements we will cover in this unit?
   A. Make changes only to the claims-made form
   B. Broaden or restrict various coverages
   C. Tailor either the claims-made or the occurrence form to meet clients' special needs
   D. Exclude coverages only

   Answer: A, B, and C are correct.

NUCLEAR ENERGY LIABILITY EXCLUSION ENDORSEMENT

2. Early in this course, you were introduced to the *mandatory* **Nuclear Energy Liability Exclusion** endorsement (Broad Form), which *must* be attached to every CGL policy, without exception. This endorsement, which appears after the claims-made CGL policy in your Forms and Endorsements, may also be required for other commercial insurance lines. Therefore, it is identified as

an **interline** form because it can be used between various lines of insurance, and its form number suggests that use with the prefix IL, for interline.

The Nuclear Energy Liability Exclusion endorsement (Broad Form) is an interline (IL) endorsement, which means that it

A. may be used with commercial forms for different lines of insurance

B. may be used only with CGL forms

C. must be altered slightly for different lines of insurance

Answer: A is correct.

3. The Nuclear Energy Liability Exclusion endorsement essentially excludes any injuries that occur as a result of the hazardous properties of nuclear material. The risks involved in this type of operation are beyond the scope of the CGL policy. While this seems to exclude a whole spectrum of nuclear facilities, transportation systems, and others, these commercial enterprises have access to nuclear policies specifically written for the nuclear risk.

Suppose the insured is a nuclear reactor service company. In addition to the people who work directly with nuclear reactors, the insured maintains an office, warehouse, and equipment. To be adequately covered for the liability risk, this insured needs

A. an insurance policy written specifically for the nuclear hazard

B. the CGL coverage part

C. both of the above

Answer: C is correct.

ENDORSEMENTS FOR THE CLAIMS-MADE FORM ONLY

Supplemental Extended Reporting Period Endorsement

4. In the previous unit, you learned that extended reporting periods may be available with the claims-made CGL. The basic 60-day and 5-year ERPs are free and automatic. An unlimited ERP is also available. You learned in the previous unit what the insured must do to have the unlimited **supplemental extended reporting period** endorsement go into effect. Which of the following are required?

A. Nothing is required. This supplemental extended reporting period is automatic under the circumstances described in the claims-made form.

B. The insured must pay an additional premium as required by the insurance company.

C. The insured must ask for the supplemental ERP in writing.

D. The insured's request must reach the insurer within 60 days after the end of the policy period.

Answer: B, C, and D are correct.

5. Now, let's look at the supplemental extended reporting period endorsement, which appears after the Nuclear Energy Liability Exclusion endorsement in the Forms and Endorsements. This endorsement amends two sections of the claims-made CGL:

■ Section III, Limits of Insurance; and

■ Section IV, Conditions.

Because we have already discussed how the endorsement modifies the conditions section, we won't go over it again. Read through the entire endorsement before continuing. Note that the supplemental ERP endorsement is excess over any other primary insurance for which the insured has been named as an additional insured by attachment of an endorsement.

The paragraphs amending the Limits of Insurance section of the claims-made policy reflect the potential for adding supplemental aggregates as a result of the endorsement. These aggregates apply separately for the products-completed operations hazard and for all other coverage that falls within the general aggregate limits.

In either case, for the separate aggregate limits to apply, the claim must meet the requirements discussed in the previous unit.

■ The claim must be for bodily injury, property damage, or personal and advertising injury.

■ The damages must have occurred before the end of the policy period.

■ The damages must *not* have occurred before the retroactive date.

■ Claims must be first received and recorded during the supplemental extended reporting period.

Assume the insured has a claims-made policy that runs from January 1, 2002, to January 1, 2003. The retroactive date is January 1, 2001. When this policy expires, the insured requests, receives and pays for the supplemental ERP endorsement. If the damages in each claim below are otherwise covered, which are included under the supplemental ERP?

A. Claim is first made on October 3, 2007, for damages that occurred May 15, 2002

B. Claim is first made on March 15, 2006, for damages that occurred December 4, 1998

C. Claim is first made on July 12, 2008, for damages that occurred February 1, 2003

D. Claim is first made on May 9, 2007, for damages that occurred September 10, 2002

Answer: A and D are correct. B is not correct because the damages occurred before the retroactive date. C is not correct because the damages occurred after the policy expired.

Exclusion of Specific Accidents, Products, Work, or Location Endorsement

6. You have learned that when the claims-made form retroactive date is the same as the policy inception, all incidents before the policy takes effect are excluded even when the claim is first made during the policy period. This can pose a difficult situation for the insured, who might be left uninsured in some cases. One way to remedy the situation is for the insurer to issue an endorsement that excludes not *everything* that occurs before the policy is in effect, but only *specific* things, such as:

■ accidents;

■ products;

■ work; and

■ locations.

For example, an otherwise acceptable insured might have experienced an incident for which no claims have been filed, but that has the potential for substantial liability. The insurance company, using a special endorsement, could exclude that one accident only. The same is true of certain products, work, or locations.

This option is open not only to the insurance company, but also to the insured. For example, an insured might prefer to self-insure a certain location, but maintain CGL coverage for all other locations.

The endorsement used to exclude designated items under Coverage A is the **exclusion of specific accidents, products, work, or location**. Which of the following could be excluded with this endorsement?

A. An insurer writing a policy for a plumbing contractor is aware of a job the plumber has completed that has potential for liability suits. Aside from this job, the plumbing contractor is a good risk, so the insurer wants to exclude only this particular job.

B. Among her other products, the insured has one for which she believes her liability risk is best handled by self-insurance. She wants the insurance company to exclude this one product from her claims-made CGL.

C. An insurer writing a new claims-made form wants to exclude any bodily injury or property damage that occurred before the policy's retroactive date.

D. An insurance company is willing to write a claims-made CGL for all but two of an insured's 12 business locations.

Answer: A, B, and D are correct. C is not correct because this does not refer to a specific item and should be handled by using a retroactive date that is the same as the policy inception date.

7. Locate the Exclusion of Specific Accidents, Products, Work, or Location endorsement in your Forms and Endorsements. Just review the top section, titled "Schedule," for now.

On the Schedule portion of this endorsement, the precise items to be excluded are listed, including identifying information. Refer to this section as you answer the following questions.

A. If an accident is excluded, what specific information must be provided about it? _____

_____

B. What information is required about a location that will be excluded?

_____

_____

C. When the insured's product or work is excluded, what information is required? _____

_____

Answer: A. Date, location and description; B. The location, its address and a description; C. A description of the product or work and the date of manufacture, sale, distribution, disposal, or completion

8. This endorsement defines a new term. Refer to Item C for the definition of **location**.

Based on the endorsement definition, which of the following represents a single location?

A. An insured has two buildings on a single lot, but they are separated by an alley running between them.

B. An insured has a business located at 611–615 North Elm Street. West Ridge Street runs between the 613 and 615 buildings.

C. An insured has a business location in St. Paul, Minnesota and another branch location doing the same type of business in Minneapolis.

D. The insured has a single fenced lot on which seven small buildings are located.

Answer: A, B, and D are correct. In C, the interruption in connection between the businesses is greater than those specified in the definition.

9. Read Item A of the endorsement.

    This item states what is excluded in general, referring to the accident, location, product, or work—whatever is listed in the schedule. The coverage is excluded for

    A. bodily injury and property damage
    B. personal and advertising injury
    C. medical payments coverage
    D. all of the above

    Answer: A is correct.

10. Item B. provides for extended reporting periods. The insurance company *must* make ERPs available to the insured when the exclusion endorsement is *first* issued on *renewal* of a claims-made policy. Read Items B.1 and 2 and the first paragraph following Item 2

    The insured is JB Associations, which has a claims-made policy with Greater City Insurance Company. When the policy expires, Greater City renews the coverage, but attaches the exclusion of specific accidents, products, work, or location endorsement to exclude a specific accident.

    A. Must Greater City provide an ERP under the expiring policy?
        ( ) Yes   ( ) No

    B. The ERP described will cover bodily injury or property damage that occurred during the policy period of the (expiring/renewal) _____ policy.

    C. If the expiring claims-made policy had been issued by State Insurance Company, is Greater City required to provide an ERP?
        ( ) Yes   ( ) No   Why? _____
        _____

    Answer: A. Yes; B. expiring; C. No. This provision applies to Greater City Insurance only if the insurance is a renewal of a previous claims-made policy issued by Greater City.

11. Read the final paragraph of Item B, which describes how the ERP will be provided.

    The purpose of the extended reporting period provision of the exclusion endorsement is to close any coverage gaps that could occur for the accident, product, work, or location that has been excluded. The endorsement mentioned provides for the ERP coverage you have learned about. We will look at that endorsement soon.

Let's conclude our discussion of this endorsement by considering circumstances where an insurance company might want to use it. At least three situations would call for it:

■ replacing an occurrence policy with a claims-made policy when a potentially risky incident is known to have occurred under the occurrence policy;

■ renewing a claims-made policy when the insurer does not want to subject the new limits to a specific occurrence under the expiring policy; and

■ renewing a claims-made policy that also had the exclusion endorsement attached, ensuring that coverage is not reinstated for previously excluded claims.

If the insurer wants to use the exclusion endorsement, it must be attached at policy inception. This is true whether the policy to which it is attached provides new, renewal, or replacement insurance.

A. Suppose an insurer renews a claims-made policy for one of its insureds. Three months into the new policy, an underwriter realizes that the expired policy had the exclusion endorsement attached to it. The new policy does not. At this point, the insurance company (may/may not) _____ immediately attach the exclusion endorsement because

_____

_____.

B. Suppose the expired policy in the previous question had been an occurrence policy instead of a claims-made policy. Now, three months into the claims-made policy, the insurer wants to exclude a certain event that happened during the expired occurrence policy. At this point, the insurer (may/may not) _____ add the exclusion endorsement for this event because _____

_____

_____.

C. Finally, a claims-made policy renewing coverage that also had the exclusion endorsement should include the exclusion as well. What might happen if the exclusion endorsement were not attached to all subsequent renewals? _____

_____

_____

Answer: A. may not, because the endorsement must be attached at policy inception; B. may not, because the endorsement must be added at policy inception; C. Coverage would no longer be excluded for the specific items, and the policy would be required to pay if claims were first made under any renewed policy periods.

Amendment of Section V—Extended Reporting Periods for Specific Accidents, Products, Work, or Location Endorsement

12. This is the endorsement that must be offered to an insured if the insurer first attaches at renewal the exclusion endorsement we just discussed. This endorsement provides the 60-day or 5-year basic extended reporting periods for whatever items are otherwise excluded by the exclusion endorsement.

    Suppose the insurer is renewing a claims-made policy with one of its insureds. On renewal, the company is attaching the exclusion of specific accidents, products, work, or location endorsement. Specifically excluded is one of the insured's locations—1515 Market Street. To protect the insured for any accidents that occurred during the previous claims-made policy at this location, and for which claims might be made now that the policy has expired, the insurance company must issue the **amendment of Section V—extended reporting periods for specific accidents, products, work, or location** endorsement. Read through this endorsement in your Forms and Endorsements.

    A. This endorsement provides the insured with ERP coverage at the excluded location for damage that occurred (before/after) _____ the end of the previous policy period.

    B. For this coverage to apply, the claim must be made during
       1. the period of the expiring policy
       2. the period of the renewal policy
       3. either the 60-day or 5-year period, depending on the circumstances
       4. any of these time periods

    C. When this endorsement is attached to the renewal policy for this insured, it applies to events that occurred
       1. anywhere in the coverage territory
       2. only at the location specifically excluded by the exclusion endorsement
       3. during the period of the renewal policy

    D. This amendment also offers the insured the option of purchasing a supplemental ERP endorsement for the excluded items. According to Item C, what is the name of the endorsement the insured may purchase for the otherwise excluded item? _____
    _____
    _____

Answer: A. before; B. 3 is correct; C. 2 is correct; D. supplemental extended reporting period endorsement for specific accidents, products, work, or locations

Supplemental ERP Endorsement for Specific Accidents, Products, Work, or Locations

13. Turn to the **Supplemental Extended Reporting Period Endorsement for Specific Accidents, Products, Work, or Locations** in your Forms and Endorsements and read it before continuing.

    This is practically a duplicate of the earlier supplemental ERP endorsement, except it states that the endorsement applies specifically to the policy as amended by the endorsement we just discussed.

    Similar to the basic supplemental ERP endorsement discussed earlier in this unit, this endorsement is excess over any other primary insurance for which the insured has been named as an additional insured by attachment of an endorsement.

    A. This endorsement is used when the insured wants the (basic/supplemental) _____ extension of the reporting period for (all/specific) _____ events.

    B. Is the insured required to pay a premium for this unlimited ERP?
        ( ) Yes   ( ) No

    Answer: A. supplemental, specific; B. Yes

ENDORSEMENTS FOR BOTH CLAIMS-MADE AND OCCURRENCE FORMS

Employment-Related Practices Exclusion Endorsement

14. An endorsement is available to specifically exclude **employment-related practices** liability from both Coverages A and B. This endorsement is mandatory with the CGL policy whenever a separate employment-related practices policy is being written.

    Locate this endorsement in the Forms and Endorsements and read it before continuing.

    A. The employment-related practices exclusion endorsement is an

        1. entirely new addition to the exclusions in the coverage forms.

        2. amendment to existing exclusions in the coverage forms.

    B. According to Item A, this endorsement excludes what type of injury resulting from the various practices mentioned? _____

    C. According to Item B, this endorsement excludes what type of injury resulting from the practices listed? _____

    D. An insured with the employment-related practices exclusion endorsement attached to the CGL fires an employee who later, as a nonemployee, sues the insured for damages based on humiliation. The insured's CGL (will/will not) _____ defend such a suit.

Answer: A. 1 is correct; B. Bodily injury; C. Personal and advertising injury; D. will not

Amendment of Liquor Liability Exclusion Endorsement

15. You'll recall that the liquor liability exclusion in the CGL refers to insureds in the business of dealing with alcoholic beverages. Some courts have used this wording to contend the exclusion does not apply to certain nonprofit organizations that furnish alcoholic beverages. For example, a group sponsoring a social event to raise funds for charitable purposes is not exactly in the business of furnishing liquor, but certainly might sell or serve alcoholic beverages at the event. Some courts have held that the exclusion does not apply to such groups.

    A separate endorsement is available for insureds and insurers who want to very specifically exclude this type of coverage. Read the **Amendment of Liquor Liability Exclusion** endorsement in the Forms and Endorsements. As you do so, compare it with the liquor liability exclusion in the commercial general liability coverage form.

    A. This endorsement

        1. is an additional exclusion for Coverage A

        2. replaces the existing liquor liability exclusion for Coverage A

    B. If the insured is not required to have a license to serve or furnish alcoholic beverages, does the endorsement exclusion still apply?
    ( ) Yes   ( ) No

    C. If the insured is required to have a license and serves or furnishes liquor, but does not do so for monetary gain, does the endorsement exclusion apply? ( ) Yes   ( ) No

    D. If the insured is in the business of manufacturing, selling, or distributing liquor, does the endorsement exclusion apply?
    ( ) Yes   ( ) No

    E. If the insured is required to have a license, but still does not charge for furnishing liquor, does the exclusion apply?   ( ) Yes   ( ) No

    F. When this endorsement is attached to the CGL, what activities involving liquor are **not** excluded? _____

    _____

Answer: A. 2 is correct; B. Yes; C. Yes; D. Yes; E. Yes; F. None. There is no liability coverage for any activity involving liquor.

Amendment of Liquor Liability Exclusion—Exception for Scheduled Activities Endorsement

16. While the previous endorsement effectively eliminates liability coverage for every activity or event involving liquor handling, another endorsement is available to do essentially the same thing, but allow limited coverage for certain *specified* events.

    Read the **Amendment of Liquor Liability Exclusion—Exception for Scheduled Activities** endorsement in the Forms and Endorsements.

    Only the provision excluding specified activities is different in this liquor liability endorsement. According to the form, there are two ways the excluded activities might be listed. What are they?

    A. _____

    B. _____

    Answer: (In either order) A. Activities may be described in the Schedule at the top of the endorsement; B. Activities may be described in the declarations.

Total Pollution Exclusion Endorsement

17. The discussion of the pollution exclusion in the CGL indicated that extremely limited pollution coverage exists. Insurers or insureds who want to eliminate even this small amount of coverage may attach the **total pollution exclusion** endorsement to the CGL. Read this endorsement in the Forms and Endorsements before continuing.

    A. Attaching the total pollution exclusion endorsement to the CGL causes the pollution exclusion to be

       1. replaced by an even more restrictive provision.
       2. amended by adding an additional restriction to the existing provision.

    B. With this endorsement attached, the CGL provides

       1. minimal pollution liability coverage
       2. complete pollution liability coverage
       3. no pollution liability coverage

    Answer: A. 1 is correct; B. 3 is correct.

Limited Pollution Liability Extension Endorsement

18. While the previous endorsement eliminates all pollution liability coverage, another endorsement is available to provide limited pollution liability. Read the **Limited Pollution Liability Extension** endorsement in the Forms

and Endorsements. Then, compare it with the CGL's pollution exclusion and limits of insurance provisions.

A. Unlike the exclusion in the CGL form, **on-premises** pollution coverage for certain pollution incidents (is/is not) _____ available with this endorsement.

B. Property damage that occurs when pollutants escape from an underground storage tank owned by an insured and cause a hostile fire (is/is not) _____ covered.

C. With this endorsement attached, the general aggregate limits of insurance (do/do not) _____ apply to pollution liability.

D. The limits of insurance available to pay damages for the pollution liability coverage under this endorsement are

1. the same as the general aggregate limits of the policy.

2. the same as the products-completed operations aggregate limit.

3. a separate limited pollution liability extension aggregate limit as listed separately in the declarations.

Answer: A. is; B. is; C. do not; D. 3 is correct.

Fungi or Bacteria Exclusion Endorsement

19. ISO has introduced endorsements in recent years to limit or exclude coverage for losses related to mold. Read the **Fungi or Bacteria Exclusion endorsement** in your Forms and Endorsements.

This endorsement excludes all mold-related losses under both Coverage A Bodily Injury and Property Damage Liability and Coverage B Personal and Advertising Injury Liability.

You may be wondering why mold losses are excluded under Coverage B. Personal and advertising injury coverage insures against injury arising out of wrongful entry or eviction or other invasion of the right of private occupancy. This coverage becomes particularly important in "sick building" cases. Claimants may allege that the presence of mold has interfered with their ability to occupy the building and they've been forced to leave. Without this endorsement, Coverage B might cover those allegations.

Or, suppose remediation of a mold-infested apartment building takes months and millions of dollars to complete. The residents may need to vacate the premises for an extended period, which might be construed as an eviction.

The fungi or bacteria exclusion endorsement expressly excludes cleanup and remediation costs. The exclusion applies to construction and completed operations exposures. As a result of this endorsement, building owners or contractors will not have coverage for claims against them for cleaning up, removing, containing, treating, detoxifying, neutralizing, remediating, or disposing of mold.

The fungi or bacteria exclusion endorsement excludes all mold-related losses under

A. Coverage A

B. Coverage B

C. Coverage A and Coverage B

D. Coverage A, Coverage B, and Coverage C

Answer: C is correct.

Limited Fungi or Bacteria Coverage Endorsement

20. Now read the **Limited Fungi or Bacteria Coverage** endorsement in your Forms and Endorsements.

    This endorsement allows the insured to schedule a limited amount of coverage under Coverages A and C for bodily injury, property damage, or medical payments resulting from fungi or bacteria for which the insured is legally liable. Note that losses under Coverage B are still excluded.

    The limited fungi or bacteria coverage endorsement provides a limited amount of coverage for mold losses under

A. Coverage A

B. Coverage B

C. Coverage C

D. both Coverage A and Coverage C

Answer: D is correct.

Terrorism Endorsements

21. After the terrorist attacks on the United States on September 11, 2001, insurers started to attach terrorism exclusion endorsements to commercial property and casualty policies. They did not want to assume the potential catastrophic losses that might result from future attacks. But without insurance for such losses, business owners who were no more capable of assuming such losses would have to bear the risk. This situation created a lot of uncertainty in the US economy, which could have many negative consequences.

    As a result, the federal Terrorism Risk Insurance Act of 2002 (TRIA) was enacted. This federal law provides a backstop for defined acts of terrorism and imposes certain obligations on insurers. It is designed to limit the exposure of individual insurers and the insurance industry as a whole, and to make insurance available and affordable, under a system where the federal government participates and shares the risk of loss. The act voids terrorism exclusions in property and casualty insurance contracts to the extent that they exclude losses that would otherwise be insured losses.

The types of commercial general liability insurance endorsements that have been issued in response to TRIA are summarized in the following table. Due to the volume of endorsements available, we have not included sample copies in your Forms and Endorsements.

Type of Endorsement	Important Provisions
Excludes defined acts of terrorism	■ Eliminates coverage for terrorism losses covered under TRIA ■ Insured must reject federal terrorism coverage in writing or fail to pay required premium for terrorism coverage
Excludes defined acts of terrorism with exception for fire losses	■ Same as above, but includes exception for fire losses arising out of terrorism as required by certain state laws
Modifies policy to conform with TRIA	■ Adds TRIA definition for act of terrorism ■ Eliminates policy's terrorism exclusion for defined acts of terrorism ■ Limits coverage for defined act of terrorism as prescribed by TRIA
Eliminates policy exclusions for terrorism	■ Broadens coverage by eliminating policy exclusions for terrorism losses and covering acts of terrorism that are not limited by TRIA definition

Under what circumstances can terrorism losses covered under TRIA be excluded by a commercial general liability policy?

A. Insured must reject coverage in writing or fail to pay required premium

B. Endorsement excluding defined acts of terrorism must be attached to the policy

C. None of the above; coverage for terrorism losses is mandatory

Answer: A and B are correct.

Professional Liability Exclusions

22. While professional liability exposures are generally excluded from coverage as you learned earlier, several endorsements are available to very specifically name those that are excluded. Medical and legal professional exposures come readily to mind, but there actually are a variety of types of professional exposures. Some of the specific exclusionary endorsements that are typically used are listed in the following table.

Endorsements to Exclude Specific Professional Liability Exposures

Endorsement Name	Endorsement Number
Exclusion—Designated Professional Services	CG 21 16
Exclusion—Inspection, Appraisal and Survey Companies	CG 22 24
Exclusion—Professional Services—Blood Banks	CG 22 32
Exclusion—Products and Professional Services (Druggists)*	CG 22 36
Exclusion—Products and Professional Services (Optical and Hearing Aid Establishments)*	CG 22 37
Exclusion—Engineers, Architects or Surveyors—Professional Liability	CG 22 43
Exclusion—Services Furnished By Health Care Providers	CG 22 44
Professional Liability Exclusion—Computer Software	CG 22 75
Professional Liability Exclusion—Health or Exercise Clubs or Commercially Operated Health or Exercise Facilities	CG 22 76
Professional Liability Exclusion—Computer Data Processing	CG 22 77
Exclusion—Contractors—Professional Liability	CG 22 79

*Exposure may be covered with a different endorsement

A. An insurer covering an optician with a CGL wants to specifically exclude the professional optical services. The endorsement used for this purpose is _____.

B. Now suppose this optician wants coverage for the professional optical services. Is such coverage available?   ( ) Yes   ( ) No   Explain.

_____

C. According to the table, which of the following exposures can be covered by an alternate endorsement?
1. Blood banks
2. Druggists
3. Hearing aid companies
4. Computer software

Answer: A. Exclusion—Products & Professional Services (Optical & Hearing Aid Establishments); B. Yes. The footnote indicates a different endorsement can be used for this purpose; C. 2 and 3 are correct.

Endorsements to Restrict Standard Coverages

23. You have seen that the CGL form includes a broad range of standard coverages. Some insureds, however, may want a more limited scope of coverage than is provided by the CGL. In addition, an insurer might want to limit or exclude certain coverages for underwriting purposes.

Endorsements are available to limit or exclude standard coverages to meet specific needs. The following table lists some of these commonly used endorsements.

Endorsements to Limit or Exclude Standard Coverages

Endorsement Name	Number	Purpose
Exclusion—Products-Completed Operations Hazard	CG 21 04	Eliminates all BI and PD coverage for products-completed operations
Exclusion—Coverage C— Medical Payments	CG 21 35	Eliminates Coverage C
Exclusion—Personal and Advertising Injury	CG 21 38	Eliminates Coverage B
Contractual Liability Limitation	CG 21 39	Replaces broad form coverage with limited contractual coverage that applies only to leasing of premises, sidetrack and easement agreements and other specified contracts
Exclusion—Damage to Premises Rented to You	CG 21 45	Eliminates BI and PD liability for damage to rented premises
Exclusion—Year 2000 Computer-Related Problems	CG 21 60	Eliminates all BI, PD, personal and advertising injury from computer malfunction or failure related to Year 2000 problems

Which of the following needs can be accomplished by using one of the endorsements listed in the table?

A. The insured wants to eliminate only property damage liability for damage to rented premises.

B. Rather than the broad contractual coverage provided by the CGL, the insured wants to limit contractual liability coverage.

C. An insured does not want her policy to include Coverages B and C.

D. Because an insured's business does not include the products-completed operations hazard, he wants to exclude coverage for this hazard.

Answer: B, C, and D are correct. Choice A is not correct because there is no endorsement to eliminate only property damage liability for damage to rented premises. However, both PD and BI liability could be excluded with CG 21 45.

Endorsements to Broaden Standard Coverages

24. A number of endorsements are also available to either:

- extend existing coverages; or
- give back excluded coverages.

Ask your supervisor or trainer for copies of all CGL endorsements used by your company.

The following table lists some common endorsements used to broaden CGL coverage.

Endorsements to Extend or Give Back Coverages

Endorsement Name	Number	Purpose
Pollution Liability Coverage Extension	CG 04 22	Eliminates the BI and PD portion of the pollution exclusion, but retains exclusion for clean-up costs
Coverage for Injury to Leased Workers	CG 04 24	Provides employers liability coverage for leased and temporary workers by modifying the definition of "employee" used in the Employers Liability exclusion
Lawn Care Services Coverage	CG 22 93	Provides liability coverage for the incidental application of "over the counter" herbicides or pesticides on lawns under the insured's regular care
Products-Completed Operations Hazard Redefined	CG 24 07	Redefines products-completed operations to eliminate need for BI or PD to occur away from insured's premises
Liquor Liability	CG 24 08	Provides liquor liability coverage by deleting the liquor liability exclusion
Boats	CG 24 12	Gives back coverage for watercraft excluded in the Aircraft, Auto and Watercraft exclusion

A. An insurer is willing to provide some pollution liability coverage by giving back the BI and PD portion of the pollution exclusion. However, the insurer is *not* willing to provide coverage for clean-up costs. What endorsement might be used? _____

B. An insured in the business of furnishing alcoholic beverages can have liquor liability coverage by using what endorsement? _____

C. In the CGL, the products-completed operations hazard definition requests these events to occur away from the insured's premises. This requirement (may/may not) _____ be eliminated by endorsement.

Answer: A. Pollution Liability Coverage Extension; B. Liquor Liability; C. may

In the final unit, you will learn about separate coverage forms available to meet special liability insurance needs.

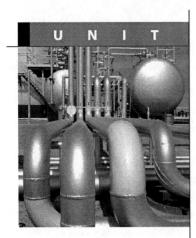

U N I T

12

Other Liability
Coverage Forms

INTRODUCTION

1. You have seen that many very specialized types of coverages are excluded from the CGL. Examples are liquor liability, for those whose business involves selling, serving, or furnishing liquor, and pollution liability, which might be needed for certain types of risks. However, these greater risks simply are not contemplated by the CGL policy. To meet the needs of such businesses, a number of optional coverage forms are available to cover other liability risks, just as certain limited coverages were available by endorsement.

    In this unit, we will consider separate coverage forms used to meet some of those needs. However, rather than reading and analyzing the forms, you will study a summary table similar to the one used for endorsements in the previous unit. Once you have looked over the table on the next page, complete the questions that follow.

Special Purpose Liability Coverage Forms

Coverage Form	Number	Purpose	Special Features

Liquor Liability Coverage Form
  Occurrence
  Claims-Made
	
	CG 00 33
	CG 00 34
		Covers liability for damages that result from selling, serving or furnishing any alcoholic beverages; overrides the liquor liability exclusion in the CGL.	ERP endorsement available

Pollution Liability Coverage Form	CG 00 39	Covers BI or PD arising from a pollution incident as specifically defined in the form. Clean-up costs as defined are also covered.	Claims-made form only ERP endorsement available
Pollution Liability Limited Coverage Form	CG 00 40	Similar to previous form. Clean-up costs are omitted.	Claims-made form only ERP endorsement available

Products-Completed Operations Liability Coverage Form
  Occurrence
  Claims-Made
	
	CG 00 37
	CG 00 38
		Covers BI and PD arising from the products-completed operations hazard only and involving the insured's business.	ERP endorsement available

Owners and Contractors Protective Liability Coverage Form for Operations of Designated Contractor	CG 00 09	Covers BI and PD liability arising from operations of independent contractors performed for or on behalf of the insured.	Used when contractor or subcontractor is required to provide protective liability coverage Personal injury liability endorsement available to provide limited additional coverage
Railroad Protective Liability Coverage Form	CG 00 35	Covers BI and PD for physical damage to specified property of the insured from operations performed by the designated contractor.	Provides liability coverage specifically excluded in the CGL coverage form
Underground Storage Tank Liability Coverage Form for Designated Tanks	CG 00 42	Covers BI and PD liability and corrective action costs for damage arising from an underground storage tank incident as specifically defined in the form.	Claims-made form only ERP endorsement available Medical payments coverage endorsement available
Employment-Related Practices Liability Coverage Form	EP 00 01	Covers damages and defense expenses for specified injuries arising out of work- and employment-related activities.	Claims-made form only ERP endorsement available
Electronic Data Liability Coverage Form	CG 00 65	Covers specified damages because of loss of electronic data	Claims-made form only ERP endorsement available
Product Withdrawal Coverage Form	CG 00 66	Covers damages incurred due to withdrawal of named insured's product from the market	Contains two insuring agreements: Coverage A Product Withdrawal Expense and Coverage B Product Withdrawal Liability

LIQUOR LIABILITY COVERAGE FORM

2. The **liquor liability coverage form** closes the gap imposed by the CGL coverage form liquor liability exclusion. This form provides coverage for insureds who are in the business of handling alcoholic beverages in a number of ways.

    According to the table, the liquor liability coverage form is available as

    A. a claims-made form only

    B. an occurrence form only

    C. either an occurrence form or a claims-made form

    Answer: C is correct

POLLUTION LIABILITY COVERAGE FORM

3. An insured who needs more pollution protection than is offered by the very restricted coverage of the CGL, and even more than the extended coverage in the pollution liability extension endorsement, may purchase the **pollution liability coverage form**. This form is available only as a *claims-made* form.

    Not only does this form cover BI and PD arising from the pollution hazard as defined in the form, it also provides for certain clean-up costs. Clean-up costs covered by the form are for operations required because of:

    ■ statutory orders of the US or Canadian governments; and

    ■ environmental damage resulting from a pollution incident.

    An insured's business has significant potential for pollution injury to people and property, as well as for damage to nearby natural resources. The insured has been ordered by the US government to take steps to clean up certain related problems. Which one of the following would best meet the insurance needs of this business?

    A. The CGL coverage form with the pollution liability extension endorsement

    B. The CGL plus the pollution liability coverage form

    Answer: B is correct.

POLLUTION LIABILITY LIMITED COVERAGE FORM

4. The **pollution liability limited coverage form** covers the pollution risk on a more limited basis. It offers the same protection as the pollution liability coverage form *except* that it excludes coverage for clean-up costs.

   Decide whether each statement below applies to the pollution liability coverage form *only* (**P**), the pollution liability limited coverage form *only* (**PL**), or to both (**B**).

   A. Available only as a claims-made form

   B. Covers bodily injury and property damage liability as well as certain clean-up costs

   C. Covers bodily injury and property damage liability only

   Answer: A-B; B-P; C-PL

PRODUCTS-COMPLETED OPERATIONS LIABILITY COVERAGE FORM

5. An endorsement is available to delete products-completed operations coverage from the CGL, but there is no similar endorsement to retain this coverage and eliminate the premises-operations coverage. For insureds who do not want the premises-operations coverage, the **products-completed operations liability coverage form** is available.

   In either the occurrence or the claims-made versions, this form includes the same broad form contractual liability coverage as the CGL. By endorsement, the broad form contractual liability can be eliminated from the products-completed operations coverage form.

   Suppose an insured likes the broad coverage of the CGL, but needs only to protect herself against the completed operations hazard. She should have the

   A. CGL with the products-completed operations coverage eliminated by endorsement

   B. CGL with the premises-operations coverage eliminated

   C. products-completed operations liability coverage form

   D. products-completed operations liability coverage form with the endorsement to eliminate broad form contractual liability coverage

   Answer: C is correct.

OWNERS AND CONTRACTORS PROTECTIVE LIABILITY COVERAGE FORM

6. Another type of liability coverage is called a **protective policy**. It differs from other types of liability insurance in that it:

- is purchased by someone other than the named insured;
- to protect the named insured;
- from liability because of the other person's actions;
- being made on the insured's behalf.

One type is the **owners and contractors protective (OCP) liability coverage form**. Here is an example of how it works.

Melinda Nichols owns an office building known as the One Hundred Building. She has hired a building contractor, Construct Corporation, for extensive remodeling on one floor of the building, which is partially occupied. Construct Corporation purchases an OCP to protect Nichols from any liability that might arise out of the remodeling operations Construct Corporation is making on Nichols' behalf.

A. As described above, who would pay the premium for the OCP policy? (Construct Corporation/Nichols) _____

B. If Construct's remodeling results in BI to a visitor in the One Hundred Building, does the OCP provide protection? ( ) Yes ( ) No   Why?

_____

C. Suppose while Construct's remodeling is going on, someone slips and falls on the rain-slick front steps of the One Hundred Building and sues Nichols. Would the OCP cover this loss? ( ) Yes ( ) No Explain your answer. _____

Answer: A. Construct Corporation; B. Yes. The injury arose from operations performed by the independent contractor; C. No. The injury did not arise from the contractor's operations.

RAILROAD PROTECTIVE LIABILITY COVERAGE FORM

7. A second type of protective policy is the **railroad protective liability coverage forms**. This is a specialized form specifically designed to protect railroads. Again, the liability would arise from a contractor's work. Generally, the work would take place somewhere along railroad tracks, such as highways or bridge construction.

Both the owners and contractors protective liability coverage form and the railroad protective liability coverage form are available only in the occurrence version.

The primary difference between the railroad protective liability coverage form and the OCP is

A. under the railroad protective liability form, the liability arises from the railroad rather than from another party.

B. the party purchasing the railroad protective liability coverage form is not a contractor, while a contractor purchases the OCP.

C. the railroad protective liability coverage form has special considerations in the form concerning railroads.

D. under the railroad protective policy, the liability arises from a contractor, but under the OCP, the liability arises from the named insured.

Answer: C is correct.

UNDERGROUND STORAGE TANK LIABILITY COVERAGE FORM FOR DESIGNATED TANKS

8. The **underground storage tank (UST) liability coverage form for designated tanks** is designed to protect insureds who store petroleum in underground tanks. In addition to bodily injury and property damage liability coverage, this form provides **corrective action costs**, the costs for the reasonable and necessary clean-up after an incident where petroleum spills, leaks, or is discharged into ground water, surface water, or subsurface soil. Corrective actions are specifically regulated by the Federal Environmental Protection Agency and other government agencies.

A. Would UST liability coverage pay for the cost of repairing a damaged storage tank?   ( ) Yes   ( ) No

B. Consider this example. An oil tanker runs off the road and spills oil on the ground's surface. Would this incident be covered by the UST liability coverage form?   ( ) Yes   ( ) No   Explain. _____

_____

_____

Answer: A. No. Maintaining the storage tank is the responsibility of the insured; B. No. The UST liability coverage form does not cover spills on the ground's surface. It covers only underground spills from underground storage tanks.

EMPLOYMENT-RELATED PRACTICES LIABILITY COVERAGE FORM

9. Cases involving work-or employment-related injuries, such as alleged discrimination, wrongful termination, abuse, coercion to commit an unlawful act, and harassment, can be very costly for companies. The **employment-related practices liability (ERPL) coverage form** can provide an insured with protection against skyrocketing damage claims and defense expenses that may result from such cases, up to the limit of insurance specified in the declarations.

    The insured retains responsibility to act legally and ethically with regard to work-related matters. The ERPL excludes intentional criminal, fraudulent, or malicious acts or omissions on the part of the insured. However, the ERPL will defend the insured up until guilt is established, if that is the case.

    A. ERPL coverage includes bodily injury and property damage arising from the offenses listed in the form.   ( ) True   ( ) False

    B. Suppose an insured has ERPL coverage with a $500,000 limit. When defense costs for a work-related harassment case reach $500,000, will the insurance company continue to cover the costs?   ( )Yes   ( ) No

    C. If an insured knowingly commits an unlawful act and is sued for damages, will ERPL coverage provide for defense costs?
        ( ) Yes   ( ) No   Explain. _____

Answer: A. False. The employment-related injuries specified in this form do not involve BI or PD; B. No. When the limit of insurance is reached, the insured takes over responsibility for these costs; C. Yes. ERPL coverage will provide for defense costs until the insured's guilt is established.

ELECTRONIC DATA LIABILITY COVERAGE FORM

10. The **electronic data liability coverage form** is a claims-made policy that covers specified damages because of loss of electronic data caused by an electronic data incident. Loss of electronic data is defined as damage to, loss of, loss of use of, corruption of, inability to access, or inability to properly manipulate electronic data. An electronic data incident is defined as an accident, negligent act, error, or omission that results in loss of electronic data. The electronic data incident must take place in the coverage territory and not occur before any retroactive date on the policy or after the end of the policy period.

    An employee in the insured's computer software company deliberately adds a virus to the company's software programs after he learns his job is being eliminated. Several customers who purchased copies of the infected program before the tampering was discovered sue the insured. Would this loss be considered an electronic data incident under the electronic data liability coverage?   ( ) Yes   ( ) No   Explain your answer. _____

_____

_____

Answer: No. An electronic data incident is an accident, negligent act, error, or omission that results in loss of electronic data. Deliberate tampering would not be considered an accident.

PRODUCT WITHDRAWAL COVERAGE FORM

11. Coverage A of the CGL excludes coverage for losses, costs, or expenses arising out of the withdrawal of the named insured's product from the market. Insureds that need coverage for these expenses can purchase the **product withdrawal coverage form**. It covers expenses incurred by the insured due to a covered product withdrawal and provides liability coverage for damages the insured becomes legally obligated to pay arising out of a covered product withdrawal.

A pharmaceutical company incurs significant expenses when one of the prescription drugs it manufactures must be taken off the market because it has potentially serious side effects. The expenses arising out of this product withdrawal could be covered under the

A. claims-made version of the CGL

B. occurrence version of the CGL

C. product withdrawal coverage form

Answer: C is correct.

Ask your supervisor or trainer for copies of all specialized commercial liability forms used by your company.

This completes your study of the commercial general liability coverage forms. For those who will be underwriting general liability insurance, we have included a checklist with this course that lists considerations for underwriting new applicants.

When you are ready, take the examination that accompanies this course. You may want to review the Glossary before you do so. Good luck.

Review Test

Important Information Regarding This Review Test

This exam was designed to provide accurate and authoritative information in regard to the subject matter covered. It is sold with the understanding that the publisher is not engaged in rendering legal, accounting, or other professional service. If legal advice or other expert assistance is required, the services of a competent professional person should be sought.

This text is updated periodically to reflect changes in laws and regulations. To verify that you have the most recent update, you may call Kaplan Financial Education at 1-800-423-4723.

1. Which one of the following examples illustrates contract law?

   A. Monroe goes on a shopping spree and puts over $5,000 in charges on his credit card. After Monroe fails to pay his bill for several months, the credit card company revokes his card.
   B. Peter turns his head to look at a shop window while driving down a busy street. While his attention is diverted, he strikes and seriously injures a child.
   C. Mark sends a written request to the Ace Fuel Company for a delivery of furnace fuel, which never arrives. Mark holds Ace liable for damage when his water pipes freeze and break.
   D. Susan goes to a baseball game and sits in the front row. During the second inning, she is struck on the head by a foul ball and seriously injured. She sues the baseball team for negligence.

2. Invasion of the right of private occupancy is an example of

   A. property damage
   B. personal and advertising injury
   C. disparagement
   D. bodily injury

3. Which one of the following represents an intentional tort?

   A. Beth is sensitive about her advancing age. When someone tells Beth she's looking quite old, she slaps him.
   B. Talia keeps a caged leopard in her oversized garage. One day it escapes and injures a neighbor.
   C. Patrick enjoys his hobby of chemistry. While he is experimenting with several new chemicals, deadly chlorine gas escapes, and the neighborhood must be evacuated.
   D. Ted is driving the posted speed limit through a residential neighborhood. A small child chases a ball into the street and runs directly into the path of Ted's car. Ted is unable to stop in time to keep from hitting the child.

4. Which one of the following examples of bodily injury or property damage falls within the products-completed operations hazard?

   A. Maria uses a home hair preparation kit to perm her hair. The product is said to give natural-looking curly hair in 30 minutes. Instead, her hair falls out.
   B. Mark is touring a computer hardware manufacturing plant. He picks up a half-finished keyboard to examine it more closely and cuts his finger on a sharp edge.
   C. In a factory showroom, Chan is invited to try a new red pen. The pen leaks red ink on Chan's new suit.
   D. A salesperson from the Nifty Spot Removing Company comes to the Janasiak home to demonstrate samples of a new spot remover. A large hole appears in the carpet immediately after the remover is applied.

5. Which one of the following illustrates the concept of absolute liability?

   A. During a heavy windstorm, the roof of a restaurant blows off. Parts of the roof strike a nearby furniture store, damaging the siding and breaking the windows.
   B. Jim keeps a police-trained German shepherd in his men's clothing store to ward off burglars. One day, after Jim forgets to feed him, the dog escapes and attacks a passerby.
   C. Fred's farm property contains a small natural pond. One winter day, when the pond is frozen, a neighbor's child wanders out onto the ice, falls, and breaks her arm.
   D. Rick is a master mechanic, but careless with his tools. A trespasser trips over a hammer Rick left lying in the driveway and is injured.

6. Preston Plumbing contracts with Coleville Dry Cleaning Store to install the plumbing for a new restroom at the dry cleaner's premises. In 2 days, the work is completed according to the contract and Coleville's owner approves it. This is an example of

   A. impaired property
   B. your product
   C. completed operations
   D. an occurrence

7. Negligence is alleged in each of the following situations. Which one appears to be valid?

   A. Lightning hit Sue's large oak tree and severed a large limb, which remained suspended across two other limbs. Four months later, the limb fell and hit a neighbor's car. Sue is charged with negligence.
   B. Jon has an auto accident. A nearby farmer is distracted by the sound of the accident while he is plowing and injures his foot in the plow. The farmer holds Jon accountable for his injury.
   C. Jan sues Kathy because Kathy playfully threatened her with a toy gun.
   D. During a rainstorm, topsoil washes from Clyde's property onto Dawn's driveway, blocking the entrance to Dawn's garage. Clyde is charged for damages.

8. An explosion in the heating system on the insured's premises spreads debris over property owned by 2 neighboring businesses. The businesses are prevented from opening for business because of the debris. The loss of use of their property suffered by these firms is an example of

   A. impaired property
   B. completed operations
   C. property damage
   D. your work

9. The failure to use even the slightest degree of care with regard to the safety of others is considered

   A. breach of duty
   B. an assumption of risk
   C. gross negligence
   D. contributory negligence

10. According to the definition in the CGL, which one of the following would be considered electronic data?

    A. A printout of data from a computer file
    B. A computer keyboard
    C. Systems software stored on a computer's hard drive
    D. A new box of floppy disks

11. Josie suffers a loss because of Richard's actions. However, because Josie fails to take proper care following this incident to protect herself from further damage, Richard is not held liable for any additional damage. This ruling is based on the fact that Josie is responsible for

    A. avoidable consequences
    B. absolute liability
    C. mediation of damages
    D. litigation of damages

12. In liability insurance transactions, the one who has been wronged is called the _____ party, the party causing injury is the _____ _____ party, and the settlement is paid by the _____ party.

    A. second, first, third
    B. third, first, second
    C. first, third, second
    D. first, second, third

13. The type of exposure covered by commercial general liability insurance without special endorsement is

    A. personal liability
    B. business liability
    C. professional liability
    D. employers liability

14. All of the following are elements that may be present in the business liability exposure EXCEPT

    A. ownership, maintenance, or use of business premises
    B. rendering professional services
    C. defects in products or operations
    D. vicarious responsibility for employee acts

15. The purpose of liability insurance is to protect an insured from financial loss

    A. arising out of liability claims by shifting the legal liability from the individual to the insurance company
    B. caused by a third party, and for which that third party has either been found legally liable or has agreed on a settlement with the insured and the insurance company
    C. arising out of physical damage or bodily injury to the insured and employees of the insured while conducting the responsibilities of employment
    D. arising out of liability claims by transferring the burden of financial loss from the individual to the insurance company

16. The term that refers to the combination of forms and endorsements for a specific line of insurance is the

    A. package part
    B. coverage part
    C. policy part
    D. endorsement part

17. A commercial package policy must contain

    A. 3 or more coverage parts
    B. a commercial general liability coverage form
    C. 2 or more coverage parts
    D. optional endorsements

18. Which component of a commercial package policy contains information about who is insured, when he is insured, and how he is insured?

    A. Line of insurance coverage form
    B. Common policy conditions
    C. Common policy declarations
    D. Interline endorsements

19. Which one of the common policy conditions includes a provision allowing only the first named insured to alter the terms of coverage with the insurer's consent?

    A. Inspections and surveys
    B. Changes
    C. Examination of your books and records
    D. Transfer of your rights and duties under this policy

20. A feature of the commercial package policy that may allow a reduction in the premium is the

    A. premium reduction factor
    B. premium condition of the common policy conditions
    C. policy writing minimum premium
    D. package modification factor

21. Which one of the following is ALWAYS included in the commercial general liability coverage part?

    A. Interline endorsements
    B. Nuclear energy liability exclusion endorsement (Broad Form)
    C. Amendment of liquor liability exclusion endorsement
    D. Claims-made form

22. Which one of the following is an auto?

    A. Glider
    B. Motorcycle
    C. All-terrain vehicle
    D. Barge-mounted crane

23. Which one of the following is considered mobile equipment?

    A. Bulldozer
    B. Motorcycle
    C. Glider
    D. Four-wheel drive vehicle with a permanently attached snow shovel

24. Which one of the following illustrates bodily injury?

    A. Mr. Palette says he has lost his ability for creative painting because of negative comments made about his work by an art critic.
    B. A railing in the insured's building gives way as a customer leans on it. The railing breaks, but the customer escapes injury.
    C. A kennel containing several dogs suffers fire damage as a result of a faulty furnace. Ten dogs die in the fire.
    D. While riding the escalator in a shopping mall, a man catches his foot on a loose tread and falls to one level below. He eventually dies as a result of his injuries.

25. Which one of the following best describes an occurrence?

    A. Every evening, florist Jane pours ice water on her competitor's rose bushes, resulting in their stunted growth.
    B. Tired of her boyfriend's constant criticisms, Gail tricks him into falling off the Golden Gate Bridge. He is never seen again.
    C. Lyle accidentally drops a burning cigarette on the premises of a business. The business burns to the ground.
    D. Ethel gets into an argument with a salesclerk and slaps the clerk in the face.

26. Which one of the following would be considered personal and advertising injury?

    A. Jack's Used Cars runs a television advertisement accusing a competitor of rebuilding automobiles that have been involved in accidents and representing them as being in mint condition.
    B. A printer misprints an advertisement for a clothing store's advertising flier, stating all items are 100% off rather than 10% off.
    C. A newspaper overcharges a person for placing an advertisement.
    D. An announcer taping an advertisement for a local television station trips over his microphone cord and breaks his leg.

27. Which one of the following is an example of a personal and advertising injury?

    A. Janet was arrested after stealing a blouse from a department store.
    B. Indira died after battling cancer.
    C. While John was at work, his landlord entered his apartment and watched television.
    D. Patrick was bitten by a German shepherd.

28. Which one of the following situations would be covered under Coverage A of the CGL?

    A. A third party is extremely embarrassed, but not injured, when she slips on an icy step in front of the insured's store.
    B. One of the insured's competitors sues the insured for slander.
    C. The insured incurs costs while administering first aid to a customer who has fainted and has injured his head.
    D. A third party becomes ill after eating a meal catered by the insured.

29. Which one of the following is NOT one of the insurer's rights and duties listed in the Coverage A insuring agreement?

    A. Pay any valid claim made during the policy period even if the policy limits have been exhausted
    B. Settle claims or suits
    C. Investigate occurrences
    D. Defend suits

30. Which one of the following statements correctly describes how coverage is triggered under the occurrence form?

    A. The event that triggered the coverage occurred during the policy period of the policy covering the loss.
    B. The event that triggered the coverage occurred during the policy year in which the claim was made.
    C. Coverage is triggered by any event that occurs after the retroactive date and before the expiration date of the current policy.
    D. Recovery for the loss must occur during the policy period of the policy that covers the loss.

31. Which one of the following is NOT one of the stipulations listed in the Coverage A insuring agreement of the occurrence version of the CGL for paying BI and PD claims?

    A. There must be a legal obligation for the insured to pay the damages.
    B. BI or PD must occur in the coverage territory.
    C. Claims for death, care, or loss of services resulting from BI must be made during the policy period to be covered.
    D. Damages must arise out of an occurrence as defined in the policy.

32. When will Coverage A of the CGL provide coverage for an insured who is found liable for causing an intentional injury?

    A. Only if the insured caused property damage while using reasonable force to protect persons or property
    B. Never
    C. Always
    D. Only if the insured caused bodily injury while using reasonable force to protect persons or property

33. Under a CGL occurrence form, an occurrence that is continuous in nature
    A. may be covered only if it was known to the insured before the policy period
    B. may never be covered
    C. may not be covered if it was known to the insured before the policy period
    D. is always covered

34. Which one of the following is generally excluded from Coverage A?
    A. Damages resulting from the insured's having assumed liability under an insured contract
    B. Damages resulting from the insured's having assumed liability in any contract or agreement
    C. Damages for which the insured would be liable whether or not any contract existed
    D. Damages occurring after an insured's contract has been executed

35. With regard to liquor liability, which one of the following situations would NOT be covered by the CGL?
    A. Ed, the insured, is relaxing in the office of his clothing store after working hours when his 14-year-old son and a friend of the same age join him. Ed gives each boy a few beers. When the 14-year-old friend leaves Ed's place, he picks up several rocks and hurls them through the windshield of a parked car. Ed is found liable.
    B. Halfmoon Distillery is the insured. Each holiday season, Halfmoon distributes samples to visitors who tour the distillery. One visitor, Adam, consumes too many samples and leaves in an intoxicated state. As he drives across Halfmoon's parking lot, Adam crashes into another visitor's car, badly damaging it. The car's owner sues Halfmoon.
    C. The insured buys a drink for a client who is already inebriated. After leaving the insured's business, the client causes an accident resulting in property damage and bodily injury.
    D. The insured has a party for several employees who are retiring. The spouse of one of the employees drinks too many of the cocktails the insured is serving and becomes unruly, slugging several other partygoers. The insured is sued for the injuries.

36 Coverage A never applies to damages
    A. that arise as a result of serving alcohol
    B. under employers liability or workers' compensation obligations
    C. that arise out of valet parking
    D. under an insured contract

37. The employers liability exclusion applies to
    A. temporary workers only
    B. regular employees only
    C. leased workers only
    D. both regular employees and leased workers

38. Which one of the following pollution liability situations is covered by Coverage A?
    A. Waste being transported from the insured's premises to a treatment plant escapes when the transporter's truck (not the insured's truck) overturns on an embankment. The insured is one of those held liable for the resulting damages.
    B. The insured incurs considerable expense cleaning up and removing pollutants at the direction of the federal Environmental Protection Agency.
    C. An accident at the insured's chemical manufacturing plant threatens citizens in the surrounding area with the potential of toxic fumes being released into the atmosphere. There is substantial monetary loss when the area is evacuated. The insured is held liable for this loss in a class action suit, even though no toxic fumes were actually released.
    D. A subcontractor of the insured is draining a creek at the insured's direction. There is a pipeline beneath the creek that runs between a refinery and an oil site. The subcontractor's equipment damages the pipeline, and the resulting spill causes extensive injury to persons and property. The insured is held liable.

39. The Coverage A exclusion regarding aircraft, auto, and watercraft applies to
    A. valet parking arrangements, provided the insured has not bought, rented or borrowed the auto involved
    B. the insured's watercraft being used to entertain business clients
    C. a watercraft the insured does not own, provided it is less than 26 feet long and is not being used for hire
    D. liability assumed under an insured contract for the ownership, maintenance, or use of aircraft or watercraft

40. Bodily injury or property damage due to war is
    A. covered only when it occurs in the continental United States
    B. always excluded
    C. covered only when it occurs outside the policy's coverage territory
    D. always covered

41. While bodily injury and property damage arising out of the use of mobile equipment are generally included in Coverage A, such damages are NOT covered when
    A. the equipment is permanently attached to one of the various specified types of other equipment
    B. they occurred because of an accident that happened while the mobile equipment was being transported across the state line by thieves
    C. they result from using mobile equipment in any stunting activity, regardless of whether the activity was prearranged or not
    D. they result from using mobile equipment for a prearranged race

42. All of the following are excluded under Coverage A EXCEPT
    A. damage arising from a condition existing at a house a speculative builder has just completed
    B. damage to personal property in the insured's custody
    C. damage to an entire batch of the insured's soup product resulting from improper formulation
    D. the costs to repair property in order to prevent injuries

43. Property damage to an insured's work that arises out of the work and is part of the products-completed operations hazard is
    A. excluded from Coverage A unless there is bodily injury involved
    B. never excluded under Coverage A
    C. always excluded under Coverage A
    D. excluded from Coverage A unless the work out of which the damage arose was done by a subcontractor instead of the insured

44. Property damage to impaired property that results from a defect in the insured's work is
    A. excluded from Coverage A unless a sudden and accidental injury to the insured's work occurred after it was put to its intended use
    B. covered by Coverage A under any circumstances
    C. covered by Coverage A if an insured contract exists
    D. excluded from Coverage A unless the insured's work has been withdrawn or recalled because of a known or suspected defect

45. The recall of products, work, or impaired property exclusion applies to losses arising out of product recall situations
    A. only when a government agency orders the recall
    B. only when the insured voluntarily recalls the product, work, or impaired property from the market
    C. only if it is discovered that the item recalled from the market was not defective
    D. under any circumstances, regardless of who is responsible for the recall

46. The expected or intended injury exclusion and the contractual liability exclusion are the only exclusions that apply to a certain type of fire damage. What type of fire damage is it?
    A. Damage to the insured's work
    B. Damage to premises rented to the insured or temporarily occupied by the insured with the permission of the owner
    C. Damage to impaired property
    D. Damage to the insured's product

47. Which one of the following situations is covered under Coverage B?

    A. Reba, the insured, owns several rental housing units. In spite of Reba's written warnings, Bill, a tenant, fails to pay his rent for 3 months in a row. After Reba serves Bill with an official eviction notice, he gets angry and sues her for wrongful eviction.

    B. The insured claims in a television advertisement that his product will allow dieters to lose 5 pounds per week without changing their eating habits. A customer sues the insured when she fails to lose weight while using the product.

    C. The insured's occurrence policy becomes effective July 22. On July 30, the insured is sued for personal and advertising injury for an article in a local newspaper that quotes the insured making derogatory statements about another business. The newspaper article appeared on July 3.

    D. The insured is sued for knowingly allowing its advertising agency to make untrue statements about a competitor in an advertisement for the insured's product.

48. What type of injury is NOT covered if the insured's business is advertising, publishing, broadcasting, or telecasting?

    A. Copyright infringement
    B. False imprisonment
    C. Violation of right of privacy
    D. Malicious prosecution

49. In connection with which one of the following might an insured, a hardware business, find coverage under the CGL's Coverage B: Personal and Advertising Injury Liability?

    A. The catalog of hardware products the insured maintains on the Internet
    B. A misleading email address the insured uses to lure customers from the competition
    C. The insured's use of another company's logo
    D. An electronic chatroom the insured hosts

50. An insured locks the door to the conference room so that visitors cannot leave during the insured's 3-hour product demonstration. After one visitor tried unsuccessfully to leave, she fainted and bumped her head when she fell, resulting in a concussion. Under what part of the insured's CGL might the visitor's injuries be covered?

    A. Coverage B
    B. Coverage C
    C. Coverage A
    D. No coverage is available under the CGL for these injuries.

51. Which one of the following situations would be covered under Coverage C?

    A. A tenant falls off the roof of the insured's apartment building and is injured.
    B. A customer is injured while shopping in the insured's store.
    C. An individual is injured by using the insured's product.
    D. A marathon runner is injured while passing the insured's premises.

52. Medical payments coverage is available for expenses incurred and reported to the insurer within how many years of the accident date?

    A. 1
    B. 2
    C. 3
    D. 4

53. Who of the following might be covered for bodily injury under Coverage C: Medical Payments, while performing duties related to the insured's business?

    A. The named insured
    B. The insured's partner
    C. A volunteer worker
    D. The insured's spouse

54. Supplementary payments for Coverages A and B are limited by

    A. the Coverage A and B limits
    B. any limitations specifically stated in the supplementary payments section
    C. the general aggregate policy limits, unless the loss falls within the products-completed operations hazard
    D. the general aggregate policy limits as well as the individual sublimits and the per occurrence limit

55. When are stockholders of an insured organization other than a partnership, joint venture, or limited liability company considered insureds?

    A. Always
    B. Only in connection with conducting the business
    C. Never
    D. Only in connection with liability as stockholders

56. If the insured is designated as an individual in the declarations, who are insureds in connection with a business of which the insured is the sole owner?

    A. The insured and the insured's spouse as well as all of the business's employees and their spouses
    B. The insured and the insured's spouse acting in regard to the business
    C. The insured and the insured's spouse as well as any stockholders and their spouses
    D. The insured and the insured's spouse as well as any partners and their spouses

57. If the insured is a trust company, what must be listed in the CGL's declarations?

    A. Only the name of the trust company
    B. Neither the name of the trust company nor the names of the trustees
    C. Both the name of the trust company and the names of the trustees
    D. Only the names of the company's trustees

58. When are executive officers of an insured organization other than a partnership, joint venture, or limited liability company considered insureds?

    A. Always
    B. Only for obligations imposed by workers' compensation and employers liability laws
    C. Only in connection with duties as officers or directors
    D. Never

59. An insured's employees are only considered insureds for

    A. property damage to property owned by the employee
    B. acts arising out of providing professional health care services
    C. bodily injury or personal and advertising injury to a coworker
    D. acts within the scope of their employment or while performing duties related to the conduct of the business

60. Which one of the following describes circumstances under which an individual is considered an insured under the CGL?

    A. A child of the insured's employee suffers severe emotional distress when she sees her mother being attacked by another employee in the employer's parking lot.
    B. An employee of the insured injures another employee while driving the insured's forklift.
    C. The brother of a deceased insured has temporary legal custody of the insured's business property.
    D. Personal property belonging to a partner in the insured business is damaged.

61. The insured has a newly acquired partnership over which she has ownership. No other insurance is available. Is this new partnership a named insured?

    A. Yes, but only for 90 days.
    B. No. Partnerships are excluded from this provision.
    C. Yes, but only for the earlier of 90 days or the end of the policy period.
    D. Yes, but only until the end of the policy period.

62. All of the following reduce the general aggregate limit EXCEPT

    A. the medical expense sublimit
    B. the products-completed operations limit
    C. the damage to premises rented to you sublimit
    D. the personal and advertising injury limit.

63. An insured has a CGL with a $200,000 general aggregate and a $100,000 personal and advertising injury limit. During the first policy year, the general aggregate is reduced by a $50,000 personal and advertising injury judgment. How much will be available in the personal and advertising injury limit at the beginning of the second policy year?

    A. $50,000
    B. $100,000
    C. $150,000
    D. $200,000

64. An insured has a CGL with a $200,000 products-completed operations limit. During the third year of a 3-year policy, this limit was reduced to $80,000. The insured asks for and receives a 2-month extension of the policy. During this 2-month period, a $140,000 products-completed operations judgment is awarded against the insured. How much is available under the products-completed operations limit to pay this loss?

    A. $60,000
    B. $80,000
    C. $140,000
    D. $200,000

65. The personal and advertising injury limit applies

    A. per offense
    B. per occurrence
    C. only as limited by the general aggregate
    D. per person or organization

66. Disregarding supplementary payments and damages covered by the products-completed operations hazard, the general aggregate limit

    A. is the most that will be paid for the sum of Coverages A, B, and C
    B. applies separately to Coverage C, but is the most that will be paid for the sum of Coverages A and B
    C. applies separately to Coverages A, B, and C
    D. is the most that will be paid for Coverage A

67. An insured increases her CGL's general aggregate limit to $400,000, the products-completed operations aggregate to $300,000, and the per occurrence limit to $200,000. The limit for personal and advertising injury will

    A. automatically increase to $200,000
    B. automatically increase to $300,000
    C. automatically increase to $400,000
    D. not increase unless the insured specifically requests an increase from the insurer

68. If an insured under a CGL policy files for bankruptcy during the policy period, the insurance company

    A. may limit payment of covered losses under the policy
    B. may cancel the policy on 10 days' notice
    C. must continue its obligations under the policy until the end of the policy period
    D. may void policy coverage immediately

69. To qualify as an agreed settlement, who must sign the release of liability?

    A. The insurance company, the insured, and the claimant or the claimant's legal representative
    B. The insurance company and the claimant
    C. The insured and the claimant
    D. The insured and the insurance company

70. If other insurance covers the insured for loss arising from the use of aircraft, autos, or watercraft, the CGL coverage is

    A. either primary or excess depending on the inception dates of both policies
    B. excess
    C. excess unless no other insurer defends, in which case it is primary
    D. primary

71. Which one of the following correctly describes what is meant by contribution by equal shares?

    A. Whether primary or excess, each insurer contributes equal amounts until the loss is paid or the limit of liability is exhausted.
    B. An insurer will pay a covered loss up to the policy's limit of liability; the insured is responsible for any costs left over after the insurer pays.
    C. When the insurer provides excess insurance, payment is based on the ratio of its applicable insurance limits to the total limits of all insurance.
    D. When more than one insurer is a primary insurer, each contributes equal amounts until the loss is paid or the limit of liability is exhausted.

72. An insured purchases liability coverage as a tenant for the rental of a party house. If the insured also has CGL coverage, the CGL would be _____ and the liability coverage for the rental would be

    _____.

    A. excess, contingent
    B. primary, excess
    C. excess, primary
    D. other, excess

73. Which one of the following statements concerning the premium audit condition is correct?

    A. The named insured may eventually be required to pay more than the advance premium shown on the policy.
    B. The insurer is responsible for recording and maintaining the information used to compute premiums.
    C. The premium shown on the policy as the advance premium is the exact amount the insured will pay for the coverage.
    D. The named insured will never pay less than the advance premium indicated on the policy.

74. After a claim has been paid under a policy, any recovery rights belong to

    A. both the insurance company and the insured
    B. the insurance company
    C. either the insurance company or the insured, depending on which one paid the greater share of the loss
    D. the insured

75. If an insurance company decides not to renew coverage under the CGL, it must provide notice of nonrenewal at least how many days before the expiration date of the policy?

    A. 10
    B. 30
    C. 45
    D. 60

76. For Coverages A and B to apply under a claims-made policy,

    A. the first notice of the claim must be made during the policy period
    B. a claim for actual damages must be made before the retroactive date of the policy
    C. the first notice of the claim must be made after the policy expires
    D. the damage or injury must occur during the policy period

77. Which one of the following is true under the claims-made form?

    A. An actual claim made to either the insured or the insurer during the policy period will trigger Coverages A and B.
    B. Written notice by the insured of a claim is not required as long as the insurer is notified immediately in some way.
    C. The first notice of a claim during the policy period will trigger Coverage C.
    D. Notice of an occurrence is the same as notice of a claim.

78. For Coverage C to apply under a claims-made policy,

    A. the first notice of the claim must be made after the policy expires
    B. the first notice of the claim must be made during the policy period
    C. the event must occur during the policy period
    D. a claim for actual damages must be made before the retroactive date of the policy

79. The retroactive date indicated on the declarations provides that coverage will be

    A. excluded for events occurring after that date
    B. included for events occurring before that date under all circumstances
    C. excluded for events occurring before that date
    D. included for events occurring before that date if the supplemental extended reporting period endorsement has been purchased

80. Coverage over the longest period of time is provided when

    A. there is no retroactive date indicated on the declarations
    B. the retroactive date is before the policy inception date
    C. the retroactive date is after the policy inception date
    D. the retroactive date is the same as the policy inception date

81. An insurer is only allowed to advance the retroactive date under certain circumstances. Which of the following is always required before any of the others are permitted?

    A. There must be a material increase in hazard.
    B. The insured must fail to provide adequate information about the nature of the business.
    C. The insured must change insurance companies.
    D. The insured must agree in writing to advance the retroactive date.

82. Continuous coverage with no overlap or gap in coverage for all insured claims can be provided when an insured has a series of claims-made policies if each policy

    A. has a supplemental extended reporting period endorsement attached
    B. has the inception date of the preceding policy as its retroactive date
    C. uses the same date for its inception date and retroactive date
    D. has the inception date of the first policy as its retroactive date

83. In a series of claims-made policies, when each policy has the same retroactive date as the first claims-made policy, the rate at which the premium is charged

    A. gradually increases
    B. gradually decreases
    C. remains constant
    D. is the same in the fifth year as it is in the first year

84. The aggregate limits of an expiring claims-made policy are reinstated under

    A. the 5-year basic extended reporting period
    B. the supplemental extended reporting period
    C. the 60-day basic extended reporting period
    D. both the 60-day and the 5-year extended reporting periods

85. All of the following are true concerning the basic extended reporting period EXCEPT

    A. no separate endorsement is required
    B. it becomes effective automatically if needed when a claims-made policy expires
    C. the insured must request it in writing within 60 days after the policy expires
    D. there is no additional premium required

86. A supplemental ERP becomes effective

    A. on the date specified in the endorsement
    B. when the policy expires
    C. no earlier than the policy's retroactive date
    D. at the end of the basic extended reporting period

87. For the 5-year basic extended reporting period to apply, the insured must

    A. purchase the supplemental extended reporting period endorsement
    B. notify the insurer within 60 days of the policy expiration of an occurrence or offense that might lead to a claim
    C. receive notice of any late claim within 60 days of the policy expiration
    D. have been in the claims-made program for 5 years

88. Which one of the following statements concerning the premium charged for the supplemental ERP endorsement is correct?

    A. There is no premium charged for this endorsement.
    B. The premium depends on the separate limits of insurance selected for the supplemental ERP endorsement.
    C. The most an insurer may charge is 200% of the previous year's annual premium for the coverage part to which the supplemental ERP endorsement is attached.
    D. There is no maximum limit set on the amount an insurer can charge for this endorsement.

89. Which one of the extended reporting periods provides excess insurance coverage when other insurance also covers a loss?

    A. 5-year basic extended reporting period
    B. Both the 60-day and 5-year basic extended reporting periods
    C. Supplemental extended reporting period
    D. 60-day basic extended reporting period

90. Which endorsement provides an unlimited extended reporting period?

    A. Supplemental extended reporting period endorsement
    B. Basic extended reporting period endorsement
    C. Total pollution exclusion endorsement
    D. Exclusion of specific accidents, products, work, or location endorsement

91. Which endorsement allows certain specified items to be excluded from protection under Coverage A of the claims-made CGL?

    A. Supplemental extended reporting period endorsement
    B. Supplemental ERP endorsement for specific accidents, products, work, or locations
    C. Exclusion of specific accidents, products, work, or location endorsement
    D. Amendment of Section V—extended reporting periods for specific accidents, products, work, or location

92. Which endorsement must be offered to the insured if the exclusion of specific accidents, products, work, or location endorsement is first attached to the policy when it is renewed?

    A. Exclusion of specific accidents, products, work, or location endorsement
    B. Supplemental extended reporting period endorsement
    C. Supplemental ERP endorsement for specific accidents, products, work, or locations
    D. Amendment of Section V—extended reporting periods for specific accidents, products, work, or location

93. An insurer who wants to specifically exclude coverage for injury arising from actions such as harassment, employment termination, demotions, or discrimination needs the

    A. employment-related practices exclusion endorsement.
    B. coverage for injury to leased workers endorsement.
    C. Exclusion—personal injury and advertising injury endorsement.
    D. Exclusion—designated professional services endorsement.

94. How can an insured who is not in the alcoholic beverage business specifically exclude liquor liability?

    A. Attach the employment-related practices exclusion endorsement to the policy.
    B. Attach the amendment of liquor liability exclusion endorsement to the policy.
    C. No action is needed because it is already excluded by the CGL.
    D. Attach the liquor liability coverage form to the policy.

95. The limited pollution liability extension endorsement extends the CGL to include

    A. pollution clean-up costs only
    B. some pollution coverage, including clean-up costs
    C. some pollution coverage, excluding clean-up costs
    D. unlimited pollution coverage

96. The liquor liability coverage form is designed to
    A. provide liquor liability coverage for those who are not in the business of handling alcoholic beverages
    B. provide liquor liability coverage for those who are in the alcoholic beverage business, thereby overriding the exclusion in the CGL coverage form
    C. eliminate liquor liability coverage for those who are not in the business of handling alcoholic beverages
    D. eliminate liquor liability coverage for those in the business of handling alcoholic beverages

97. An insured wants pollution liability coverage against the possibility of bodily injury and property damage claims, but is not interested in coverage for clean-up costs. This insured needs
    A. the pollution liability limited coverage form
    B. the pollution liability coverage form
    C. only the pollution liability endorsement
    D. the pollution liability coverage form plus the limited coverage form to eliminate the coverage for clean-up costs

98. All of the following are correct about the products-completed operations liability coverage form EXCEPT
    A. it covers BI and PD arising from the product-completed operations hazard involving the insured's business
    B. it is available in only the claims-made version
    C. it provides the same broad form contractual liability coverage as the CGL
    D. it eliminates premises-operations coverage

99. Which one of the following statements describes a protective policy, such as the owners and contractors protective liability coverage form and the railroad protective liability coverage form?
    A. Someone other than the named insured purchases a policy to protect the named insured from liability because of the other person's actions made on the insured's behalf.
    B. The named insured purchases a policy to protect someone else from liability because of the insured's actions or actions made on the insured's behalf.
    C. Someone other than the named insured purchases a policy to protect someone else from liability because of the insured's actions or actions made on the insured's behalf.
    D. The named insured purchases a policy for protection from liability because of personal actions or actions made by others on the insured's behalf.

100. Which one of the following provides corrective action costs?
    A. Employment-related practices liability coverage form
    B. Underground storage tank liability coverage form for designated tanks
    C. Liquor liability coverage form
    D. Pollution liability limited coverage form

ANSWERS AND RATIONALES

1. **A.** There is no contract between Mark and the Ace Fuel Company because there was no agreement made. The other answer choices illustrate possible cases of negligence, which fall under tort law.

2. **B.** Invasion of the right of private occupancy is one of the many offenses listed in the policy's definition of personal and advertising injury.

3. **A.** An intentional tort is a civil violation of another's natural right that involves a deliberate intent to do harm.

4. **A.** The situation involving the Nifty Spot Removing Company is not correct because the product was still in the insured's possession. The scenarios involving Chan and Mark are not correct because the injuries occurred on the insured's premises.

5. **B.** Absolute liability may result when an individual deliberately acts in a way that is potentially hazardous, even though there was no intent to harm others. It is most frequently applied when dangerous materials, hazardous operations, or animals are involved, regardless of the skills or precautions used to prevent harm from occurring.

6. **C.** Work is considered a completed operation when all work called for in the insured's contract has been completed.

7. **A.** This situation includes the 4 conditions that must exist for a charge of negligence to be established: a legal duty owed, a breach of the legal duty owed, actual damages, and proximate cause. The other answer choices do not include all 4 conditions.

8. **C.** The definition of property damage includes loss of use of tangible property that is not physically injured. In this case, the 2 businesses suffered economic loss because, although their property was not physically injured, it could not be used.

9. **C.** Breach of duty is one of the conditions required to establish a charge of negligence. Assumption of risk and contributory negligence are both possible defenses against a charge of negligence.

10. **C.** According to the definition, electronic data is not tangible property. The computer keyboard, printout, and floppy disks are all tangible.

11. **A.** The law assumes that when a reasonable person experiences a loss, she will take every precaution to prevent further damages. If that person does not take such precautions and further loss occurs, the principle of avoidable consequences is introduced. The principle is that a person should not recover for loss that results because the individual failed to take appropriate action to avoid further loss.

12. **B.** The wronged party is the third party, who brings a charge of negligence against the first party, who caused the injury. The first party's insurance company, as the second party, pays the settlement.

13. **B.** The exposures listed in the other answer choices must be covered under other policies.

14. **B.** Liability for rendering professional services is an element of the professional liability exposure.

15. **D.** This is the basic function that liability insurance serves.

16. **B.** A CGL coverage part includes the mandatory and optional forms and endorsements needed to provide the coverage desired by the insured. Two or more coverage parts can be combined into a commercial package policy.

17. **C.** To qualify as a package policy, at least 2 coverage parts are required.

18. **C.** The Common policy conditions describe the terms on which the contract is issued. A line of insurance coverage form describes the coverage applicable to the line of insurance purchased. Interline endorsements modify the policy in some way and may be used for 2 or more lines of insurance.

19. **B.** The inspections and surveys condition gives the insurer the right to inspect the insured's premises. The examination of your books and records condition allows the insurer to examine the insured's books and records as they relate to the policy. The transfer of your rights and duties under this policy condition sets out the terms under which the insured may assign the policy.

20. **D.** Only certain CPPs are eligible for a package modification factor. The package modification factor used depends on the type of coverage included in the CPP and the type of risk covered by the policy.

21. **B.** This endorsement is mandatory. Common policy conditions and interline endorsements are part of a commercial package policy. The amendment of liquor liability exclusion is an optional endorsement for modifying coverage.

22. **B.** The policy defines an auto as a land motor vehicle designed for travel on public roads or a land vehicle that is subject to compulsory or financial responsibility laws. The other answer choices listed do not fit this definition.

23. **A.** A motorcycle and a four-wheel drive vehicle with a permanently attached snow shovel are considered autos. A glider is an aircraft.

24. **D.** The policy defines bodily injury as bodily injury, sickness, or disease sustained by a person, including death resulting from any of these at any time.

25. **C.** The events described in the other answer choices are deliberate, not accidental.

26. **A.** Personal and advertising injury includes false arrest or imprisonment, malicious prosecution, wrongful eviction or entry, slander, libel, violation of personal privacy, use of another's advertising idea, or copyright infringement.

27. **C.** The dog bite and death are bodily injuries, not personal and advertising injuries. The arrest would have been a personal and advertising injury only if Janet was falsely accused.

28. **D.** The situation involving slander would be covered under Coverage B. The example involving first aid would be covered under Coverage C. The case involving the woman who fell but was not injured would not be covered under the CGL.

29. **A.** After the limits of insurance are exhausted, the insurer is no longer obligated to pay claims.

30. **A.** Under an occurrence form, BI or PD must occur during the policy period. The policy in effect when the loss occurred then pays the claim, even if the claim is not made until after the policy expires.

31. **C.** Under the occurrence version of the CGL, the bodily injury or property damage must occur during the policy period, but the claim for damages does not have to be made during the policy period.

32. **D.** While BI or PD must arise out of an accident to be covered, the policy does allow the insured to use reasonable force to protect property or persons without losing coverage. The use of reasonable force is exempted only for bodily injury; property damage is excluded.

33. **C.** Although coverage may apply when an occurrence is continuous in nature, the CGL occurrence form does NOT cover losses of a continuous or ongoing nature that were, before the policy period, known to the insured or employees authorized to report losses.

34. **B.** Contractual liability is generally not covered. However, liability for bodily injury or property damage assumed under contract is covered when the contract meets the policy's definition of an insured contract, and the BI or PD occurs after the contract is executed, or if there is no contract, but the insured would be liable anyway.

35. **B.** The liquor liability exclusion applies only to insureds in the business of manufacturing, distributing, selling, serving, or furnishing alcoholic beverages. It does not apply when liquor is provided as an incidental part of a business.

36. **B.** This exposure is specifically excluded by the policy.

37. **D.** The policy's definition of an employee includes leased workers, but not temporary workers.

38. **D.** Coverage is available because the pipeline that was the source of the pollution causing bodily injury was not brought to the site by the insured or subcontractor.

39. **B.** Injury arising from use of the insured's own watercraft is excluded.

40. **B.** The war exclusion applies to BI or PD arising out of war and various warlike actions. There are no exceptions to this exclusion.

41. **D.** BI or PD arising out of the use of mobile equipment is excluded only if the damage occurs while the mobile equipment is transported by an auto owned or operated by an insured or involved in a prearranged stunting activity.

42. **A.** An exception to the damage to property exclusion permits coverage for building contractors who build on speculation, provided the builder has never occupied, rented, or held the property for rental.

43. **D.** The damage to your work exclusion does not apply if the work out of which the damage arises is performed by a subcontractor for the insured.

44. **A.** The damage to impaired property exclusion does not apply when a sudden and accidental injury to the insured's work occurred after it was put to its intended use.

45. **D.** This exclusion, which is sometimes called the sistership exclusion, categorically excludes coverage for losses, costs, or expenses resulting from product recall situations, regardless of who is responsible for the recall.

46. **B.** This coverage is for legal liability for fire damage to premises rented to the insured or temporarily occupied by the insured with the permission of the owner.

47. **A.** The insurer will defend Reba in the wrongful eviction suit because she hasn't actually violated the tenant's rights. Coverage is excluded if the advertisement was first published before the policy's effective date, the loss arises out of the failure of products to conform with advertised quality, or the insured knowingly publishes something that is false.

48. **A.** The CGL's personal and advertising injury coverage is not designed for the media because its chance of loss is much greater than that of other business risks. Advertising agencies, publishers, broadcasters, and telecasters must purchase specialized insurance protection for this liability exposure.

49. **A.** The other answer choices are specifically excluded under the CGL's Coverage B.

50. **A.** The visitor's injuries are considered consequential bodily injuries resulting from a personal and advertising injury (false detention). Therefore, they are covered under Coverage B: Personal and Advertising Injury Liability.

51. **B.** The policy exclusions that apply to the other answer choices include injury on normally occupied premises, products-completed operations hazards, and athletics activities.

52. **A.** Also, the accident must take place within the coverage territory and during the policy period.

53. **C.** Insureds, except for volunteer workers, are excluded for bodily injury expenses.

54. **B.** Supplementary payments are not subject to aggregate limits. The only limitations that apply are those stipulated in the supplementary payments section of the form.

55. **D.** Stockholders are never considered insureds in connection with conducting the business.

56. **B.** The insured's business partners and their spouses would be insureds if the insured was designated as a partnership or joint venture. Stockholders' and employees' spouses are never considered insureds; employees are only considered insureds under special circumstances.

57. **A.** Because trustees are automatically insureds with respect to their duties as trustees, only the name of the trust company must be listed in the declarations.

58. **C.** Obligations imposed by workers' compensation and employers liability laws are excluded by the policy.

59. **D.** The situations described in the other answer choices are specifically excluded.

60. **C.** The brother is an insured until a legal representative is appointed.

61. **B.** Newly acquired or formed partnerships, joint ventures, and limited liability companies cannot be covered under the CGL.

62. **B.** Products-completed operations has its own aggregate limit. The other limits mentioned fall under the general aggregate limit.

63. **B.** The full policy limits are restored at the beginning of each policy year, unless the policy period is extended for an additional period of less than 12 months. In that case, the additional period is considered an extension of the last policy year for the purpose of determining liability limits.

64. **B.** The full policy limits are restored at the beginning of each policy year, unless the policy period is extended for an additional period of less than 12 months. In that case, the additional period is considered an extension of the last policy year for the purpose of determining liability limits.

65. **D.** The personal and advertising injury limit has a per person or organization limit instead of a per occurrence limit.

66. **A.** The general aggregate for Coverages A, B, and C is the largest amount that will be paid in any one policy period. The aggregate does not apply separately; when the aggregate is used up, no further payments will be made.

67. **A.** The personal and advertising injury limit automatically increases to the same amount as the per occurrence increase.

68. **C.** An insured's bankruptcy or insolvency does not relieve the insurer of its obligations under the policy.

69. **A.** An agreed settlement is a settlement and release of liability signed by the insurer, the insured, and the claimant or the claimant's legal representative.

70. **B.** This is one of the situations in which the CGL policy is always excess when other insurance exists.

71. **D.** All companies divide the loss equally. If a company uses up its limits before the loss is paid, the other companies share equally in the unpaid portion up to their policy limits.

72. **C.** The CGL is excess over any other insurance the insured purchases when temporarily renting property or occupying a premises with the permission of the owner.

73. **A.** The advance premium listed in the declarations is adjusted periodically to determine the earned premium for that period. If it is greater than the advance premium, the insured must pay the difference. If it is less, the insured receives a refund.

74. **B.** If the company pays a claim under the policy, the insured's recovery rights are transferred to the company. At the company's request, the insured must help the company enforce those rights.

75. **B.** In addition, nonrenewal notices must be in writing and may be delivered only to the first named insured.

76. **A.** This describes the trigger for Coverages A and B under the claims-made form.

77. **A.** If the insured receives the claim, he must record the specifics of the claim and the date it was received and notify the insurer as soon as possible.

78. **C.** For Coverages A and B, a claim for damages must first be made during the policy period. For Coverage C, the loss must occur during the policy period.

79. **C.** The purpose of the retroactive date is to stipulate a date before which the company is not liable for occurrences that might result in claims under the claims-made policy. The policy stipulates that the insurance does not apply to injury or damage that occurs before any retroactive date shown in the declarations.

80. **A.** The other two optional uses of the retroactive date are the same date as the policy inception and an earlier date than the policy inception. Both of these choices exclude some prior occurrences. By not imposing a retroactive date, if a valid claim is made during the current policy term, there will be coverage no matter when the occurrence happened.

81. **D.** Advancing the retroactive date can leave an insured without coverage for certain claims. To avoid this situation, the insured must give written consent to advancing the retroactive date.

82. **D.** If the retroactive date is not advanced any further than the inception date of the first claims-made policy written for the insured, no coverage gap can occur. Any of the other options listed could result in claims for losses that no policy would cover if the retroactive date is changed.

83. **A.** The rate is lowest in the first year of a claims-made policy because the chance of loss is the lowest. For the second year, if the retroactive date is kept the same, the premium is slightly more because the insurer is now liable for reported claims over a two-year period. The premium gradually increases as long as the retroactive date of each policy stays the same as that for the first-year policy.

84. **B.** Neither of the basic extended reporting periods reinstates the policy limits, so if they are greatly reduced, payment under the policy still might not be possible. The supplemental extended reporting period reinstates limits equal to the dollar amounts shown in the declarations.

85. **C.** The basic extended reporting period is automatic and free, and the insured does not have to apply for it.

86. **D.** An insured who wants more than the 60-day or 5-year basic periods for reporting unknown claims may write to the insurer requesting that a supplemental ERP endorsement be attached to the expiring policy.

87. **B.** If the insured is aware of an event that took place before the policy expired but suspects that claims won't come in until after the 60-day ERP expires, he should report the occurrence or offense to the insurer to take advantage of the 5-year ERP.

88. **C.** When determining the additional premium, the insurer may take into account the exposures insured, previous types and amounts of insurance, and the limits of insurance available under the policy.

89. **C.** Neither of the basic extended reporting periods provides excess insurance.

90. **A.** While the 60-day and 5-year basic ERPs are available automatically at no additional charge, the insured must specifically request and pay for supplemental extended reporting period coverage.

91. **C.** When the retroactive date is the same as the policy inception date, all incidents before the policy takes effect are excluded even when the claim is first made during the policy period. This can leave the insured without coverage in some cases. This endorsement allows the insurer to exclude only specific items from coverage.

92. **D.** This endorsement provides the 60-day or 5-year basic extended reporting periods for whatever items are otherwise excluded by the exclusion of specific accidents, products, work, or location endorsement.

93. **A.** This endorsement specifically excludes liability for such employment-related practices from both Coverages A and B.

94. **B.** Liquor liability coverage is provided under an unendorsed CGL as long as the insured is not engaged in the alcoholic beverage business. Insureds who want to specifically exclude this coverage should purchase this endorsement.

95. **C.** On-premises pollution coverage for certain pollution incidents is available through this endorsement.

96. **B.** Insureds who are not in the business of handling alcoholic beverages have liquor liability coverage under an unendorsed CGL.

97. **A.** The pollution liability limited coverage form is the same as the pollution liability coverage form except it excludes clean-up costs.

98. **B.** While several coverage forms are available in only the claims-made version, this one is provided in occurrence and claims-made versions.

99. **A.** The owners and contractors protective liability coverage form and the railroad protective liability coverage form are designed to protect the named insured-owner from liability arising from a contractor's work.

100. **B.** Corrective action costs are the costs for reasonable and necessary clean-up after an incident. The underground storage tank liability coverage form for designated tanks provides clean-up after petroleum spills, leaks, or is discharged from a tank into ground water, surface water, or subsurface soil. The other coverages do not provide clean-up.

Glossary

A

Absolute Liability Refers to liability that arises from deliberately pursuing actions that are potentially hazardous.

Accident An event that is unexpected and not intended from the insured's standpoint. See also *Occurrence*

Advertisement* A broadcast or published notice about the insured's goods, products, or services.

Aggregate Limits The overall limits of insurance that will be paid during a specified policy period.

Aircraft, Auto, or Watercraft Exclusion** An exclusion in the CGL forms that prohibits coverage for bodily injury or property damage resulting from owning, maintaining, using, or entrusting to someone else any aircraft, auto, or watercraft. Certain exceptions apply.

Amendment of Liquor Liability Exclusion—Exception for Scheduled Activities Endorsement A CGL endorsement that eliminates all liability coverage for activities involving alcohol, except for those activities specifically listed in the endorsement or the policy declarations.

Amendment of Liquor Liability Exclusion Endorsement A CGL endorsement that eliminates all liability coverage for any activity involving alcohol.

Amendment of Section V—Extended Reporting Periods for Specific Accidents, Products, Work, or Locations Endorsement An endorsement used with the CGL claims-made form to provide 60-day or 5-year basic extended reporting periods for items excluded by the exclusion of specific accidents, products, work, or location endorsement.

Assumption of Risk The willing and knowledgeable exposure of oneself or one's property to the possibility of injury. This is used as a defense in negligence cases and is valid when the plaintiff knows the danger, but voluntarily takes the risk.

Attractive Nuisance A structure or artificial condition that is especially attractive to trespassing children, usually those under the age of 14, and which might result in danger to them. The owner of an attractive nuisance has the legal duty to take unusual care to guard children from the danger.

Auto* Motorized vehicles meant to be used on public roads, but not certain specifically defined mobile equipment.

Avoidable Consequences Consequences that are caused by a lack of care on the part of an individual, and that could have been avoided had the individual exercised proper care. Generally refers to events that occur following a loss as the result of a person's failure to take steps to prevent the consequences.

B

Bankruptcy Condition A condition in the CGL forms that provides that the insurer's obligations under the policy are not relieved if the insured files for bankruptcy or becomes insolvent.

Basic Extended Reporting Period One of two periods following the expiration of a CGL claims-made policy during which claims may be made against the policy or notification of potential claims may be made. Depending on the circumstances, the period is either 60 days or 5 years. *Basic* means that the periods are provided at no additional cost to the insured. See also *Extended Reporting Period* and *Supplemental Extended Reporting Period Endorsement*

Basic Policy Limits The minimum amount of insurance coverage a policy will provide. Can be increased for additional premium or decreased under certain circumstances.

BI See *Bodily Injury*

Bodily Injury (BI)* Injuries to a person as well as sickness, disease, and death.

Breach of Contract Failure to perform a contract without legal excuse.

Bulletin Board, Electronic A computer medium that allows users to read and post public notices as electronic messages.

Business Liability Exposure Liability exposure that arises from the conduct of business. The CGL covers this exposure.

C

Cancellation Termination of insurance before the end of the policy period as specified in the declarations, either by the insured or the insurer, under provisions contained in the policy.

CGL Popular abbreviation for the commercial general liability coverage forms.

---

* This term is specifically defined in the policy. See the Commercial General Liability Coverage Forms and Endorsements for the exact wording.

** Refer to the Commercial General Liability Coverage Forms and Endorsements for the exact wording of CGL policy exclusions.

Chatroom, Electronic A virtual room where computer users can communicate online in real time.

Civil Law The area of law where one or more individuals take legal action against another party or parties to recover for damages suffered from a negligent act or omission. Damages are generally awarded in the form of money, including punitive damages.

Claim A demand to recover under an insurance policy for a loss. In CGL insurance, the claim may be against the insured by a third party under the insurance policy held by the insured. In this case, claims are referred to the insurer to handle on behalf of the insured in accordance with the terms of the policy.

Claims-Made Form A CGL coverage form that pays for events that occur during a specified period and for which a claim is made during the policy period, subject to stipulated limitations and extensions.

Claims-Made Trigger See *Coverage Trigger*

Clean-Up Costs Expenses incurred to remove or neutralize pollutants.

Commercial General Liability Insurance A line of insurance available to commercial organizations that provides coverage on behalf of insureds for sums they may be legally required to pay to others as a result of the insureds' actions or negligence. May include coverage for bodily injury, property damage, personal and advertising injury, medical payments, and certain supplemental payments specified in the policy.

Commercial Package Policy (CPP) The Insurance Services Office (ISO) commercial lines policy that contains two or more lines of insurance or two or more coverage parts. It will include some forms and/or endorsements that are common to all lines of insurance or coverage parts as well as the individual forms and endorsements required for the individual coverages selected.

Common Policy Conditions Written conditions that are common to all coverage parts contained in a commercial policy and that specify the duties and responsibilities of both the insured and the insurer. In a commercial package policy, the common conditions form has to be included only once, regardless of how many different coverage parts or lines of insurance are included.

Common Policy Declarations Information about who is an insured, where he is insured, and how he is an insured, all summarized in a single document. In a commercial package policy, the common policy declarations form has to be included only once, regardless of how many different coverage parts or lines of insurance are included. In some cases, line of insurance declarations may be combined with the common policy declarations in one document.

Comparative Negligence In negligence cases, refers to the relative degree of negligence by each party involved. Recovery by the plaintiff will be increased or decreased depending on the degree of negligence of each party.

Consequential Damage Type of damage that is the result or consequence of direct damage.

Contract A legal agreement between two or more parties. An insurance policy is a contract.

Contract Law Type of civil law involving a written or stated agreement between two or more parties for some specific promise of action. The promise of action constitutes a valid contractual agreement.

Contractual Liability Type of liability that is assumed in a contract or agreement.

Contractual Liability Exclusion** An exclusion in the CGL forms that prohibits coverage for liability the insured assumes under a contract or agreement. Certain exceptions apply.

Contribution by Equal Shares A method used to pay a loss covered by more than one insurance policy. All insurers divide the loss equally. If one or more companies use up their limits of liability before the loss is completely paid, then the other companies share equally in the unpaid portion, up to their policy limits.

Contribution by Limits A method used to pay a loss covered by more than one insurance policy. Each policy covers a portion of the loss in proportion to the relationship its limit of liability bears to the total limit of liability under all applicable policies.

Contributory Negligence Refers to negligence on the part of both parties or individuals involved in a suit. Under the concept of contributory negligence, if a plaintiff is found to have contributed to the loss in any way, she cannot collect damages.

Coverage In insurance, the guarantee to pay for specific losses as provided under the terms of the policy. Coverage means the same as protection and is often used synonymously with the word *insurance*.

Coverage A In the CGL coverage forms, the coverage that pays for bodily injury and property damage liability.

Coverage B In the CGL coverage forms, the coverage that pays for personal and advertising injury liability.

Coverage C In the CGL coverage forms, the coverage that pays for medical payments for bodily injury caused by an accident under specified circumstances.

Coverage Part All the forms and endorsements used in a certain line of insurance to provide the desired coverage.

Coverage Territory* The specific geographical area within which damage must occur in order to be

---

* This term is specifically defined in the policy. See the Commercial General Liability Coverage Forms and Endorsements for the exact wording.

** Refer to the Commercial General Liability Coverage Forms and Endorsements for the exact wording of CGL policy exclusions.

covered by an insurance policy. The precise area is always defined in a policy.

Coverage Trigger Refers to the event that triggers or activates coverage under a certain insurance policy. In an occurrence policy, coverage is triggered according to when an event occurs. In a claims-made policy, coverage is triggered when a claim is first made.

CPP See *Commercial Package Policy*

Criminal Law The area of law concerned with the state prosecuting an individual in the interest of society, generally for violating a written law or statute. Penalties may include fines, imprisonment, or both.

D

Damage to Impaired Property or Property not Physically Injured Exclusion** An exclusion in the CGL forms that prohibits coverage for property damage to impaired property or property that is not physically injured due to specifically listed causes, such as defects or deficiencies in the insured's product or work and failure by the insured to perform a contract.

Damage to Premises Rented to You Legal Liability Coverage Coverage in CGL forms that pays for legal liability for property damage to rented premises covered by the CGL or for fire damage to premises temporarily rented or occupied with the owner's permission.

Damage to Premises Rented to You Legal Liability Sublimit A separate sublimit of insurance provided in CGL forms for payment of legal liability for property damage to rented premises covered by the CGL or for fire damage liability for premises temporarily rented or occupied with the owner's permission. Subject to the per occurrence limit and the general aggregate.

Damage to Property Exclusion** An exclusion in the CGL forms that denies coverage for property damage to property specifically listed in the form, such as property owned, rented, or occupied by the insured and property in the insured's care, custody, or control. Certain exceptions apply.

Damage to Your Product Exclusion** An exclusion in the CGL forms that prohibits coverage for property damage to the insured's product that results because there is a defect in all or any part of the product.

Damage to Your Work Exclusion** An exclusion in the CGL forms that prohibits coverage for property damage to the insured's work arising from it or any part of it. Applies only to work that falls within the products-completed operations hazard.

Data, Electronic Information, facts, or programs that are stored, created, or transmitted via computer software. May include systems and applications software, hard or floppy disks, CD-ROMS, tapes, drives, cells, data processing devices, and other media used with electronically controlled equipment.

Defense Costs Certain amounts an insurance company might spend to defend a claim or suit. Most defense costs are paid by the insurer in addition to the policy's limits of liability.

Duties in the Event of Occurrence, Offense, Claim, or Suit Condition A condition in the CGL forms that spells out the insured's obligations for notifying the insurer of events that may result in a liability claim, or of actual suits or claims filed under the policy.

Duty Owed A legal duty owed to the plaintiff by the defendant in a suit.

E

Effective Date In an insurance policy, the date on which protection under the policy begins. Also called *inception date*.

Electronic See *Bulletin Board, Electronic; Chatroom, Electronic; Data, Electronic*

Employee* Someone who is employed by the insured. Includes leased workers, but not temporary workers.

Employers Liability Exclusion** An exclusion in the CGL forms that denies coverage to an insured's employee for bodily injury that arises out of employment by the insured. Also excludes consequential damages to the employee's relatives and dual capacity claims.

Employment-Related Practices Exclusion Endorsement A CGL endorsement that excludes coverage for bodily injury or personal and advertising injury arising out of specified employment-related practices such as termination of employment, discrimination, and harassment.

Employment-Related Practices Liability (ERPL) Coverage Form A special purpose liability coverage form, available only in claims-made form, which covers damages and defense expenses for specified injuries arising out of work- and employment-related activities.

Endorsement An amendment in writing added to and made a part of an insurance policy to modify its original terms.

Endorsement, Interline An endorsement that can be used for two or more lines of insurance.

Endorsement, Line of Insurance An endorsement that modifies one or more coverage forms within a single line of insurance.

ERP See *Extended Reporting Period*

Excess Insurance Insurance coverage that pays only after other insurance, called primary insurance, has been exhausted.

---

* This term is specifically defined in the policy. See the Commercial General Liability Coverage Forms and Endorsements for the exact wording.

** Refer to the Commercial General Liability Coverage Forms and Endorsements for the exact wording of CGL policy exclusions.

Exclusion Anything specifically stated in an insurance policy as not covered by the policy.

Exclusion of Specific Accidents, Products, Work, or Location Endorsement An endorsement for the CGL claims-made form that excludes coverage for specified accidents, products, work, or locations.

Executive Officer* A person holding an officer's position created by the insured's charter, bylaws, constitution, or other governing document.

Expected or Intended Injury Exclusion** An exclusion in the CGL forms that prohibits coverage for bodily injury or property damage that is expected or intended from the insured's standpoint. Does not apply to bodily injury resulting from the use of reasonable force to protect persons or property.

Expiration Date In an insurance policy, the date on which protection under the policy ends.

Extended Reporting Period (ERP) Under a CGL claims-made form, a period following policy expiration during which claims may be made or during which the insurer may be notified that an event has occurred that could result in a claim. If the claim or notification is made during the ERP, the insurer considers the claim as if it had been made during the policy period. Extends the reporting period but not the time during which covered events may occur. See also *Basic Extended Reporting Period* and *Supplemental Extended Reporting Period Endorsement*

F

Fire Damage Exception Coverage A exception to the CGL forms that permits limited fire legal liability coverage.

First Named Insured The insured individual or organization named first in the policy declarations. Under the CGL forms, the first named insured has rights and responsibilities not specifically assigned to other named insureds. See also *Named Insured*

First Party In liability insurance claims, the party who causes injury to another.

G

General Aggregate Limit In the CGL forms, the total limit of insurance coverage that will be paid in one policy for all coverages except the products-completed operations hazard, which has its own aggregate limit.

General Liability Insurance See *Commercial General Liability Insurance*

Gross Negligence Failure to use ordinary care; total disregard for the safety of others; reckless, wanton, and willful misconduct; or breach of the standard of due care of a reasonably prudent person.

H

Hostile Fire* A fire that has escaped from the place it was intended to be or is uncontrolled.

I

Impaired Property* Tangible property that fits neither the definition of the insured's product nor the insured's work, but involves either of those. As a result of that involvement, the property is either less useful or not capable of being used for its intended purpose. To fit the definition of impaired property, the property must be able to be restored to use.

Implied Contract An agreement between two or more parties that is inferred from the conduct of the parties.

Inception Date See *Effective Date*

Increased/Decreased Limits Policy limits (increased) above or (decreased) below the basic policy limits.

Indemnitee A party who is not an insured but who is under contract to provide goods or services to an insured.

Insurance Services Office (ISO) An organization established for the benefit of its member insurance companies and other subscriber companies. The ISO gathers statistics, provides loss costs, drafts policy forms and coverage provisions, and conducts inspections for rate-making purposes.

Insured The person or organization covered by an insurance company. See also *First Named Insured* and *Named Insured*

Insured Contract* Any one of several very specifically defined contracts that do not invalidate coverage under the CGL forms. Not all contracts entered into by an insured are insured contracts.

Insurer The insurance company that issues a particular insurance policy and agrees to provide the coverage the policy describes.

Insuring Agreement The portion of an insurance policy that expresses the insurer's agreement to provide coverage.

Intentional Tort A wrong performed by one party with the deliberate attempt to harm another.

Invitee A person on another's property with express or implied permission of the property owner and for the benefit of the property owner.

L

Leased Worker* A person leased to the insured's business by a labor leasing firm to perform duties related to the conduct of the insured's business. Does not include temporary workers.

Legal Action Against The Insurer Condition A condition in the CGL forms that spells out the conditions

---

* This term is specifically defined in the policy. See the Commercial General Liability Coverage Forms and Endorsements for the exact wording.

** Refer to the Commercial General Liability Coverage Forms and Endorsements for the exact wording of CGL policy exclusions.

under which legal actions may be brought against the insurer.

Legal Liability Type of liability imposed by law, as opposed to liability arising out of a contract or agreement.

Liability Exposure The possibility of financial loss due to a claim by a third party. The three categories of liability exposure are personal, professional, and business.

Liability Insurance See *Commercial General Liability Insurance*

Licensee A visitor on another's property for the sole benefit of the visitor.

Limited Liability Company (LLC) A company that is structured like a corporation, but which has additional tax and liability advantages for its members.

Limited Pollution Liability Extension Endorsement An endorsement used with the CGL forms to provide more pollution liability coverage than is normally available in the CGL.

Limit of Insurance The greatest amount of insurance a policy will provide; the amount beyond which the insurer is no longer required to pay.

Liquor Liability Coverage Form A special purpose liability coverage form that eliminates the liquor liability exclusion in the CGL.

Liquor Liability Exclusion** A CGL exclusion that prohibits liability coverage for insureds involved in the business of manufacturing, selling, distributing, serving, or furnishing alcoholic beverages.

Loading or Unloading* The handling of property in the precise ways described in the policy. The term excludes movement of property in ways specifically described in the policy.

M

Mandatory Endorsement An endorsement that must be included in an insurance policy. The nuclear energy liability exclusion endorsement (Broad Form) is an example of a mandatory endorsement for CGL forms.

Mature Claims-Made Program Refers to an insured's insurance program that has included five successive years of claims-made policies that all use the first claims-made policy's retroactive date.

Medical Expense Sublimit A separate sublimit of insurance provided in the CGL forms for payment of Coverage C medical expenses. Subject to the per occurrence limit and the general aggregate.

Medical Payments Coverage C of the CGL forms. It provides reimbursement on a no-fault basis for medical expenses incurred under circumstances described in the policy.

Mobile Equipment* Certain specifically described vehicles that are used on land.

Mobile Equipment Exclusion** An exclusion in the CGL forms that prohibits coverage for bodily injury and property damage related to the transportation and use of mobile equipment in certain circumstances.

Monoline Policy An insurance policy that provides coverage under only one line of insurance.

Multiline Policy An insurance policy that provides coverage under more than one line of insurance.

N

Named Insured The individual or organization named in the declarations of an insurance policy as the insured, as opposed to someone who may have an interest in the coverage, but is not named in the policy. See also *First Named Insured* and *Insured*

Negligence Failure to use the care that is required to protect others from the unreasonable chance of harm. Negligence may be caused by acts of omission, acts of commission, or both.

Nonrenewal Condition A condition in the CGL forms that describes the insurer's responsibilities if it decides not to renew coverage.

Nuclear Energy Liability Exclusion Endorsement (Broad Form) A mandatory CGL endorsement that excludes any injuries that occur as a result of the hazardous properties of nuclear material.

O

Occurrence* An accident; includes events that occur as a result of continuous or repeated exposure to the same condition that causes the occurrence.

Occurrence Form A CGL form that pays for events that occur during its policy term, regardless of when a claim is filed. An expired occurrence policy will pay a valid claim even if the claim is made years after the policy expiration date, provided the event occurred while the policy was in effect.

Occurrence Trigger See *Coverage Trigger*

Offense An intentional action, not an accident.

Other Insurance Condition A condition in the CGL forms that indicates how the policy will pay a loss that is covered by more than one insurance policy.

Owners and Contractors Protective (OCP) Liability Coverage Form A special purpose liability coverage form that covers claims caused by the negligence of a contractor or subcontractor hired by the insured.

P

Package Modification Factor (PMF) A factor used to reduce the premium for qualified commercial package policies. The PMF used depends on the type of

---

* This term is specifically defined in the policy. See the Commercial General Liability Coverage Forms and Endorsements for the exact wording.
** Refer to the Commercial General Liability Coverage Forms and Endorsements for the exact wording of CGL policy exclusions.

coverage included in the package and the type of risk covered by the policy.

PD See *Property Damage*

Per Occurrence Limit In the CGL forms, an amount representing the maximum a policy will pay for losses attributable to a single occurrence. After each occurrence, the per occurrence limit is reinstated, up to the exhaustion of the aggregate limits.

Personal and Advertising Injury* Injury, including consequential bodily injury, that results from false arrest or imprisonment, malicious prosecution, wrongful eviction or entry, slander, libel, violation of personal privacy, use of another's advertising idea, or copyright infringement.

Personal and Advertising Injury Exclusion An exclusion in the CGL forms that prohibits bodily injury that is a consequence of personal and advertising injury to be covered by Coverage A.

Personal and Advertising Injury Limit The limit of insurance in the CGL forms for Coverage B: Personal and Advertising Injury, losses. Subject to the general aggregate limit, but not the per occurrence limit.

Personal Liability Exposure Liability exposure that arises from an individual's personal activities, such as the use of an automobile, owning a home, or participating in sports. This exposure is not covered by CGL insurance.

PMF See *Package Modification Factor*

Policywriting Minimum Premium The least amount for which an insurance company feels it can issue a policy.

Pollutant* A solid, liquid, gas, or thermal irritant or contaminant. Can include smoke, vapor, soot, fumes, acids, alkalis, chemicals, and waste. See also *Waste*

Pollution Exclusion** An exclusion in the CGL forms that denies coverage for most forms of pollution that result in property damage, bodily injury, or clean-up costs associated with pollution.

Pollution Liability Coverage Form A special purpose liability coverage form that covers BI and PD arising from a pollution incident as specifically defined in the form. Includes coverage for clean-up costs.

Pollution Liability Limited Coverage Form A special purpose liability coverage form that covers BI and PD arising from a pollution incident as specifically defined in the form. Does not cover clean-up costs.

Prejudgment Interest Interest a claimant requests in addition to the judgment for the actual claim. Based on the premise that earlier awarding of a judgment would have resulted in the claimant having earlier use of the award. Therefore, the claimant should be paid interest for the period when the judgment money was not available for use by the claimant.

Premises-Operations Liability Refers to the liability that arises from the use of the insured's premises and the operations involved in the insured's business.

Premium Audit Condition A condition in the CGL forms that explains how the policy premium is computed.

Primary Insurance The policy that applies first when two or more policies apply to the same loss.

Products-Completed Operations Aggregate Limit In the CGL forms, the total limit of insurance coverage that will be paid in one policy year for all losses that fall within the products-completed operations hazard.

Products-Completed Operations Liability Coverage Form A special purpose liability coverage form that eliminates premises-operations coverage from the CGL. Covers BI and PD arising from the products-completed operations hazard only.

Products-Completed Operations Hazard* Refers to bodily injury and property damage that occur somewhere other than the insured's premises and involve the insured's products or work, subject to the limits and parameters specified in the CGL forms.

Products-Completed Operations Liability See *Products-Completed Operations Hazard*

Products-Completed Operations per Occurrence Limit In the CGL forms, the limit of insurance for each occurrence of a loss falling under the products-completed operations hazard.

Professional Liability Exposure Liability exposure that arises from the pursuit of a profession. This exposure is not covered by the CGL.

Property Damage (PD)* Physical damage to tangible property and loss of use of tangible property regardless of whether or not it is damaged.

Protective Policy Liability insurance purchased by someone other than the named insured to protect the named insured from liability from the other person's actions performed on the insured's behalf. In liability insurance, examples of protective policies are the owners and contractors protective liability coverage form and the railroad protective liability coverage form.

Proximate Cause An action that, in a natural and continuous sequence, produces a loss.

R

Railroad Protective Liability Coverage Form A special purpose liability coverage form designed to protect railroads. Covers BI and PD for physical damage to specified property of the insured from operations performed by the designated contractor.

---

* This term is specifically defined in the policy. See the Commercial General Liability Coverage Forms and Endorsements for the exact wording.
** Refer to the Commercial General Liability Coverage Forms and Endorsements for the exact wording of CGL policy exclusions.

Reasonable Person Describes behavior of a prudent person who follows those ordinary considerations that guide human affairs.

Recall of Products, Work, or Impaired Property Exclusion** An exclusion in the CGL forms that prohibits coverage for losses, costs, or expenses resulting from the recall or withdrawal of the insured's product, work, or impaired property from the market.

Renewal Reinstatement of an insurance policy beyond the original expiration date, either by endorsement, certificate, or issuance of a new policy.

Representations Condition A condition in the CGL forms that explains that the insurer has issued the CGL form based on representations, or truthful statements, the insured has made to the insurer. An intentional misrepresentation can invalidate the policy.

Retroactive Date Under the CGL claims-made form, a date stipulated in the declarations as the first date on which an event may occur and be covered by the policy if a valid claim is filed. An occurrence before the retroactive date of a claims-made policy will not be covered even if the claim is first made during the policy period.

S

Second Party In liability insurance claims, the insurance company.

Separation of Insureds Condition A condition in the CGL forms that provides that, if more than one insured is named in a CGL, no insured will receive less protection than if there were only one named insured.

Sistership Exclusion See *Recall of Products, Work, or Impaired Property Exclusion*

Suit* Court or arbitration proceedings that request damages for bodily injury, property damage, or personal and advertising injury. Also includes any other alternative dispute resolution proceeding.

Supplemental Extended Reporting Period Endorsement An endorsement that provides an extension of unlimited duration to the basic extended reporting period provision of the CGL claims-made policy. An additional premium is required. In addition, the aggregate limits of insurance that applied to the expired policy apply during the supplemental period. See also *Basic Extended Reporting Period* and *Extended Reporting Period*

Supplemental Extended Reporting Period Endorsement for Specific Accidents, Products, Work, or Locations An endorsement that provides a supplemental extended reporting period for items specifically excluded by the exclusion of specific accidents, products, work, or location endorsement.

Supplementary Payments Under the CGL forms, certain payments that may be made to the insured in addition to the payments made for the coverages provided.

T

Temporary Worker* A person hired by the insured to meet seasonal or short-term workload conditions or to fill in for a permanent employee on leave.

Third Party In liability insurance claims, the party who is injured by another party.

Tort A civil wrong that is a violation of another's natural rights, other than wrongs that arise from breach of contract.

Tortfeasor A person who commits a tort.

Tort Liability Legal responsibility based on one of these three grounds: absolute liability, intentional tort, or negligence.

Total Pollution Exclusion Endorsement A CGL endorsement that eliminates all pollution liability coverage from the CGL.

Trade Dress The total appearance and image of a product as well as the techniques for advertising and marketing its sale.

Transfer of Recovery Rights Condition A condition in the CGL forms that states that the insurance company, but not the insured, has the right to pursue any legal action against a third party who is liable for a loss that has been paid by the insurer.

Trespasser A person who enters the premises of another without either express or implied permission from the property owner.

Trust An organization that establishes legal arrangements whereby property is held and managed by trustees for the benefit of beneficiaries. May also refer to the legal arrangement itself.

U

Underground Storage Tank (UST) Liability Coverage Form for Designated Tanks A special purpose liability coverage form, available only in claims-made form, which covers BI and PD liability and corrective action costs for damage arising from an underground storage tank incident as specifically defined in the form.

V

Volunteer Worker* A person who is not an employee, but who donates his time, and who is not paid by the insured or anyone else for work performed. A volunteer worker acts at the direction of the insured to perform duties determined by the insured.

---

* This term is specifically defined in the policy. See the Commercial General Liability Coverage Forms and Endorsements for the exact wording.

** Refer to the Commercial General Liability Coverage Forms and Endorsements for the exact wording of CGL policy exclusions.

W

War Exclusion** An exclusion in the CGL forms that prohibits coverage for bodily injury or property damage arising out of war and various warlike actions.

Waste In the context of the CGL, certain materials that will be treated and converted to fuel. Waste is considered a pollutant in the CGL forms.

Workers' Compensation and Employers Liability Insurance A type of liability insurance not included in the CGL coverage part. Workers' compensation pays benefits for injuries to, disability, or death of an employee without regard to liability. Employers liability covers the common law liability of an employer for injuries to an employee. Because these coverages are related specifically to employer-employee relationships, they are not characterized as general liability.

Workers' Compensation and Similar Laws Exclusion** An exclusion in the CGL forms that prohibits coverage for obligations of the insured arising under a workers' compensation law or any similar law.

Y

Your Product* Any goods involved in the insured's business, including handling by the insured or others acting in the insured's interest as specifically designated in the CGL forms.

Your Work* Activities the insured performs in the course of business, including those performed by others on the insured's behalf. Also includes certain specified materials that represent part of the insured's work.

---

* This term is specifically defined in the policy. See the Commercial General Liability Coverage Forms and Endorsements for the exact wording.

** Refer to the Commercial General Liability Coverage Forms and Endorsements for the exact wording of CGL policy exclusions.

Checklist for Underwriting New Applicants for General Liability Insurance

Here is a brief checklist you can use when you are considering a new prospect for general liability insurance. This is not a complete list, just a few basic considerations.

- Check the applicant's:

  - ❑ **Operations**

  - ❑ **Premises owned or occupied**

  - ❑ **Products**

  to see that the limits of insurance (especially aggregate limits) requested are high enough to cover possible losses.

- Should **additional insureds** be named under the policy, and are appropriate certificates of insurance being issued to all additional insureds that require them? Consider:

  - ❑ **Landlords**

  - ❑ **Tenants**

  - ❑ **Subsidiary companies**

  - ❑ **Partnerships**

  - ❑ **Joint ventures**

  - ❑ **Trusts**

  - ❑ **Limited liability companies**

- For claims-made policies, what **retroactive date** is being used for the quote?

- Is there a **products exposure** that might create a catastrophic loss or a latent discovery period? Examples include:

  - ❑ **Airplane parts**

  - ❑ **Machine tools**

  - ❑ **Structural materials**

  - ❑ **Drugs**

  - ❑ **Toxic chemicals**

  - ❑ **Radioactive materials**

Use the following list for requests for a competitive quote or replacement policy.

- Are all the insured's liability risks being underwritten by the same insurer?

- Are reserves set up for open claims?

- Have aggregate limits been reduced?

- Are there any past occurrences that might result in claims for damages in the future?

- Are there potential gaps in continuity of coverage?

    ❑ If this will be a claims-made form replacing a claims-made form, will the retroactive date be the same?

    ❑ Can the Supplemental Extended Reporting Period Endorsement be provided on the expiring policy to fill any coverage gap?

Index

Commercial General Liability Coverage

Supplemental Material

COMMERCIAL GENERAL LIABILITY COVERAGE
SUPPLEMENTAL MATERIAL, 7TH EDITION, REVISED
© 2007 DF Institute, Inc. All rights reserved.

Published by DF Institute, Inc.

Printed in the United States of America.

ISBN: 1-4277-6710-6

PPN: 5322-0601

07 08 10 9 8 7 6 5 4 3 2 1
J   F   M   A M J J A S O N D

POLICY NUMBER: CP 12 345 678

IL DS 00 07 02

COMMON POLICY DECLARATIONS

COMPANY NAME AREA	PRODUCER NAME AREA

NAMED INSURED: Jay's Jewelry Manufacturing Company

MAILING ADDRESS: 1110 Wishingwell Road
Indianapolis, Indiana 46222

POLICY PERIOD: FROM February 2, 2002 TO February 2, 2003 AT 12:01 A.M. STANDARD TIME AT YOUR MAILING ADDRESS SHOWN ABOVE.

BUSINESS DESCRIPTION	Manufacturing of gold and diamond jewelry

IN RETURN FOR THE PAYMENT OF THE PREMIUM, AND SUBJECT TO ALL THE TERMS OF THIS POLICY, WE AGREE WITH YOU TO PROVIDE THE INSURANCE AS STATED IN THIS POLICY.

THIS POLICY CONSISTS OF THE FOLLOWING COVERAGE PARTS FOR WHICH A PREMIUM IS INDICATED. THIS PREMIUM MAY BE SUBJECT TO ADJUSTMENT.

	PREMIUM
BOILER AND MACHINERY COVERAGE PART	$
CAPITAL ASSETS PROGRAM (OUTPUT POLICY) COVERAGE PART	$
COMMERCIAL AUTOMOBILE COVERAGE PART	$
COMMERCIAL GENERAL LIABILITY COVERAGE PART	$ 8,100
COMMERCIAL INLAND MARINE COVERAGE PART	$
COMMERCIAL PROPERTY COVERAGE PART	$ 6,900
CRIME AND FIDELITY COVERAGE PART	$ 3,450
EMPLOYMENT-RELATED PRACTICES LIABILITY COVERAGE PART	$
FARM COVERAGE PART	$
LIQUOR LIABILITY COVERAGE PART	$
POLLUTION LIABILITY COVERAGE PART	$
PROFESSIONAL LIABILITY COVERAGE PART	$
	$
TOTAL:	$ 18,450

Premium shown is payable: $ 18,450 at inception. $

FORMS APPLICABLE TO ALL COVERAGE PARTS (SHOW NUMBERS):

Common Policy Conditions IL 00 17 11 98

Common Policy Declarations IL DS 00 07 02

Countersigned:	By:
(Date)	(Authorized Representative)

NOTE

OFFICERS' FACSIMILE SIGNATURES MAY BE INSERTED HERE, ON THE POLICY COVER OR ELSEWHERE AT THE COMPANY'S OPTION.

COMMON POLICY CONDITIONS

All Coverage Parts included in this policy are subject to the following conditions.

A. Cancellation

1. The first Named Insured shown in the Declarations may cancel this policy by mailing or delivering to us advance written notice of cancellation.

2. We may cancel this policy by mailing or delivering to the first Named Insured written notice of cancellation at least:

   a. 10 days before the effective date of cancellation if we cancel for nonpayment of premium; or

   b. 30 days before the effective date of cancellation if we cancel for any other reason.

3. We will mail or deliver our notice to the first Named Insured's last mailing address known to us.

4. Notice of cancellation will state the effective date of cancellation. The policy period will end on that date.

5. If this policy is cancelled, we will send the first Named Insured any premium refund due. If we cancel, the refund will be pro rata. If the first Named Insured cancels, the refund may be less than pro rata. The cancellation will be effective even if we have not made or offered a refund.

6. If notice is mailed, proof of mailing will be sufficient proof of notice.

B. Changes

This policy contains all the agreements between you and us concerning the insurance afforded. The first Named Insured shown in the Declarations is authorized to make changes in the terms of this policy with our consent. This policy's terms can be amended or waived only by endorsement issued by us and made a part of this policy.

C. Examination Of Your Books And Records

We may examine and audit your books and records as they relate to this policy at any time during the policy period and up to three years afterward.

D. Inspections And Surveys

1. We have the right to:

   a. Make inspections and surveys at any time;

   b. Give you reports on the conditions we find; and

   c. Recommend changes.

2. We are not obligated to make any inspections, surveys, reports or recommendations and any such actions we do undertake relate only to insurability and the premiums to be charged. We do not make safety inspections. We do not undertake to perform the duty of any person or organization to provide for the health or safety of workers or the public. And we do not warrant that conditions:

   a. Are safe or healthful; or

   b. Comply with laws, regulations, codes or standards.

3. Paragraphs 1. and 2. of this condition apply not only to us, but also to any rating, advisory, rate service or similar organization which makes insurance inspections, surveys, reports or recommendations.

4. Paragraph 2. of this condition does not apply to any inspections, surveys, reports or recommendations we may make relative to certification, under state or municipal statutes, ordinances or regulations, of boilers, pressure vessels or elevators.

E. Premiums

The first Named Insured shown in the Declarations:

1. Is responsible for the payment of all premiums; and

2. Will be the payee for any return premiums we pay.

F. Transfer Of Your Rights And Duties Under This Policy

Your rights and duties under this policy may not be transferred without our written consent except in the case of death of an individual named insured.

If you die, your rights and duties will be transferred to your legal representative but only while acting within the scope of duties as your legal representative. Until your legal representative is appointed, anyone having proper temporary custody of your property will have your rights and duties but only with respect to that property.

COMMERCIAL GENERAL LIABILITY DECLARATIONS

COMPANY NAME AREA	PRODUCER NAME AREA

NAMED INSURED: Jay's Jewelry Manufacturing Company

MAILING ADDRESS: 1110 Wishingwell Road

Indianapolis, Indiana 46222

POLICY PERIOD: FROM February 2, 2002 TO February 2, 2003 AT 12:01 A.M. TIME AT YOUR MAILING ADDRESS SHOWN ABOVE

IN RETURN FOR THE PAYMENT OF THE PREMIUM, AND SUBJECT TO ALL THE TERMS OF THIS POLICY, WE AGREE WITH YOU TO PROVIDE THE INSURANCE AS STATED IN THIS POLICY.

LIMITS OF INSURANCE

EACH OCCURRENCE LIMIT	$ 100,000	
DAMAGE TO PREMISES RENTED TO YOU LIMIT	$ 100,000	Any one premises
MEDICAL EXPENSE LIMIT	$,000	Any one person
PERSONAL & ADVERTISING INJURY LIMIT	$ 100,000	Any one person or organization
GENERAL AGGREGATE LIMIT	$ 500,000	
PRODUCTS/COMPLETED OPERATIONS AGGREGATE LIMIT	$ 500,000	

RETROACTIVE DATE (CG 00 02 ONLY)

THIS INSURANCE DOES NOT APPLY TO "BODILY INJURY", "PROPERTY DAMAGE" OR "PERSONAL AND ADVERTISING INJURY" WHICH OCCURS BEFORE THE RETROACTIVE DATE, IF ANY, SHOWN BELOW.

RETROACTIVE DATE: None

(ENTER DATE OR "NONE" IF NO RETROACTIVE DATE APPLIES)

DESCRIPTION OF BUSINESS

FORM OF BUSINESS:

☐ INDIVIDUAL ☐ PARTNERSHIP ☐ JOINT VENTURE ☐ TRUST

☐ LIMITED LIABILITY COMPANY ☐ ORGANIZATION, INCLUDING A CORPORATION (BUT NOT IN-CLUDING A PARTNERSHIP, JOINT VENTURE OR LIMITED LIABILITY COMPANY)

BUSINESS DESCRIPTION: Manufacturing of gold and diamond jewelry

ALL PREMISES YOU OWN, RENT OR OCCUPY	
LOCATION NUMBER	ADDRESS OF ALL PREMISES YOU OWN, RENT OR OCCUPY
1	1110 Wishingwell Road Indianapolis, Indiana 46222

CLASSIFICATION AND PREMIUM							
LOCATION NUMBER	CLASSIFICATION	CODE NO.	PREMIUM BASE	RATE		ADVANCE PREMIUM	
				Prem/ Ops	Prod/Comp Ops	Prem/ Ops	Prod/Comp Ops
1	Jewelry Manufacturing	55802	$6,000,000 (s)	$ .20	$1.15	$1,200	$ 6,900

	STATE TAX OR OTHER (if applicable) $ _____
	TOTAL PREMIUM (SUBJECT TO AUDIT) $ 8,100
PREMIUM SHOWN IS PAYABLE:	AT INCEPTION $ 8,100
	AT EACH ANNIVERSARY $ _____
	(IF POLICY PERIOD IS MORE THAN ONE YEAR AND PREMIUM IS PAID IN ANNUAL INSTALLMENTS)
AUDIT PERIOD (IF APPLICABLE)	☐ ANNUALLY ☐ SEMI-ANNUALLY ☐ QUARTERLY ☐ MONTHLY

ENDORSEMENTS
ENDORSEMENTS ATTACHED TO THIS POLICY:
IL 02 21 07 02 Nuclear Energy Liability Exclusion (Broad Form)
_____
_____

THESE DECLARATIONS, TOGETHER WITH THE COMMON POLICY CONDITIONS AND COVERAGE FORM(S) AND ANY ENDORSEMENT(S), COMPLETE THE ABOVE NUMBERED POLICY.

Countersigned:	By:
(Date)	(Authorized Representative)

NOTE

OFFICERS' FACSIMILE SIGNATURES MAY BE INSERTED HERE, ON THE POLICY COVER OR ELSEWHERE AT THE COMPANY'S OPTION.

COMMERCIAL GENERAL LIABILITY COVERAGE FORM

Various provisions in this policy restrict coverage. Read the entire policy carefully to determine rights, duties and what is and is not covered.

Throughout this policy the words "you" and "your" refer to the Named Insured shown in the Declarations, and any other person or organization qualifying as a Named Insured under this policy. The words "we", "us" and "our" refer to the company providing this insurance.

The word "insured" means any person or organization qualifying as such under Section **II** – Who Is An Insured.

Other words and phrases that appear in quotation marks have special meaning. Refer to Section **V** – Definitions.

SECTION I – COVERAGES

COVERAGE A BODILY INJURY AND PROPERTY DAMAGE LIABILITY

1. Insuring Agreement

a. We will pay those sums that the insured becomes legally obligated to pay as damages because of "bodily injury" or "property damage" to which this insurance applies. We will have the right and duty to defend the insured against any "suit" seeking those damages. However, we will have no duty to defend the insured against any "suit" seeking damages for "bodily injury" or "property damage" to which this insurance does not apply. We may, at our discretion, investigate any "occurrence" and settle any claim or "suit" that may result. But:

(1) The amount we will pay for damages is limited as described in Section **III** – Limits Of Insurance; and

(2) Our right and duty to defend ends when we have used up the applicable limit of insurance in the payment of judgments or settlements under Coverages **A** or **B** or medical expenses under Coverage **C**.

No other obligation or liability to pay sums or perform acts or services is covered unless explicitly provided for under Supplementary Payments – Coverages **A** and **B**.

b. This insurance applies to "bodily injury" and "property damage" only if:

(1) The "bodily injury" or "property damage" is caused by an "occurrence" that takes place in the "coverage territory";

(2) The "bodily injury" or "property damage" occurs during the policy period; and

(3) Prior to the policy period, no insured listed under Paragraph **1.** of Section **II** – Who Is An Insured and no "employee" authorized by you to give or receive notice of an "occurrence" or claim, knew that the "bodily injury" or "property damage" had occurred, in whole or in part. If such a listed insured or authorized "employee" knew, prior to the policy period, that the "bodily injury" or "property damage" occurred, then any continuation, change or resumption of such "bodily injury" or "property damage" during or after the policy period will be deemed to have been known prior to the policy period.

c. "Bodily injury" or "property damage" which occurs during the policy period and was not, prior to the policy period, known to have occurred by any insured listed under Paragraph **1.** of Section **II** – Who Is An Insured or any "employee" authorized by you to give or receive notice of an "occurrence" or claim, includes any continuation, change or resumption of that "bodily injury" or "property damage" after the end of the policy period.

d. "Bodily injury" or "property damage" will be deemed to have been known to have occurred at the earliest time when any insured listed under Paragraph **1.** of Section **II** – Who Is An Insured or any "employee" authorized by you to give or receive notice of an "occurrence" or claim:

(1) Reports all, or any part, of the "bodily injury" or "property damage" to us or any other insurer;

(2) Receives a written or verbal demand or claim for damages because of the "bodily injury" or "property damage"; or

(3) Becomes aware by any other means that "bodily injury" or "property damage" has occurred or has begun to occur.

e. Damages because of "bodily injury" include damages claimed by any person or organization for care, loss of services or death resulting at any time from the "bodily injury".

2. Exclusions

This insurance does not apply to:

a. Expected Or Intended Injury

"Bodily injury" or "property damage" expected or intended from the standpoint of the insured. This exclusion does not apply to "bodily injury" resulting from the use of reasonable force to protect persons or property.

b. Contractual Liability

"Bodily injury" or "property damage" for which the insured is obligated to pay damages by reason of the assumption of liability in a contract or agreement. This exclusion does not apply to liability for damages:

(1) That the insured would have in the absence of the contract or agreement; or

(2) Assumed in a contract or agreement that is an "insured contract", provided the "bodily injury" or "property damage" occurs subsequent to the execution of the contract or agreement. Solely for the purposes of liability assumed in an "insured contract", reasonable attorney fees and necessary litigation expenses incurred by or for a party other than an insured are deemed to be damages because of "bodily injury" or "property damage", provided:

(a) Liability to such party for, or for the cost of, that party's defense has also been assumed in the same "insured contract"; and

(b) Such attorney fees and litigation expenses are for defense of that party against a civil or alternative dispute resolution proceeding in which damages to which this insurance applies are alleged.

c. Liquor Liability

"Bodily injury" or "property damage" for which any insured may be held liable by reason of:

(1) Causing or contributing to the intoxication of any person;

(2) The furnishing of alcoholic beverages to a person under the legal drinking age or under the influence of alcohol; or

(3) Any statute, ordinance or regulation relating to the sale, gift, distribution or use of alcoholic beverages.

This exclusion applies only if you are in the business of manufacturing, distributing, selling, serving or furnishing alcoholic beverages.

d. Workers' Compensation And Similar Laws

Any obligation of the insured under a workers' compensation, disability benefits or unemployment compensation law or any similar law.

e. Employer's Liability

"Bodily injury" to:

(1) An "employee" of the insured arising out of and in the course of:

(a) Employment by the insured; or

(b) Performing duties related to the conduct of the insured's business; or

(2) The spouse, child, parent, brother or sister of that "employee" as a consequence of Paragraph **(1)** above.

This exclusion applies:

(1) Whether the insured may be liable as an employer or in any other capacity; and

(2) To any obligation to share damages with or repay someone else who must pay damages because of the injury.

This exclusion does not apply to liability assumed by the insured under an "insured contract".

 CG 00 01 12 04

f. Pollution

(1) "Bodily injury" or "property damage" arising out of the actual, alleged or threatened discharge, dispersal, seepage, migration, release or escape of "pollutants":

(a) At or from any premises, site or location which is or was at any time owned or occupied by, or rented or loaned to, any insured. However, this subparagraph does not apply to:

(i) "Bodily injury" if sustained within a building and caused by smoke, fumes, vapor or soot produced by or originating from equipment that is used to heat, cool or dehumidify the building, or equipment that is used to heat water for personal use, by the building's occupants or their guests;

(ii) "Bodily injury" or "property damage" for which you may be held liable, if you are a contractor and the owner or lessee of such premises, site or location has been added to your policy as an additional insured with respect to your ongoing operations performed for that additional insured at that premises, site or location and such premises, site or location is not and never was owned or occupied by, or rented or loaned to, any insured, other than that additional insured; or

(iii) "Bodily injury" or "property damage" arising out of heat, smoke or fumes from a "hostile fire";

(b) At or from any premises, site or location which is or was at any time used by or for any insured or others for the handling, storage, disposal, processing or treatment of waste;

(c) Which are or were at any time transported, handled, stored, treated, disposed of, or processed as waste by or for:

(i) Any insured; or

(ii) Any person or organization for whom you may be legally responsible; or

(d) At or from any premises, site or location on which any insured or any contractors or subcontractors working directly or indirectly on any insured's behalf are performing operations if the "pollutants" are brought on or to the premises, site or location in connection with such operations by such insured, contractor or subcontractor. However, this subparagraph does not apply to:

(i) "Bodily injury" or "property damage" arising out of the escape of fuels, lubricants or other operating fluids which are needed to perform the normal electrical, hydraulic or mechanical functions necessary for the operation of "mobile equipment" or its parts, if such fuels, lubricants or other operating fluids escape from a vehicle part designed to hold, store or receive them. This exception does not apply if the "bodily injury" or "property damage" arises out of the intentional discharge, dispersal or release of the fuels, lubricants or other operating fluids, or if such fuels, lubricants or other operating fluids are brought on or to the premises, site or location with the intent that they be discharged, dispersed or released as part of the operations being performed by such insured, contractor or subcontractor;

(ii) "Bodily injury" or "property damage" sustained within a building and caused by the release of gases, fumes or vapors from materials brought into that building in connection with operations being performed by you or on your behalf by a contractor or subcontractor; or

(iii) "Bodily injury" or "property damage" arising out of heat, smoke or fumes from a "hostile fire".

(e) At or from any premises, site or location on which any insured or any contractors or subcontractors working directly or indirectly on any insured's behalf are performing operations if the operations are to test for, monitor, clean up, remove, contain, treat, detoxify or neutralize, or in any way respond to, or assess the effects of, "pollutants".

 □

(2) Any loss, cost or expense arising out of any:

(a) Request, demand, order or statutory or regulatory requirement that any insured or others test for, monitor, clean up, remove, contain, treat, detoxify or neutralize, or in any way respond to, or assess the effects of, "pollutants"; or

(b) Claim or "suit" by or on behalf of a governmental authority for damages because of testing for, monitoring, cleaning up, removing, containing, treating, detoxifying or neutralizing, or in any way responding to, or assessing the effects of, "pollutants".

However, this paragraph does not apply to liability for damages because of "property damage" that the insured would have in the absence of such request, demand, order or statutory or regulatory requirement, or such claim or "suit" by or on behalf of a governmental authority.

g. Aircraft, Auto Or Watercraft

"Bodily injury" or "property damage" arising out of the ownership, maintenance, use or entrustment to others of any aircraft, "auto" or watercraft owned or operated by or rented or loaned to any insured. Use includes operation and "loading or unloading".

This exclusion applies even if the claims against any insured allege negligence or other wrongdoing in the supervision, hiring, employment, training or monitoring of others by that insured, if the "occurrence" which caused the "bodily injury" or "property damage" involved the ownership, maintenance, use or entrustment to others of any aircraft, "auto" or watercraft that is owned or operated by or rented or loaned to any insured.

This exclusion does not apply to:

(1) A watercraft while ashore on premises you own or rent;

(2) A watercraft you do not own that is:

(a) Less than 26 feet long; and

(b) Not being used to carry persons or property for a charge;

(3) Parking an "auto" on, or on the ways next to, premises you own or rent, provided the "auto" is not owned by or rented or loaned to you or the insured;

(4) Liability assumed under any "insured contract" for the ownership, maintenance or use of aircraft or watercraft; or

(5) "Bodily injury" or "property damage" arising out of:

(a) The operation of machinery or equipment that is attached to, or part of, a land vehicle that would qualify under the definition of "mobile equipment" if it were not subject to a compulsory or financial responsibility law or other motor vehicle insurance law in the state where it is licensed or principally garaged; or

(b) the operation of any of the machinery or equipment listed in Paragraph **f.(2)** or **f.(3)** of the definition of "mobile equipment".

h. Mobile Equipment

"Bodily injury" or "property damage" arising out of:

(1) The transportation of "mobile equipment" by an "auto" owned or operated by or rented or loaned to any insured; or

(2) The use of "mobile equipment" in, or while in practice for, or while being prepared for, any prearranged racing, speed, demolition, or stunting activity.

i. War

"Bodily injury" or "property damage", however caused, arising, directly or indirectly, out of:

(1) War, including undeclared or civil war;

(2) Warlike action by a military force, including action in hindering or defending against an actual or expected attack, by any government, sovereign or other authority using military personnel or other agents; or

(3) Insurrection, rebellion, revolution, usurped power, or action taken by governmental authority in hindering or defending against any of these.

j. Damage To Property

"Property damage" to:

(1) Property you own, rent, or occupy, including any costs or expenses incurred by you, or any other person, organization or entity, for repair, replacement, enhancement, restoration or maintenance of such property for any reason, including prevention of injury to a person or damage to another's property;

(2) Premises you sell, give away or abandon, if the "property damage" arises out of any part of those premises;

(3) Property loaned to you;

(4) Personal property in the care, custody or control of the insured;

(5) That particular part of real property on which you or any contractors or subcontractors working directly or indirectly on your behalf are performing operations, if the "property damage" arises out of those operations; or

(6) That particular part of any property that must be restored, repaired or replaced because "your work" was incorrectly performed on it.

Paragraphs **(1)**, **(3)** and **(4)** of this exclusion do not apply to "property damage" (other than damage by fire) to premises, including the contents of such premises, rented to you for a period of 7 or fewer consecutive days. A separate limit of insurance applies to Damage To Premises Rented To You as described in Section **III** – Limits Of Insurance.

Paragraph **(2)** of this exclusion does not apply if the premises are "your work" and were never occupied, rented or held for rental by you.

Paragraphs **(3)**, **(4)**, **(5)** and **(6)** of this exclusion do not apply to liability assumed under a sidetrack agreement.

Paragraph **(6)** of this exclusion does not apply to "property damage" included in the "products-completed operations hazard".

k. Damage To Your Product

"Property damage" to "your product" arising out of it or any part of it.

l. Damage To Your Work

"Property damage" to "your work" arising out of it or any part of it and included in the "products-completed operations hazard".

This exclusion does not apply if the damaged work or the work out of which the damage arises was performed on your behalf by a subcontractor.

m. Damage To Impaired Property Or Property Not Physically Injured

"Property damage" to "impaired property" or property that has not been physically injured, arising out of:

(1) A defect, deficiency, inadequacy or dangerous condition in "your product" or "your work"; or

(2) A delay or failure by you or anyone acting on your behalf to perform a contract or agreement in accordance with its terms.

This exclusion does not apply to the loss of use of other property arising out of sudden and accidental physical injury to "your product" or "your work" after it has been put to its intended use.

n. Recall Of Products, Work Or Impaired Property

Damages claimed for any loss, cost or expense incurred by you or others for the loss of use, withdrawal, recall, inspection, repair, replacement, adjustment, removal or disposal of:

(1) "Your product";

(2) "Your work"; or

(3) "Impaired property";

if such product, work, or property is withdrawn or recalled from the market or from use by any person or organization because of a known or suspected defect, deficiency, inadequacy or dangerous condition in it.

o. Personal And Advertising Injury

"Bodily injury" arising out of "personal and advertising injury".

p. Electronic Data

Damages arising out of the loss of, loss of use of, damage to, corruption of, inability to access, or inability to manipulate electronic data.

As used in this exclusion, electronic data means information, facts or programs stored as or on, created or used on, or transmitted to or from computer software, including systems and applications software, hard or floppy disks, CD-ROMS, tapes, drives, cells, data processing devices or any other media which are used with electronically controlled equipment.

Exclusions **c.** through **n.** do not apply to damage by fire to premises while rented to you or temporarily occupied by you with permission of the owner. A separate limit of insurance applies to this coverage as described in Section **III** – Limits Of Insurance.

COVERAGE B PERSONAL AND ADVERTISING INJURY LIABILITY

1. Insuring Agreement

a. We will pay those sums that the insured becomes legally obligated to pay as damages because of "personal and advertising injury" to which this insurance applies. We will have the right and duty to defend the insured against any "suit" seeking those damages. However, we will have no duty to defend the insured against any "suit" seeking damages for "personal and advertising injury" to which this insurance does not apply. We may, at our discretion, investigate any offense and settle any claim or "suit" that may result. But:

(1) The amount we will pay for damages is limited as described in Section **III** – Limits Of Insurance; and

(2) Our right and duty to defend end when we have used up the applicable limit of insurance in the payment of judgments or settlements under Coverages **A** or **B** or medical expenses under Coverage **C**.

No other obligation or liability to pay sums or perform acts or services is covered unless explicitly provided for under Supplementary Payments – Coverages **A** and **B**.

b. This insurance applies to "personal and advertising injury" caused by an offense arising out of your business but only if the offense was committed in the "coverage territory" during the policy period.

2. Exclusions

This insurance does not apply to:

a. Knowing Violation Of Rights Of Another

"Personal and advertising injury" caused by or at the direction of the insured with the knowledge that the act would violate the rights of another and would inflict "personal and advertising injury".

b. Material Published With Knowledge Of Falsity

"Personal and advertising injury" arising out of oral or written publication of material, if done by or at the direction of the insured with knowledge of its falsity.

c. Material Published Prior To Policy Period

"Personal and advertising injury" arising out of oral or written publication of material whose first publication took place before the beginning of the policy period.

d. Criminal Acts

"Personal and advertising injury" arising out of a criminal act committed by or at the direction of the insured.

e. Contractual Liability

"Personal and advertising injury" for which the insured has assumed liability in a contract or agreement. This exclusion does not apply to liability for damages that the insured would have in the absence of the contract or agreement.

f. Breach Of Contract

"Personal and advertising injury" arising out of a breach of contract, except an implied contract to use another's advertising idea in your "advertisement".

g. Quality Or Performance Of Goods – Failure To Conform To Statements

"Personal and advertising injury" arising out of the failure of goods, products or services to conform with any statement of quality or performance made in your "advertisement".

h. Wrong Description Of Prices

"Personal and advertising injury" arising out of the wrong description of the price of goods, products or services stated in your "advertisement".

i. Infringement Of Copyright, Patent, Trademark Or Trade Secret

"Personal and advertising injury" arising out of the infringement of copyright, patent, trademark, trade secret or other intellectual property rights.

However, this exclusion does not apply to infringement, in your "advertisement", of copyright, trade dress or slogan.

j. Insureds In Media And Internet Type Businesses

"Personal and advertising injury" committed by an insured whose business is:

(1) Advertising, broadcasting, publishing or telecasting;

(2) Designing or determining content of websites for others; or

(3) An Internet search, access, content or service provider.

However, this exclusion does not apply to Paragraphs **14.a., b.** and **c.** of "personal and advertising injury" under the Definitions Section.

For the purposes of this exclusion, the placing of frames, borders or links, or advertising, for you or others anywhere on the Internet, is not by itself, considered the business of advertising, broadcasting, publishing or telecasting.

k. Electronic Chatrooms Or Bulletin Boards

"Personal and advertising injury" arising out of an electronic chatroom or bulletin board the insured hosts, owns, or over which the insured exercises control.

l. Unauthorized Use Of Another's Name Or Product

"Personal and advertising injury" arising out of the unauthorized use of another's name or product in your e-mail address, domain name or metatag, or any other similar tactics to mislead another's potential customers.

 CG 00 01 12 04 □

m. Pollution

"Personal and advertising injury" arising out of the actual, alleged or threatened discharge, dispersal, seepage, migration, release or escape of "pollutants" at any time.

n. Pollution-Related

Any loss, cost or expense arising out of any:

(1) Request, demand, order or statutory or regulatory requirement that any insured or others test for, monitor, clean up, remove, contain, treat, detoxify or neutralize, or in any way respond to, or assess the effects of, "pollutants"; or

(2) Claim or suit by or on behalf of a governmental authority for damages because of testing for, monitoring, cleaning up, removing, containing, treating, detoxifying or neutralizing, or in any way responding to, or assessing the effects of, "pollutants".

o. War

"Personal and advertising injury", however caused, arising, directly or indirectly, out of:

(1) War, including undeclared or civil war;

(2) Warlike action by a military force, including action in hindering or defending against an actual or expected attack, by any government, sovereign or other authority using military personnel or other agents; or

(3) Insurrection, rebellion, revolution, usurped power, or action taken by governmental authority in hindering or defending against any of these.

COVERAGE C MEDICAL PAYMENTS

1. Insuring Agreement

a. We will pay medical expenses as described below for "bodily injury" caused by an accident:

(1) On premises you own or rent;

(2) On ways next to premises you own or rent; or

(3) Because of your operations;

provided that:

(1) The accident takes place in the "coverage territory" and during the policy period;

(2) The expenses are incurred and reported to us within one year of the date of the accident; and

(3) The injured person submits to examination, at our expense, by physicians of our choice as often as we reasonably require.

b. We will make these payments regardless of fault. These payments will not exceed the applicable limit of insurance. We will pay reasonable expenses for:

(1) First aid administered at the time of an accident;

(2) Necessary medical, surgical, x-ray and dental services, including prosthetic devices; and

(3) Necessary ambulance, hospital, professional nursing and funeral services.

2. Exclusions

We will not pay expenses for "bodily injury":

a. Any Insured

To any insured, except "volunteer workers".

b. Hired Person

To a person hired to do work for or on behalf of any insured or a tenant of any insured.

c. Injury On Normally Occupied Premises

To a person injured on that part of premises you own or rent that the person normally occupies.

d. Workers Compensation And Similar Laws

To a person, whether or not an "employee" of any insured, if benefits for the "bodily injury" are payable or must be provided under a workers' compensation or disability benefits law or a similar law.

e. Athletics Activities

To a person injured while practicing, instructing or participating in any physical exercises or games, sports, or athletic contests.

f. Products-Completed Operations Hazard

Included within the "products-completed operations hazard".

g. Coverage A Exclusions

Excluded under Coverage **A**.

SUPPLEMENTARY PAYMENTS – COVERAGES A AND B

1. We will pay, with respect to any claim we investigate or settle, or any "suit" against an insured we defend:

a. All expenses we incur.

b. Up to $250 for cost of bail bonds required because of accidents or traffic law violations arising out of the use of any vehicle to which the Bodily Injury Liability Coverage applies. We do not have to furnish these bonds.

c. The cost of bonds to release attachments, but only for bond amounts within the applicable limit of insurance. We do not have to furnish these bonds.

d. All reasonable expenses incurred by the insured at our request to assist us in the investigation or defense of the claim or "suit", including actual loss of earnings up to $250 a day because of time off from work.

e. All costs taxed against the insured in the "suit".

f. Prejudgment interest awarded against the insured on that part of the judgment we pay. If we make an offer to pay the applicable limit of insurance, we will not pay any prejudgment interest based on that period of time after the offer.

g. All interest on the full amount of any judgment that accrues after entry of the judgment and before we have paid, offered to pay, or deposited in court the part of the judgment that is within the applicable limit of insurance.

These payments will not reduce the limits of insurance.

2. If we defend an insured against a "suit" and an indemnitee of the insured is also named as a party to the "suit", we will defend that indemnitee if all of the following conditions are met:

a. The "suit" against the indemnitee seeks damages for which the insured has assumed the liability of the indemnitee in a contract or agreement that is an "insured contract";

b. This insurance applies to such liability assumed by the insured;

c. The obligation to defend, or the cost of the defense of, that indemnitee, has also been assumed by the insured in the same "insured contract";

d. The allegations in the "suit" and the information we know about the "occurrence" are such that no conflict appears to exist between the interests of the insured and the interests of the indemnitee;

e. The indemnitee and the insured ask us to conduct and control the defense of that indemnitee against such "suit" and agree that we can assign the same counsel to defend the insured and the indemnitee; and

f. The indemnitee:

(1) Agrees in writing to:

(a) Cooperate with us in the investigation, settlement or defense of the "suit";

(b) Immediately send us copies of any demands, notices, summonses or legal papers received in connection with the "suit";

(c) Notify any other insurer whose coverage is available to the indemnitee; and

(d) Cooperate with us with respect to coordinating other applicable insurance available to the indemnitee; and

(2) Provides us with written authorization to:

(a) Obtain records and other information related to the "suit"; and

(b) Conduct and control the defense of the indemnitee in such "suit".

So long as the above conditions are met, attorneys' fees incurred by us in the defense of that indemnitee, necessary litigation expenses incurred by us and necessary litigation expenses incurred by the indemnitee at our request will be paid as Supplementary Payments. Notwithstanding the provisions of Paragraph **2.b.(2)** of Section I – Coverage A – Bodily Injury And Property Damage Liability, such payments will not be deemed to be damages for "bodily injury" and "property damage" and will not reduce the limits of insurance.

Our obligation to defend an insured's indemnitee and to pay for attorneys' fees and necessary litigation expenses as Supplementary Payments ends when:

a. We have used up the applicable limit of insurance in the payment of judgments or settlements; or

b. The conditions set forth above, or the terms of the agreement described in Paragraph **f.** above, are no longer met.

SECTION II – WHO IS AN INSURED

1. If you are designated in the Declarations as:

a. An individual, you and your spouse are insureds, but only with respect to the conduct of a business of which you are the sole owner.

b. A partnership or joint venture, you are an insured. Your members, your partners, and their spouses are also insureds, but only with respect to the conduct of your business.

c. A limited liability company, you are an insured. Your members are also insureds, but only with respect to the conduct of your business. Your managers are insureds, but only with respect to their duties as your managers.

d. An organization other than a partnership, joint venture or limited liability company, you are an insured. Your "executive officers" and directors are insureds, but only with respect to their duties as your officers or directors. Your stockholders are also insureds, but only with respect to their liability as stockholders.

e. A trust, you are an insured. Your trustees are also insureds, but only with respect to their duties as trustees.

2. Each of the following is also an insured:

a. Your "volunteer workers" only while performing duties related to the conduct of your business, or your "employees", other than either your "executive officers" (if you are an organization other than a partnership, joint venture or limited liability company) or your managers (if you are a limited liability company), but only for acts within the scope of their employment by you or while performing duties related to the conduct of your business. However, none of these "employees" or "volunteer workers" are insureds for:

(1) "Bodily injury" or "personal and advertising injury":

(a) To you, to your partners or members (if you are a partnership or joint venture), to your members (if you are a limited liability company), to a co-"employee" while in the course of his or her employment or performing duties related to the conduct of your business, or to your other "volunteer workers" while performing duties related to the conduct of your business;

(b) To the spouse, child, parent, brother or sister of that co-"employee" or "volunteer worker" as a consequence of Paragraph **(1)(a)** above;

(c) For which there is any obligation to share damages with or repay someone else who must pay damages because of the injury described in Paragraphs **(1)(a)** or **(b)** above; or

(d) Arising out of his or her providing or failing to provide professional health care services.

(2) "Property damage" to property:

(a) Owned, occupied or used by,

(b) Rented to, in the care, custody or control of, or over which physical control is being exercised for any purpose by

you, any of your "employees", "volunteer workers", any partner or member (if you are a partnership or joint venture), or any member (if you are a limited liability company).

b. Any person (other than your "employee" or "volunteer worker"), or any organization while acting as your real estate manager.

c. Any person or organization having proper temporary custody of your property if you die, but only:

(1) With respect to liability arising out of the maintenance or use of that property; and

(2) Until your legal representative has been appointed.

d. Your legal representative if you die, but only with respect to duties as such. That representative will have all your rights and duties under this Coverage Part.

3. Any organization you newly acquire or form, other than a partnership, joint venture or limited liability company, and over which you maintain ownership or majority interest, will qualify as a Named Insured if there is no other similar insurance available to that organization. However:

a. Coverage under this provision is afforded only until the 90th day after you acquire or form the organization or the end of the policy period, whichever is earlier;

b. Coverage **A** does not apply to "bodily injury" or "property damage" that occurred before you acquired or formed the organization; and

c. Coverage **B** does not apply to "personal and advertising injury" arising out of an offense committed before you acquired or formed the organization.

No person or organization is an insured with respect to the conduct of any current or past partnership, joint venture or limited liability company that is not shown as a Named Insured in the Declarations.

SECTION III – LIMITS OF INSURANCE

1. The Limits of Insurance shown in the Declarations and the rules below fix the most we will pay regardless of the number of:

a. Insureds;

b. Claims made or "suits" brought; or

c. Persons or organizations making claims or bringing "suits".

2. The General Aggregate Limit is the most we will pay for the sum of:

   a. Medical expenses under Coverage **C**;

   b. Damages under Coverage **A**, except damages because of "bodily injury" or "property damage" included in the "products-completed operations hazard"; and

   c. Damages under Coverage **B**.

3. The Products-Completed Operations Aggregate Limit is the most we will pay under Coverage **A** for damages because of "bodily injury" and "property damage" included in the "products-completed operations hazard".

4. Subject to **2.** above, the Personal and Advertising Injury Limit is the most we will pay under Coverage **B** for the sum of all damages because of all "personal and advertising injury" sustained by any one person or organization.

5. Subject to **2.** or **3.** above, whichever applies, the Each Occurrence Limit is the most we will pay for the sum of:

   a. Damages under Coverage **A**; and

   b. Medical expenses under Coverage **C**

   because of all "bodily injury" and "property damage" arising out of any one "occurrence".

6. Subject to **5.** above, the Damage To Premises Rented To You Limit is the most we will pay under Coverage **A** for damages because of "property damage" to any one premises, while rented to you, or in the case of damage by fire, while rented to you or temporarily occupied by you with permission of the owner.

7. Subject to **5.** above, the Medical Expense Limit is the most we will pay under Coverage **C** for all medical expenses because of "bodily injury" sustained by any one person.

The Limits of Insurance of this Coverage Part apply separately to each consecutive annual period and to any remaining period of less than 12 months, starting with the beginning of the policy period shown in the Declarations, unless the policy period is extended after issuance for an additional period of less than 12 months. In that case, the additional period will be deemed part of the last preceding period for purposes of determining the Limits of Insurance.

SECTION IV – COMMERCIAL GENERAL LIABILITY CONDITIONS

1. Bankruptcy

Bankruptcy or insolvency of the insured or of the insured's estate will not relieve us of our obligations under this Coverage Part.

2. Duties In The Event Of Occurrence, Offense, Claim Or Suit

a. You must see to it that we are notified as soon as practicable of an "occurrence" or an offense which may result in a claim. To the extent possible, notice should include:

   (1) How, when and where the "occurrence" or offense took place;

   (2) The names and addresses of any injured persons and witnesses; and

   (3) The nature and location of any injury or damage arising out of the "occurrence" or offense.

b. If a claim is made or "suit" is brought against any insured, you must:

   (1) Immediately record the specifics of the claim or "suit" and the date received; and

   (2) Notify us as soon as practicable.

   You must see to it that we receive written notice of the claim or "suit" as soon as practicable.

c. You and any other involved insured must:

   (1) Immediately send us copies of any demands, notices, summonses or legal papers received in connection with the claim or "suit";

   (2) Authorize us to obtain records and other information;

   (3) Cooperate with us in the investigation or settlement of the claim or defense against the "suit"; and

   (4) Assist us, upon our request, in the enforcement of any right against any person or organization which may be liable to the insured because of injury or damage to which this insurance may also apply.

d. No insured will, except at that insured's own cost, voluntarily make a payment, assume any obligation, or incur any expense, other than for first aid, without our consent.

3. Legal Action Against Us

No person or organization has a right under this Coverage Part:

a. To join us as a party or otherwise bring us into a "suit" asking for damages from an insured; or

b. To sue us on this Coverage Part unless all of its terms have been fully complied with.

A person or organization may sue us to recover on an agreed settlement or on a final judgment against an insured; but we will not be liable for damages that are not payable under the terms of this Coverage Part or that are in excess of the applicable limit of insurance. An agreed settlement means a settlement and release of liability signed by us, the insured and the claimant or the claimant's legal representative.

4. Other Insurance

If other valid and collectible insurance is available to the insured for a loss we cover under Coverages **A** or **B** of this Coverage Part, our obligations are limited as follows:

a. Primary Insurance

This insurance is primary except when **b.** below applies. If this insurance is primary, our obligations are not affected unless any of the other insurance is also primary. Then, we will share with all that other insurance by the method described in **c.** below.

b. Excess Insurance

This insurance is excess over:

(1) Any of the other insurance, whether primary, excess, contingent or on any other basis:

(a) That is Fire, Extended Coverage, Builder's Risk, Installation Risk or similar coverage for "your work";

(b) That is Fire insurance for premises rented to you or temporarily occupied by you with permission of the owner;

(c) That is insurance purchased by you to cover your liability as a tenant for "property damage" to premises rented to you or temporarily occupied by you with permission of the owner; or

(d) If the loss arises out of the maintenance or use of aircraft, "autos" or watercraft to the extent not subject to Exclusion **g.** of Section **I** – Coverage **A** – Bodily Injury And Property Damage Liability.

(2) Any other primary insurance available to you covering liability for damages arising out of the premises or operations, or the products and completed operations, for which you have been added as an additional insured by attachment of an endorsement.

When this insurance is excess, we will have no duty under Coverages **A** or **B** to defend the insured against any "suit" if any other insurer has a duty to defend the insured against that "suit". If no other insurer defends, we will undertake to do so, but we will be entitled to the insured's rights against all those other insurers.

When this insurance is excess over other insurance, we will pay only our share of the amount of the loss, if any, that exceeds the sum of:

(1) The total amount that all such other insurance would pay for the loss in the absence of this insurance; and

(2) The total of all deductible and self-insured amounts under all that other insurance.

We will share the remaining loss, if any, with any other insurance that is not described in this Excess Insurance provision and was not bought specifically to apply in excess of the Limits of Insurance shown in the Declarations of this Coverage Part.

c. Method Of Sharing

If all of the other insurance permits contribution by equal shares, we will follow this method also. Under this approach each insurer contributes equal amounts until it has paid its applicable limit of insurance or none of the loss remains, whichever comes first.

If any of the other insurance does not permit contribution by equal shares, we will contribute by limits. Under this method, each insurer's share is based on the ratio of its applicable limit of insurance to the total applicable limits of insurance of all insurers.

5. Premium Audit

a. We will compute all premiums for this Coverage Part in accordance with our rules and rates.

b. Premium shown in this Coverage Part as advance premium is a deposit premium only. At the close of each audit period we will compute the earned premium for that period and send notice to the first Named Insured. The due date for audit and retrospective premiums is the date shown as the due date on the bill. If the sum of the advance and audit premiums paid for the policy period is greater than the earned premium, we will return the excess to the first Named Insured.

c. The first Named Insured must keep records of the information we need for premium computation, and send us copies at such times as we may request.

6. Representations

By accepting this policy, you agree:

a. The statements in the Declarations are accurate and complete;

b. Those statements are based upon representations you made to us; and

c. We have issued this policy in reliance upon your representations.

7. Separation Of Insureds

Except with respect to the Limits of Insurance, and any rights or duties specifically assigned in this Coverage Part to the first Named Insured, this insurance applies:

a. As if each Named Insured were the only Named Insured; and

b. Separately to each insured against whom claim is made or "suit" is brought.

8. Transfer Of Rights Of Recovery Against Others To Us

If the insured has rights to recover all or part of any payment we have made under this Coverage Part, those rights are transferred to us. The insured must do nothing after loss to impair them. At our request, the insured will bring "suit" or transfer those rights to us and help us enforce them.

9. When We Do Not Renew

If we decide not to renew this Coverage Part, we will mail or deliver to the first Named Insured shown in the Declarations written notice of the nonrenewal not less than 30 days before the expiration date.

If notice is mailed, proof of mailing will be sufficient proof of notice.

SECTION V – DEFINITIONS

1. "Advertisement" means a notice that is broadcast or published to the general public or specific market segments about your goods, products or services for the purpose of attracting customers or supporters. For the purposes of this definition:

a. Notices that are published include material placed on the Internet or on similar electronic means of communication; and

b. Regarding web-sites, only that part of a website that is about your goods, products or services for the purposes of attracting customers or supporters is considered an advertisement.

2. "Auto" means:

a. A land motor vehicle, trailer or semitrailer designed for travel on public roads, including any attached machinery or equipment; or

b. Any other land vehicle that is subject to a compulsory or financial responsibility law or other motor vehicle insurance law in the state where it is licensed or principally garaged.

However, "auto" does not include "mobile equipment".

3. "Bodily injury" means bodily injury, sickness or disease sustained by a person, including death resulting from any of these at any time.

4. "Coverage territory" means:

a. The United States of America (including its territories and possessions), Puerto Rico and Canada;

b. International waters or airspace, but only if the injury or damage occurs in the course of travel or transportation between any places included in **a.** above; or

c. All other parts of the world if the injury or damage arises out of:

(1) Goods or products made or sold by you in the territory described in **a.** above;

(2) The activities of a person whose home is in the territory described in **a.** above, but is away for a short time on your business; or

(3) "Personal and advertising injury" offenses that take place through the Internet or similar electronic means of communication

provided the insured's responsibility to pay damages is determined in a "suit" on the merits, in the territory described in **a.** above or in a settlement we agree to.

5. "Employee" includes a "leased worker". "Employee" does not include a "temporary worker".

6. "Executive officer" means a person holding any of the officer positions created by your charter, constitution, by-laws or any other similar governing document.

7. "Hostile fire" means one which becomes uncontrollable or breaks out from where it was intended to be.

8. "Impaired property" means tangible property, other than "your product" or "your work", that cannot be used or is less useful because:

a. It incorporates "your product" or "your work" that is known or thought to be defective, deficient, inadequate or dangerous; or

b. You have failed to fulfill the terms of a contract or agreement;

if such property can be restored to use by:

a. The repair, replacement, adjustment or removal of "your product" or "your work"; or

b. Your fulfilling the terms of the contract or agreement.

9. "Insured contract" means:

   a. A contract for a lease of premises. However, that portion of the contract for a lease of premises that indemnifies any person or organization for damage by fire to premises while rented to you or temporarily occupied by you with permission of the owner is not an "insured contract";

   b. A sidetrack agreement;

   c. Any easement or license agreement, except in connection with construction or demolition operations on or within 50 feet of a railroad;

   d. An obligation, as required by ordinance, to indemnify a municipality, except in connection with work for a municipality;

   e. An elevator maintenance agreement;

   f. That part of any other contract or agreement pertaining to your business (including an indemnification of a municipality in connection with work performed for a municipality) under which you assume the tort liability of another party to pay for "bodily injury" or "property damage" to a third person or organization. Tort liability means a liability that would be imposed by law in the absence of any contract or agreement.

   Paragraph **f.** does not include that part of any contract or agreement:

   (1) That indemnifies a railroad for "bodily injury" or "property damage" arising out of construction or demolition operations, within 50 feet of any railroad property and affecting any railroad bridge or trestle, tracks, roadbeds, tunnel, underpass or crossing;

   (2) That indemnifies an architect, engineer or surveyor for injury or damage arising out of:

   (a) Preparing, approving, or failing to prepare or approve, maps, shop drawings, opinions, reports, surveys, field orders, change orders or drawings and specifications; or

   (b) Giving directions or instructions, or failing to give them, if that is the primary cause of the injury or damage; or

   (3) Under which the insured, if an architect, engineer or surveyor, assumes liability for an injury or damage arising out of the insured's rendering or failure to render professional services, including those listed in **(2)** above and supervisory, inspection, architectural or engineering activities.

10. "Leased worker" means a person leased to you by a labor leasing firm under an agreement between you and the labor leasing firm, to perform duties related to the conduct of your business. "Leased worker" does not include a "temporary worker".

11. "Loading or unloading" means the handling of property:

    a. After it is moved from the place where it is accepted for movement into or onto an aircraft, watercraft or "auto";

    b. While it is in or on an aircraft, watercraft or "auto"; or

    c. While it is being moved from an aircraft, watercraft or "auto" to the place where it is finally delivered;

    but "loading or unloading" does not include the movement of property by means of a mechanical device, other than a hand truck, that is not attached to the aircraft, watercraft or "auto".

12. "Mobile equipment" means any of the following types of land vehicles, including any attached machinery or equipment:

    a. Bulldozers, farm machinery, forklifts and other vehicles designed for use principally off public roads;

    b. Vehicles maintained for use solely on or next to premises you own or rent;

    c. Vehicles that travel on crawler treads;

    d. Vehicles, whether self-propelled or not, maintained primarily to provide mobility to permanently mounted:

    (1) Power cranes, shovels, loaders, diggers or drills; or

    (2) Road construction or resurfacing equipment such as graders, scrapers or rollers;

    e. Vehicles not described in **a.**, **b.**, **c.** or **d.** above that are not self-propelled and are maintained primarily to provide mobility to permanently attached equipment of the following types:

    (1) Air compressors, pumps and generators, including spraying, welding, building cleaning, geophysical exploration, lighting and well servicing equipment; or

    (2) Cherry pickers and similar devices used to raise or lower workers;

    f. Vehicles not described in **a.**, **b.**, **c.** or **d.** above maintained primarily for purposes other than the transportation of persons or cargo.

    However, self-propelled vehicles with the following types of permanently attached equipment are not "mobile equipment" but will be considered "autos":

(1) Equipment designed primarily for:

  (a) Snow removal;

  (b) Road maintenance, but not construction or resurfacing; or

  (c) Street cleaning;

(2) Cherry pickers and similar devices mounted on automobile or truck chassis and used to raise or lower workers; and

(3) Air compressors, pumps and generators, including spraying, welding, building cleaning, geophysical exploration, lighting and well servicing equipment.

However, "mobile equipment" does not include any land vehicles that are subject to a compulsory or financial responsibility law or other motor vehicle insurance law in the state where it is licensed or principally garaged. Land vehicles subject to a compulsory or financial responsibility law or other motor vehicle insurance law are considered "autos".

13. "Occurrence" means an accident, including continuous or repeated exposure to substantially the same general harmful conditions.

14. "Personal and advertising injury" means injury, including consequential "bodily injury", arising out of one or more of the following offenses:

  a. False arrest, detention or imprisonment;

  b. Malicious prosecution;

  c. The wrongful eviction from, wrongful entry into, or invasion of the right of private occupancy of a room, dwelling or premises that a person occupies, committed by or on behalf of its owner, landlord or lessor;

  d. Oral or written publication, in any manner, of material that slanders or libels a person or organization or disparages a person's or organization's goods, products or services;

  e. Oral or written publication, in any manner, of material that violates a person's right of privacy;

  f. The use of another's advertising idea in your "advertisement"; or

  g. Infringing upon another's copyright, trade dress or slogan in your "advertisement".

15. "Pollutants" mean any solid, liquid, gaseous or thermal irritant or contaminant, including smoke, vapor, soot, fumes, acids, alkalis, chemicals and waste. Waste includes materials to be recycled, reconditioned or reclaimed.

16. "Products-completed operations hazard":

  a. Includes all "bodily injury" and "property damage" occurring away from premises you own or rent and arising out of "your product" or "your work" except:

  (1) Products that are still in your physical possession; or

  (2) Work that has not yet been completed or abandoned. However, "your work" will be deemed completed at the earliest of the following times:

    (a) When all of the work called for in your contract has been completed.

    (b) When all of the work to be done at the job site has been completed if your contract calls for work at more than one job site.

    (c) When that part of the work done at a job site has been put to its intended use by any person or organization other than another contractor or subcontractor working on the same project.

  Work that may need service, maintenance, correction, repair or replacement, but which is otherwise complete, will be treated as completed.

  b. Does not include "bodily injury" or "property damage" arising out of:

  (1) The transportation of property, unless the injury or damage arises out of a condition in or on a vehicle not owned or operated by you, and that condition was created by the "loading or unloading" of that vehicle by any insured;

  (2) The existence of tools, uninstalled equipment or abandoned or unused materials; or

  (3) Products or operations for which the classification, listed in the Declarations or in a policy schedule, states that products-completed operations are subject to the General Aggregate Limit.

17. "Property damage" means:

  a. Physical injury to tangible property, including all resulting loss of use of that property. All such loss of use shall be deemed to occur at the time of the physical injury that caused it; or

© ISO Properties, Inc., 2003   **CG 00 01 12 04**   □

b. Loss of use of tangible property that is not physically injured. All such loss of use shall be deemed to occur at the time of the "occurrence" that caused it.

For the purposes of this insurance, electronic data is not tangible property.

As used in this definition, electronic data means information, facts or programs stored as or on, created or used on, or transmitted to or from computer software, including systems and applications software, hard or floppy disks, CD-ROMS, tapes, drives, cells, data processing devices or any other media which are used with electronically controlled equipment.

18. "Suit" means a civil proceeding in which damages because of "bodily injury", "property damage" or "personal and advertising injury" to which this insurance applies are alleged. "Suit" includes:

a. An arbitration proceeding in which such damages are claimed and to which the insured must submit or does submit with our consent; or

b. Any other alternative dispute resolution proceeding in which such damages are claimed and to which the insured submits with our consent.

19. "Temporary worker" means a person who is furnished to you to substitute for a permanent "employee" on leave or to meet seasonal or short-term workload conditions.

20. "Volunteer worker" means a person who is not your "employee", and who donates his or her work and acts at the direction of and within the scope of duties determined by you, and is not paid a fee, salary or other compensation by you or anyone else for their work performed for you.

21. "Your product":

a. Means:

(1) Any goods or products, other than real property, manufactured, sold, handled, distributed or disposed of by:

(a) You;

(b) Others trading under your name; or

(c) A person or organization whose business or assets you have acquired; and

(2) Containers (other than vehicles), materials, parts or equipment furnished in connection with such goods or products.

b. Includes

(1) Warranties or representations made at any time with respect to the fitness, quality, durability, performance or use of "your product"; and

(2) The providing of or failure to provide warnings or instructions.

c. Does not include vending machines or other property rented to or located for the use of others but not sold.

22. "Your work":

a. Means:

(1) Work or operations performed by you or on your behalf; and

(2) Materials, parts or equipment furnished in connection with such work or operations.

b. Includes

(1) Warranties or representations made at any time with respect to the fitness, quality, durability, performance or use of "your work", and

(2) The providing of or failure to provide warnings or instructions.

COMMERCIAL GENERAL LIABILITY COVERAGE FORM

**COVERAGES A AND B PROVIDE
CLAIMS-MADE COVERAGE
PLEASE READ THE ENTIRE FORM CAREFULLY**

Various provisions in this policy restrict coverage. Read the entire policy carefully to determine rights, duties and what is and is not covered.

Throughout this policy the words "you" and "your" refer to the Named Insured shown in the Declarations, and any other person or organization qualifying as a Named Insured under this policy. The words "we", "us" and "our" refer to the Company providing this insurance.

The word "insured" means any person or organization qualifying as such under Section **II** – Who Is An Insured.

Other words and phrases that appear in quotation marks have special meaning. Refer to Section **VI** – Definitions.

SECTION I – COVERAGES

COVERAGE A BODILY INJURY AND PROPERTY DAMAGE LIABILITY

1. Insuring Agreement

a. We will pay those sums that the insured becomes legally obligated to pay as damages because of "bodily injury" or "property damage" to which this insurance applies. We will have the right and duty to defend the insured against any "suit" seeking those damages. However, we will have no duty to defend the insured against any "suit" seeking damages for "bodily injury" or "property damage" to which this insurance does not apply. We may, at our discretion, investigate any "occurrence" and settle any claim or "suit" that may result. But:

(1) The amount we will pay for damages is limited as described in Section **III** – Limits Of Insurance; and

(2) Our right and duty to defend ends when we have used up the applicable limit of insurance in the payment of judgments or settlements under Coverages **A** or **B** or medical expenses under Coverage **C**.

No other obligation or liability to pay sums or perform acts or services is covered unless explicitly provided for under Supplementary Payments – Coverages **A** and **B**.

b. This insurance applies to "bodily injury" and "property damage" only if:

(1) The "bodily injury" or "property damage" is caused by an "occurrence" that takes place in the "coverage territory";

(2) The "bodily injury" or "property damage" did not occur before the Retroactive Date, if any, shown in the Declarations or after the end of the policy period; and

(3) A claim for damages because of the "bodily injury" or "property damage" is first made against any insured, in accordance with Paragraph **c.** below, during the policy period or any Extended Reporting Period we provide under Section **V** – Extended Reporting Periods.

c. A claim by a person or organization seeking damages will be deemed to have been made at the earlier of the following times:

(1) When notice of such claim is received and recorded by any insured or by us, whichever comes first; or

(2) When we make settlement in accordance with Paragraph **1.a.** above.

All claims for damages because of "bodily injury" to the same person, including damages claimed by any person or organization for care, loss of services, or death resulting at any time from the "bodily injury", will be deemed to have been made at the time the first of those claims is made against any insured.

All claims for damages because of "property damage" causing loss to the same person or organization will be deemed to have been made at the time the first of those claims is made against any insured.

2. Exclusions

This insurance does not apply to:

a. Expected Or Intended Injury

"Bodily injury" or "property damage" expected or intended from the standpoint of the insured. This exclusion does not apply to "bodily injury" resulting from the use of reasonable force to protect persons or property.

b. Contractual Liability

"Bodily injury" or "property damage" for which the insured is obligated to pay damages by reason of the assumption of liability in a contract or agreement. This exclusion does not apply to liability for damages:

(1) That the insured would have in the absence of the contract or agreement; or

(2) Assumed in a contract or agreement that is an "insured contract", provided the "bodily injury" or "property damage" occurs subsequent to the execution of the contract or agreement. Solely for the purposes of liability assumed in an "insured contract", reasonable attorney fees and necessary litigation expenses incurred by or for a party other than an insured are deemed to be damages because of "bodily injury" or "property damage", provided:

(a) Liability to such party for, or for the cost of, that party's defense has also been assumed in the same "insured contract"; and

(b) Such attorney fees and litigation expenses are for defense of that party against a civil or alternative dispute resolution proceeding in which damages to which this insurance applies are alleged.

c. Liquor Liability

"Bodily injury" or "property damage" for which any insured may be held liable by reason of:

(1) Causing or contributing to the intoxication of any person;

(2) The furnishing of alcoholic beverages to a person under the legal drinking age or under the influence of alcohol; or

(3) Any statute, ordinance or regulation relating to the sale, gift, distribution or use of alcoholic beverages.

This exclusion applies only if you are in the business of manufacturing, distributing, selling, serving or furnishing alcoholic beverages.

d. Workers' Compensation And Similar Laws

Any obligation of the insured under a workers' compensation, disability benefits or unemployment compensation law or any similar law.

e. Employer's Liability

"Bodily injury" to:

(1) An "employee" of the insured arising out of and in the course of:

(a) Employment by the insured; or

(b) Performing duties related to the conduct of the insured's business; or

(2) The spouse, child, parent, brother or sister of that "employee" as a consequence of Paragraph **(1)** above.

This exclusion applies:

(1) Whether the insured may be liable as an employer or in any other capacity; and

(2) To any obligation to share damages with or repay someone else who must pay damages because of the injury.

This exclusion does not apply to liability assumed by the insured under an "insured contract".

f. Pollution

(1) "Bodily injury" or "property damage" arising out of the actual, alleged or threatened discharge, dispersal, seepage, migration, release or escape of "pollutants":

(a) At or from any premises, site or location which is or was at any time owned or occupied by, or rented or loaned to, any insured. However, this subparagraph does not apply to:

(i) "Bodily injury" if sustained within a building and caused by smoke, fumes, vapor or soot produced by or originating from equipment that is used to heat, cool or dehumidify the building, or equipment that is used to heat water for personal use by the building's occupants or their guests;

(ii) "Bodily injury" or "property damage" for which you may be held liable, if you are a contractor and the owner or lessee of such premises, site or location has been added to your policy as an additional insured with respect to your ongoing operations performed for that additional insured at that premises, site or location and such premises, site or location is not or never was owned or occupied by, or rented or loaned to, any insured, other than that additional insured; or

(iii) "Bodily injury" or "property damage" arising out of heat, smoke or fumes from a "hostile fire";

(b) At or from any premises, site or location which is or was at any time used by or for any insured or others for the handling, storage, disposal, processing or treatment of waste;

(c) Which are or were at any time transported, handled, stored, treated, disposed of, or processed as waste by or for:

(i) Any insured; or

(ii) Any person or organization for whom you may be legally responsible; or

(d) At or from any premises, site or location on which any insured or any contractors or subcontractors working directly or indirectly on any insured's behalf are performing operations if the "pollutants" are brought on or to the premises, site or location in connection with such operations by such insured, contractor or subcontractor. However, this subparagraph does not apply to:

(i) "Bodily injury" or "property damage" arising out of the escape of fuels, lubricants or other operating fluids which are needed to perform the normal electrical, hydraulic or mechanical functions necessary for the operation of "mobile equipment" or its parts, if such fuels, lubricants or other operating fluids escape from a vehicle part designed to hold, store or receive them. This exception does not apply if the "bodily injury" or "property damage" arises out of the intentional discharge, dispersal or release of the fuels, lubricants or other operating fluids, or if such fuels, lubricants or other operating fluids are brought on or to the premises, site or location with the intent that they be discharged, dispersed or released as part of the operations being performed by such insured, contractor or subcontractor;

(ii) "Bodily injury" or "property damage" sustained within a building and caused by the release of gases, fumes or vapors from materials brought into that building in connection with operations being performed by you or on your behalf by a contractor or subcontractor; or

(iii) "Bodily injury" or "property damage" arising out of heat, smoke or fumes from a "hostile fire".

(e) At or from any premises, site or location on which any insured or any contractors or subcontractors working directly or indirectly on any insured's behalf are performing operations if the operations are to test for, monitor, clean up, remove, contain, treat, detoxify or neutralize, or in any way respond to, or assess the effects of, "pollutants".

(2) Any loss, cost or expense arising out of any:

(a) Request, demand, order or statutory or regulatory requirement that any insured or others test for, monitor, clean up, remove, contain, treat, detoxify or neutralize, or in any way respond to, or assess the effects of, "pollutants"; or

(b) Claim or suit by or on behalf of a governmental authority for damages because of testing for, monitoring, cleaning up, removing, containing, treating, detoxifying or neutralizing, or in any way responding to, or assessing the effects of, "pollutants".

However, this paragraph does not apply to liability for damages because of "property damage" that the insured would have in the absence of such request, demand, order or statutory or regulatory requirement, or such claim or "suit" by or on behalf of a governmental authority.

g. Aircraft, Auto Or Watercraft

"Bodily injury" or "property damage" arising out of the ownership, maintenance, use or entrustment to others of any aircraft, "auto" or watercraft owned or operated by or rented or loaned to any insured. Use includes operation and "loading or unloading".

This exclusion applies even if the claims against any insured allege negligence or other wrongdoing in the supervision, hiring, employment, training or monitoring of others by that insured, if the "occurrence" which caused the "bodily injury" or "property damage" involved the ownership, maintenance, use or entrustment to others of any aircraft, "auto" or watercraft that is owned or operated by or rented or loaned to any insured.

This exclusion does not apply to:

(1) A watercraft while ashore on premises you own or rent;

(2) A watercraft you do not own that is:

(a) Less than 26 feet long; and

(b) Not being used to carry persons or property for a charge;

(3) Parking an "auto" on, or on the ways next to, premises you own or rent, provided the "auto" is not owned by or rented or loaned to you or the insured;

(4) Liability assumed under any "insured contract" for the ownership, maintenance or use of aircraft or watercraft; or

(5) "Bodily injury" or "property damage" arising out of:

(a) The operation of machinery or equipment that is attached to, or part of, a land vehicle that would qualify under the definition of "mobile equipment" if it were not subject to a compulsory or financial responsibility law or other motor vehicle insurance law in the state where it is licensed or principally garaged; or

(b) The operation of any of the machinery or equipment listed in Paragraph **f.(2)** or **f.(3)** of the definition of "mobile equipment".

h. Mobile Equipment

"Bodily injury" or "property damage" arising out of:

(1) The transportation of "mobile equipment" by an "auto" owned or operated by or rented or loaned to any insured; or

(2) The use of "mobile equipment" in, or while in practice for, or while being prepared for, any prearranged racing, speed, demolition, or stunting activity.

i. War

"Bodily injury" or "property damage", however caused, arising, directly or indirectly, out of:

(1) War, including undeclared or civil war;

(2) Warlike action by a military force, including action in hindering or defending against an actual or expected attack, by any government, sovereign or other authority using military personnel or other agents; or

(3) Insurrection, rebellion, revolution, usurped power, or action taken by governmental authority in hindering or defending against any of these.

j. Damage To Property

"Property damage" to:

(1) Property you own, rent, or occupy, including any costs or expenses incurred by you, or any other person, organization or entity, for repair, replacement, enhancement, restoration or maintenance of such property for any reason, including prevention of injury to a person or damage to another's property;

(2) Premises you sell, give away or abandon, if the "property damage" arises out of any part of those premises;

(3) Property loaned to you;

(4) Personal property in the care, custody or control of the insured;

(5) That particular part of real property on which you or any contractors or subcontractors working directly or indirectly on your behalf are performing operations, if the "property damage" arises out of those operations; or

(6) That particular part of any property that must be restored, repaired or replaced because "your work" was incorrectly performed on it.

Paragraphs **(1)**, **(3)** and **(4)** of this exclusion do not apply to "property damage" (other than damage by fire) to premises, including the contents of such premises, rented to you for a period of 7 or fewer consecutive days. A separate limit of insurance applies to Damage To Premises Rented To You as described in Section **III** – Limits Of Insurance.

Paragraph **(2)** of this exclusion does not apply if the premises are "your work" and were never occupied, rented or held for rental by you.

Paragraphs **(3)**, **(4)**, **(5)** and **(6)** of this exclusion do not apply to liability assumed under a side-track agreement.

Paragraph **(6)** of this exclusion does not apply to "property damage" included in the "products-completed operations hazard".

k. Damage To Your Product

"Property damage" to "your product" arising out of it or any part of it.

l. Damage To Your Work

"Property damage" to "your work" arising out of it or any part of it and included in the "products-completed operations hazard".

This exclusion does not apply if the damaged work or the work out of which the damage arises was performed on your behalf by a subcontractor.

m. Damage To Impaired Property Or Property Not Physically Injured

"Property damage" to "impaired property" or property that has not been physically injured, arising out of:

(1) A defect, deficiency, inadequacy or dangerous condition in "your product" or "your work"; or

(2) A delay or failure by you or anyone acting on your behalf to perform a contract or agreement in accordance with its terms.

This exclusion does not apply to the loss of use of other property arising out of sudden and accidental physical injury to "your product" or "your work" after it has been put to its intended use.

n. Recall Of Products, Work Or Impaired Property

Damages claimed for any loss, cost or expense incurred by you or others for the loss of use, withdrawal, recall, inspection, repair, replacement, adjustment, removal or disposal of:

(1) "Your product";

(2) "Your work"; or

(3) "Impaired property";

if such product, work, or property is withdrawn or recalled from the market or from use by any person or organization because of a known or suspected defect, deficiency, inadequacy or dangerous condition in it.

o. Personal And Advertising Injury

"Bodily injury" arising out of "personal and advertising injury".

p. Electronic Data

Damages arising out of the loss of, loss of use of, damage to, corruption of, inability to access, or inability to manipulate electronic data.

As used in this exclusion, electronic data means information, facts or programs stored as or on, created or used on, or transmitted to or from computer software, including systems and applications software, hard or floppy disks, CD-ROMS, tapes, drives, cells, data processing devices or any other media which are used with electronically controlled equipment.

Exclusions **c.** through **n.** do not apply to damage by fire to premises while rented to you or temporarily occupied by you with permission of the owner. A separate limit of insurance applies to this coverage as described in Section **III** – Limits Of Insurance.

COVERAGE B PERSONAL AND ADVERTISING INJURY LIABILITY

1. Insuring Agreement

a. We will pay those sums that the insured becomes legally obligated to pay as damages because of "personal and advertising injury" to which this insurance applies. We will have the right and duty to defend the insured against any "suit" seeking those damages. However, we will have no duty to defend the insured against any "suit" seeking damages for "personal and advertising injury" to which this insurance does not apply. We may, at our discretion, investigate any offense and settle any claim or "suit" that may result. But:

(1) The amount we will pay for damages is limited as described in Section **III** – Limits Of Insurance; and

(2) Our right and duty to defend end when we have used up the applicable limit of insurance in the payment of judgments or settlements under Coverages **A** or **B** or medical expenses under Coverage **C**.

No other obligation or liability to pay sums or perform acts or services is covered unless explicitly provided for under Supplementary Payments – Coverages **A** and **B**.

b. This insurance applies to "personal and advertising injury" caused by an offense arising out of your business, but only if:

(1) The offense was committed in the "coverage territory";

(2) The offense was not committed before the Retroactive Date, if any, shown in the Declarations or after the end of the policy period; and

(3) A claim for damages because of the "personal and advertising injury" is first made against any insured, in accordance with Paragraph **c.** below, during the policy period or any Extended Reporting Period we provide under Section **V** – Extended Reporting Periods.

c. A claim made by a person or organization seeking damages will be deemed to have been made at the earlier of the following times:

(1) When notice of such claim is received and recorded by any insured or by us, whichever comes first; or

(2) When we make settlement in accordance with Paragraph **1.a.** above.

All claims for damages because of "personal and advertising injury" to the same person or organization as a result of an offense will be deemed to have been made at the time the first of those claims is made against any insured.

2. Exclusions

This insurance does not apply to:

a. Knowing Violation Of Rights Of Another

"Personal and advertising injury" caused by or at the direction of the insured with the knowledge that the act would violate the rights of another and would inflict "personal and advertising injury".

b. Material Published With Knowledge Of Falsity

"Personal and advertising injury" arising out of oral or written publication of material, if done by or at the direction of the insured with knowledge of its falsity.

c. Material Published Prior To Policy Period

"Personal and advertising injury" arising out of oral or written publication of material whose first publication took place before the Retroactive Date, if any, shown in the Declarations.

d. Criminal Acts

"Personal and advertising injury" arising out of a criminal act committed by or at the direction of the insured.

e. Contractual Liability

"Personal and advertising injury" for which the insured has assumed liability in a contract or agreement. This exclusion does not apply to liability for damages that the insured would have in the absence of the contract or agreement.

f. Breach Of Contract

"Personal and advertising injury" arising out of a breach of contract, except an implied contract to use another's advertising idea in your "advertisement".

g. Quality Or Performance Of Goods – Failure To Conform To Statements

"Personal and advertising injury" arising out of the failure of goods, products or services to conform with any statement of quality or performance made in your "advertisement".

h. Wrong Description Of Prices

"Personal and advertising injury" arising out of the wrong description of the price of goods, products or services stated in your "advertisement".

i. Infringement Of Copyright, Patent, Trademark Or Trade Secret

"Personal and advertising injury" arising out of the infringement of copyright, patent, trademark, trade secret or other intellectual property rights.

However, this exclusion does not apply to infringement, in your "advertisement", of copyright, trade dress or slogan.

j. Insureds In Media And Internet Type Businesses

"Personal and advertising injury" committed by an insured whose business is:

(1) Advertising, broadcasting, publishing or telecasting;

(2) Designing or determining content or websites for others; or

(3) An Internet search, access, content or service provider.

However, this exclusion does not apply to Paragraphs **14.a., b.** and **c.** of "personal and advertising injury" under the Definitions Section.

For the purposes of this exclusion, the placing of frames, borders or links, or advertising, for you or others anywhere on the Internet, is not by itself, considered the business of advertising, broadcasting, publishing or telecasting.

k. Electronic Chatrooms Or Bulletin Boards

"Personal and advertising injury" arising out of an electronic chatroom or bulletin board the insured hosts, owns, or over which the insured exercises control.

CG 00 02 12 04

l. Unauthorized Use Of Another's Name Or Product

"Personal and advertising injury" arising out of the unauthorized use of another's name or product in your e-mail address, domain name or metatag, or any other similar tactics to mislead another's potential customers.

m. Pollution

"Personal and advertising injury" arising out of the actual, alleged or threatened discharge, dispersal, seepage, migration, release or escape of "pollutants" at any time.

n. Pollution-Related

Any loss, cost or expense arising out of any:

(1) Request, demand, order or statutory or regulatory requirement that any insured or others test for, monitor, clean up, remove, contain, treat, detoxify or neutralize, or in any way respond to, or assess the effects of, "pollutants"; or

(2) Claim or suit by or on behalf of a governmental authority for damages because of testing for, monitoring, cleaning up, removing, containing, treating, detoxifying or neutralizing, or in any way responding to, or assessing the effects of, "pollutants".

o. War

"Personal and advertising injury", however caused, arising, directly or indirectly, out of:

(1) War, including undeclared or civil war;

(2) Warlike action by a military force, including action in hindering or defending against an actual or expected attack, by any government, sovereign or other authority using military personnel or other agents; or

(3) Insurrection, rebellion, revolution, usurped power, or action taken by governmental authority in hindering or defending against any of these.

COVERAGE C MEDICAL PAYMENTS

1. Insuring Agreement

a. We will pay medical expenses as described below for "bodily injury" caused by an accident:

(1) On premises you own or rent;

(2) On ways next to premises you own or rent; or

(3) Because of your operations;

provided that:

(1) The accident takes place in the "coverage territory" and during the policy period;

(2) The expenses are incurred and reported to us within one year of the date of the accident; and

(3) The injured person submits to examination, at our expense, by physicians of our choice as often as we reasonably require.

b. We will make these payments regardless of fault. These payments will not exceed the applicable limit of insurance. We will pay reasonable expenses for:

(1) First aid administered at the time of an accident;

(2) Necessary medical, surgical, x-ray and dental services, including prosthetic devices; and

(3) Necessary ambulance, hospital, professional nursing and funeral services.

2. Exclusions

We will not pay expenses for "bodily injury":

a. Any Insured

To any insured, except "volunteer workers".

b. Hired Person

To a person hired to do work for or on behalf of any insured or a tenant of any insured.

c. Injury On Normally Occupied Premises

To a person injured on that part of premises you own or rent that the person normally occupies.

d. Workers Compensation And Similar Laws

To a person, whether or not an "employee" of any insured, if benefits for the "bodily injury" are payable or must be provided under a workers' compensation or disability benefits law or a similar law.

e. Athletics Activities

To a person injured while practicing, instructing or participating in any physical exercises or games, sports, or athletic contests.

f. Products-Completed Operations Hazard

Included within the "products-completed operations hazard".

g. Coverage A Exclusions

Excluded under Coverage **A**.

SUPPLEMENTARY PAYMENTS – COVERAGES A AND B

1. We will pay, with respect to any claim we investigate or settle or any "suit" against an insured we defend:

   a. All expenses we incur.

   b. Up to $250 for cost of bail bonds required because of accidents or traffic law violations arising out of the use of any vehicle to which the Bodily Injury Liability Coverage applies. We do not have to furnish these bonds.

   c. The cost of bonds to release attachments, but only for bond amounts within the applicable limit of insurance. We do not have to furnish these bonds.

   d. All reasonable expenses incurred by the insured at our request to assist us in the investigation or defense of the claim or "suit", including actual loss of earnings up to $250 a day because of time off from work.

   e. All costs taxed against the insured in the "suit".

   f. Prejudgment interest awarded against the insured on that part of the judgment we pay. If we make an offer to pay the applicable limit of insurance, we will not pay any prejudgment interest based on that period of time after the offer.

   g. All interest on the full amount of any judgment that accrues after entry of the judgment and before we have paid, offered to pay, or deposited in court the part of the judgment that is within the applicable limit of insurance.

   These payments will not reduce the limits of insurance.

2. If we defend an insured against a "suit" and an indemnitee of the insured is also named as a party to the "suit", we will defend that indemnitee if all of the following conditions are met:

   a. The "suit" against the indemnitee seeks damages for which the insured has assumed the liability of the indemnitee in a contract or agreement that is an "insured contract";

   b. This insurance applies to such liability assumed by the insured;

   c. The obligation to defend, or the cost of the defense of, that indemnitee, has also been assumed by the insured in the same "insured contract";

   d. The allegations in the "suit" and the information we know about the "occurrence" are such that no conflict appears to exist between the interests of the insured and the interests of the indemnitee;

   e. The indemnitee and the insured ask us to conduct and control the defense of that indemnitee against such "suit" and agree that we can assign the same counsel to defend the insured and the indemnitee; and

   f. The indemnitee:

      (1) Agrees in writing to:

         (a) Cooperate with us in the investigation, settlement or defense of the "suit";

         (b) Immediately send us copies of any demands, notices, summonses or legal papers received in connection with the "suit";

         (c) Notify any other insurer whose coverage is available to the indemnitee; and

         (d) Cooperate with us with respect to coordinating other applicable insurance available to the indemnitee; and

      (2) Provides us with written authorization to:

         (a) Obtain records and other information related to the "suit"; and

         (b) Conduct and control the defense of the indemnitee in such "suit".

   So long as the above conditions are met, attorneys' fees incurred by us in the defense of that indemnitee, necessary litigation expenses incurred by us and necessary litigation expenses incurred by the indemnitee at our request will be paid as Supplementary Payments. Notwithstanding the provisions of Paragraph 2.b.(2) of Section I – Coverage A – Bodily Injury And Property Damage Liability, such payments will not be deemed to be damages for "bodily injury" and "property damage" and will not reduce the limits of insurance.

   Our obligation to defend an insured's indemnitee and to pay for attorneys' fees and necessary litigation expenses as Supplementary Payments ends when:

   a. We have used up the applicable limit of insurance in the payment of judgments or settlements; or

   b. The conditions set forth above, or the terms of the agreement described in Paragraph f. above, are no longer met.

SECTION II – WHO IS AN INSURED

1. If you are designated in the Declarations as:

   a. An individual, you and your spouse are insureds, but only with respect to the conduct of a business of which you are the sole owner.

   b. A partnership or joint venture, you are an insured. Your members, your partners, and their spouses are also insureds, but only with respect to the conduct of your business.

c. A limited liability company, you are an insured. Your members are also insureds, but only with respect to the conduct of your business. Your managers are insureds, but only with respect to their duties as your managers.

d. An organization other than a partnership, joint venture or limited liability company, you are an insured. Your "executive officers" and directors are insureds, but only with respect to their duties as your officers or directors. Your stockholders are also insureds, but only with respect to their liability as stockholders.

e. A trust, you are an insured. Your trustees are also insureds, but only with respect to their duties as trustees.

2. Each of the following is also an insured:

a. Your "volunteer workers" only while performing duties related to the conduct of your business, or your "employees", other than either your "executive officers" (if you are an organization other than a partnership, joint venture or limited liability company) or your managers (if you are a limited liability company), but only for acts within the scope of their employment by you or while performing duties related to the conduct of your business. However, none of these "employees" or "volunteer workers" are insureds for:

(1) "Bodily injury" or "personal and advertising injury":

(a) To you, to your partners or members (if you are a partnership or joint venture), to your members (if you are a limited liability company), to a co-"employee" while in the course of his or her employment or performing duties related to the conduct of your business, or to your other "volunteer workers" while performing duties related to the conduct of your business;

(b) To the spouse, child, parent, brother or sister of that co-"employee" or "volunteer worker" as a consequence of Paragraph **(1)(a)** above;

(c) For which there is any obligation to share damages with or repay someone else who must pay damages because of the injury described in Paragraphs **(1)(a)** or **(b)** above; or

(d) Arising out of his or her providing or failing to provide professional health care services.

(2) "Property damage" to property:

(a) Owned, occupied or used by,

(b) Rented to, in the care, custody or control of, or over which physical control is being exercised for any purpose by

you, any of your "employees", "volunteer workers", any partner or member (if you are a partnership or joint venture), or any member (if you are a limited liability company).

b. Any person (other than your "employee" or "volunteer worker") or any organization while acting as your real estate manager.

c. Any person or organization having proper temporary custody of your property if you die, but only:

(1) With respect to liability arising out of the maintenance or use of that property; and

(2) Until your legal representative has been appointed.

d. Your legal representative if you die, but only with respect to duties as such. That representative will have all your rights and duties under this Coverage Part.

3. Any organization you newly acquire or form, other than a partnership, joint venture or limited liability company, and over which you maintain ownership or majority interest, will qualify as a Named Insured if there is no other similar insurance available to that organization. However:

a. Coverage under this provision is afforded only until the 90th day after you acquire or form the organization or the end of the policy period, whichever is earlier;

b. Coverage **A** does not apply to "bodily injury" or "property damage" that occurred before you acquired or formed the organization; and

c. Coverage **B** does not apply to "personal and advertising injury" arising out of an offense committed before you acquired or formed the organization.

No person or organization is an insured with respect to the conduct of any current or past partnership, joint venture or limited liability company that is not shown as a Named Insured in the Declarations.

SECTION III – LIMITS OF INSURANCE

1. The Limits of Insurance shown in the Declarations and the rules below fix the most we will pay regardless of the number of:

a. Insureds;

b. Claims made or "suits" brought; or

c. Persons or organizations making claims or bringing "suits".

2. The General Aggregate Limit is the most we will pay for the sum of:

  a. Medical expenses under Coverage **C**;

  b. Damages under Coverage **A,** except damages because of "bodily injury" or "property damage" included in the "products-completed operations hazard"; and

  c. Damages under Coverage **B.**

3. The Products-Completed Operations Aggregate Limit is the most we will pay under Coverage **A** for damages because of "bodily injury" and "property damage" included in the "products-completed operations hazard".

4. Subject to **2.** above, the Personal and Advertising Injury Limit is the most we will pay under Coverage **B** for the sum of all damages because of all "personal and advertising injury" sustained by any one person or organization.

5. Subject to **2.** or **3.** above, whichever applies, the Each Occurrence Limit is the most we will pay for the sum of:

  a. Damages under Coverage **A**; and

  b. Medical expenses under Coverage **C**

because of all "bodily injury" and "property damage" arising out of any one "occurrence".

6. Subject to **5.** above, the Damage To Premises Rented To You Limit is the most we will pay under Coverage **A** for damages because of "property damage" to any one premises, while rented to you, or in the case of damage by fire, while rented to you or temporarily occupied by you with permission of the owner.

7. Subject to **5.** above, the Medical Expense Limit is the most we will pay under Coverage **C** for all medical expenses because of "bodily injury" sustained by any one person.

The Limits of Insurance of this Coverage Part apply separately to each consecutive annual period and to any remaining period of less than 12 months, starting with the beginning of the policy period shown in the Declarations, unless the policy period is extended after issuance for an additional period of less than 12 months. In that case, the additional period will be deemed part of the last preceding period for purposes of determining the Limits of Insurance.

SECTION IV – COMMERCIAL GENERAL LIABILITY CONDITIONS

1. Bankruptcy

Bankruptcy or insolvency of the insured or of the insured's estate will not relieve us of our obligations under this Coverage Part.

2. Duties In The Event Of Occurrence, Offense, Claim Or Suit

  a. You must see to it that we are notified as soon as practicable of an "occurrence" or offense which may result in a claim. To the extent possible, notice should include:

    (1) How, when and where the "occurrence" or offense took place;

    (2) The names and addresses of any injured persons and witnesses; and

    (3) The nature and location of any injury or damage arising out of the "occurrence" or offense.

  Notice of an "occurrence" or offense is not notice of a claim.

  b. If a claim is received by any insured, you must:

    (1) Immediately record the specifics of the claim and the date received; and

    (2) Notify us as soon as practicable.

  You must see to it that we receive written notice of the claim as soon as practicable.

  c. You and any other involved insured must:

    (1) Immediately send us copies of any demands, notices, summonses or legal papers received in connection with the claim or a "suit";

    (2) Authorize us to obtain records and other information;

    (3) Cooperate with us in the investigation or settlement of the claim or defense against the "suit"; and

    (4) Assist us, upon our request, in the enforcement of any right against any person or organization which may be liable to the insured because of injury or damage to which this insurance may also apply.

  d. No insured will, except at that insured's own cost, voluntarily make a payment, assume any obligation, or incur any expense, other than for first aid, without our consent.

3. Legal Action Against Us

No person or organization has a right under this Coverage Part:

  a. To join us as a party or otherwise bring us into a "suit" asking for damages from an insured; or

  b. To sue us on this Coverage Part unless all of its terms have been fully complied with.

A person or organization may sue us to recover on an agreed settlement or on a final judgment against an insured; but we will not be liable for damages that are not payable under the terms of this Coverage Part or that are in excess of the applicable limit of insurance. An agreed settlement means a settlement and release of liability signed by us, the insured and the claimant or the claimant's legal representative.

4. Other Insurance

If other valid and collectible insurance is available to the insured for a loss we cover under Coverages **A** or **B** of this Coverage Part, our obligations are limited as follows:

a. Primary Insurance

This insurance is primary except when **b.** below applies. If this insurance is primary, our obligations are not affected unless any of the other insurance is also primary. Then, we will share with all that other insurance by the method described in **c.** below.

b. Excess Insurance

This insurance is excess over:

(1) Any of the other insurance, whether primary, excess, contingent or on any other basis:

(a) That is effective prior to the beginning of the policy period shown in the Declarations of this insurance and applies to "bodily injury" or "property damage" on other than a claims-made basis, if:

(i) No Retroactive Date is shown in the Declarations of this insurance; or

(ii) The other insurance has a policy period which continues after the Retroactive Date shown in the Declarations of this insurance;

(b) That is Fire, Extended Coverage, Builders' Risk, Installation Risk or similar coverage for "your work";

(c) That is Fire insurance for premises rented to you or temporarily occupied by you with permission of the owner;

(d) That is insurance purchased by you to cover your liability as a tenant for "property damage" to premises rented to you or temporarily occupied by you with permission of the owner; or

(e) If the loss arises out of the maintenance or use of aircraft, "autos" or watercraft to the extent not subject to Exclusion **g.** of Section **I** – Coverage **A** – Bodily Injury And Property Damage Liability.

(2) Any other primary insurance available to you covering liability for damages arising out of the premises or operations, or the products and completed operations, for which you have been added as an additional insured by attachment of an endorsement.

When this insurance is excess, we will have no duty under Coverages **A** or **B** to defend the insured against any "suit" if any other insurer has a duty to defend the insured against that "suit". If no other insurer defends, we will undertake to do so, but we will be entitled to the insured's rights against all those other insurers.

When this insurance is excess over other insurance, we will pay only our share of the amount of the loss, if any, that exceeds the sum of:

(1) The total amount that all such other insurance would pay for the loss in the absence of this insurance; and

(2) The total of all deductible and self-insured amounts under all that other insurance.

We will share the remaining loss, if any, with any other insurance that is not described in this Excess Insurance provision and was not bought specifically to apply in excess of the Limits of Insurance shown in the Declarations of this Coverage Part.

c. Method Of Sharing

If all of the other insurance permits contribution by equal shares, we will follow this method also. Under this approach each insurer contributes equal amounts until it has paid its applicable limit of insurance or none of the loss remains, whichever comes first.

If any of the other insurance does not permit contribution by equal shares, we will contribute by limits. Under this method, each insurer's share is based on the ratio of its applicable limit of insurance to the total applicable limits of insurance of all insurers.

5. Premium Audit

a. We will compute all premiums for this Coverage Part in accordance with our rules and rates.

b. Premium shown in this Coverage Part as advance premium is a deposit premium only. At the close of each audit period we will compute the earned premium for that period and send notice to the first Named Insured. The due date for audit and retrospective premiums is the date shown as the due date on the bill. If the sum of the advance and audit premiums paid for the policy period is greater than the earned premium, we will return the excess to the first Named Insured.

c. The first Named Insured must keep records of the information we need for premium computation, and send us copies at such times as we may request.

6. Representations

By accepting this policy, you agree:

a. The statements in the Declarations are accurate and complete;

b. Those statements are based upon representations you made to us; and

c. We have issued this policy in reliance upon your representations.

7. Separation Of Insureds

Except with respect to the Limits of Insurance, and any rights or duties specifically assigned in this Coverage Part to the first Named Insured, this insurance applies:

a. As if each Named Insured were the only Named Insured; and

b. Separately to each insured against whom claim is made or "suit" is brought.

8. Transfer Of Rights Of Recovery Against Others To Us

If the insured has rights to recover all or part of any payment we have made under this Coverage Part, those rights are transferred to us. The insured must do nothing after loss to impair them. At our request, the insured will bring "suit" or transfer those rights to us and help us enforce them.

9. When We Do Not Renew

If we decide not to renew this Coverage Part, we will mail or deliver to the first Named Insured shown in the Declarations written notice of the nonrenewal not less than 30 days before the expiration date.

If notice is mailed, proof of mailing will be sufficient proof of notice.

We will provide the first Named Insured shown in the Declarations the following information relating to this and any preceding general liability claims-made Coverage Part we have issued to you during the previous three years:

a. A list or other record of each "occurrence", not previously reported to any other insurer, of which we were notified in accordance with Paragraph **2.a.** of the Section **IV** – Duties In The Event Of Occurrence, Offense, Claim Or Suit Condition. We will include the date and brief description of the "occurrence" if that information was in the notice we received.

b. A summary by policy year, of payments made and amounts reserved, stated separately, under any applicable General Aggregate Limit and Products-Completed Operations Aggregate Limit.

Amounts reserved are based on our judgment. They are subject to change and should not be regarded as ultimate settlement values.

You must not disclose this information to any claimant or any claimant's representative without our consent.

If we cancel or elect not to renew this Coverage Part, we will provide such information no later than 30 days before the date of policy termination. In other circumstances, we will provide this information only if we receive a written request from the first Named Insured within 60 days after the end of the policy period. In this case, we will provide this information within 45 days of receipt of the request.

We compile claim and "occurrence" information for our own business purposes and exercise reasonable care in doing so. In providing this information to the first Named Insured, we make no representations or warranties to insureds, insurers, or others to whom this information is furnished by or on behalf of any insured. Cancellation or non-renewal will be effective even if we inadvertently provide inaccurate information.

SECTION V – EXTENDED REPORTING PERIODS

1. We will provide one or more Extended Reporting Periods, as described below, if:

a. This Coverage Part is canceled or not renewed; or

b. We renew or replace this Coverage Part with insurance that:

(1) Has a Retroactive Date later than the date shown in the Declarations of this Coverage Part; or

(2) Does not apply to "bodily injury", "property damage" or "personal and advertising injury" on a claims-made basis.

2. Extended Reporting Periods do not extend the policy period or change the scope of coverage provided. They apply only to claims for:

a. "Bodily injury" or "property damage" that occurs before the end of the policy period but not before the Retroactive Date, if any, shown in the Declarations; or

b. "Personal and advertising injury" caused by an offense committed before the end of the policy period but not before the Retroactive Date, if any, shown in the Declarations.

Once in effect, Extended Reporting Periods may not be canceled.

3. A Basic Extended Reporting Period is automatically provided without additional charge. This period starts with the end of the policy period and lasts for:

a. Five years with respect to claims because of "bodily injury" and "property damage" arising out of an "occurrence" reported to us, not later than 60 days after the end of the policy period, in accordance with Paragraph **2.a.** of the Section **IV** – Duties In The Event Of Occurrence, Offense, Claim Or Suit Condition;

b. Five years with respect to claims because of "personal and advertising injury" arising out of an offense reported to us, not later than 60 days after the end of the policy period, in accordance with Paragraph **2.a.** of the Section **IV** – Duties In The Event Of Occurrence, Offense, Claim Or Suit Condition; and

c. Sixty days with respect to claims arising from "occurrences" or offenses not previously reported to us.

The Basic Extended Reporting Period does not apply to claims that are covered under any subsequent insurance you purchase, or that would be covered but for exhaustion of the amount of insurance applicable to such claims.

4. The Basic Extended Reporting Period does not reinstate or increase the Limits of Insurance.

5. A Supplemental Extended Reporting Period of unlimited duration is available, but only by an endorsement and for an extra charge. This supplemental period starts when the Basic Extended Reporting Period, set forth in Paragraph **3.** above, ends.

You must give us a written request for the endorsement within 60 days after the end of the policy period. The Supplemental Extended Reporting Period will not go into effect unless you pay the additional premium promptly when due.

We will determine the additional premium in accordance with our rules and rates. In doing so, we may take into account the following:

a. The exposures insured;

b. Previous types and amounts of insurance;

c. Limits of Insurance available under this Coverage Part for future payment of damages; and

d. Other related factors.

The additional premium will not exceed 200% of the annual premium for this Coverage Part.

This endorsement shall set forth the terms, not inconsistent with this Section, applicable to the Supplemental Extended Reporting Period, including a provision to the effect that the insurance afforded for claims first received during such period is excess over any other valid and collectible insurance available under policies in force after the Supplemental Extended Reporting Period starts.

6. If the Supplemental Extended Reporting Period is in effect, we will provide the supplemental aggregate limits of insurance described below, but only for claims first received and recorded during the Supplemental Extended Reporting Period.

The supplemental aggregate limits of insurance will be equal to the dollar amount shown in the Declarations in effect at the end of the policy period for such of the following limits of insurance for which a dollar amount has been entered:

General Aggregate Limit
Products-Completed Operations Aggregate Limit

Paragraphs **2.** and **3.** of Section **III** – Limits Of Insurance will be amended accordingly. The Personal and Advertising Injury Limit, the Each Occurrence Limit and the Damage To Premises Rented To You Limit shown in the Declarations will then continue to apply, as set forth in Paragraphs **4.**, **5.** and **6.** of that Section.

SECTION VI – DEFINITIONS

1. "Advertisement" means a notice that is broadcast or published to the general public or specific market segments about your goods, products or services for the purpose of attracting customers or supporters. For the purposes of this definition:

a. Notices that are published include material placed on the Internet or on similar electronic means of communication; and

b. Regarding web-sites, only that part of a web-site that is about your goods, products or services for the purposes of attracting customers or supporters is considered an advertisement.

2. "Auto" means:

a. A land motor vehicle, trailer or semitrailer designed for travel on public roads, including any attached machinery or equipment; or

b. Any other land vehicle that is subject to a compulsory or financial responsibility law or other motor vehicle insurance law in the state where it is licensed or principally garaged.

However, "auto" does not include "mobile equipment".

3. "Bodily injury" means bodily injury, sickness or disease sustained by a person, including death resulting from any of these at any time.

4. "Coverage territory" means:

a. The United States of America (including its territories and possessions), Puerto Rico and Canada;

b. International waters or airspace, but only if the injury or damage occurs in the course of travel or transportation between any places included in **a.** above; or

c. All other parts of the world if the injury or damage arises out of:

(1) Goods or products made or sold by you in the territory described in **a.** above;

(2) The activities of a person whose home is in the territory described in **a.** above, but is away for a short time on your business; or

(3) "Personal and advertising injury" offenses that take place through the Internet or similar electronic means of communication

provided the insured's responsibility to pay damages is determined in a "suit" on the merits, in the territory described in **a.** above or in a settlement we agree to.

5. "Employee" includes a "leased worker". "Employee" does not include a "temporary worker".

6. "Executive officer" means a person holding any of the officer positions created by your charter, constitution, by-laws or any other similar governing document.

7. "Hostile fire" means one which becomes uncontrollable or breaks out from where it was intended to be.

8. "Impaired property" means tangible property, other than "your product" or "your work", that cannot be used or is less useful because:

a. It incorporates "your product" or "your work" that is known or thought to be defective, deficient, inadequate or dangerous; or

b. You have failed to fulfill the terms of a contract or agreement;

if such property can be restored to use by:

a. The repair, replacement, adjustment or removal of "your product" or "your work"; or

b. Your fulfilling the terms of the contract or agreement.

9. "Insured contract" means:

a. A contract for a lease of premises. However, that portion of the contract for a lease of premises that indemnifies any person or organization for damage by fire to premises while rented to you or temporarily occupied by you with permission of the owner is not an "insured contract";

b. A sidetrack agreement;

c. Any easement or license agreement, except in connection with construction or demolition operations on or within 50 feet of a railroad;

d. An obligation, as required by ordinance, to indemnify a municipality, except in connection with work for a municipality;

e. An elevator maintenance agreement;

f. That part of any other contract or agreement pertaining to your business (including an indemnification of a municipality in connection with work performed for a municipality) under which you assume the tort liability of another party to pay for "bodily injury" or "property damage" to a third person or organization. Tort liability means a liability that would be imposed by law in the absence of any contract or agreement.

Paragraph **f.** does not include that part of any contract or agreement:

(1) That indemnifies a railroad for "bodily injury" or "property damage" arising out of construction or demolition operations, within 50 feet of any railroad property and affecting any railroad bridge or trestle, tracks, roadbeds, tunnel, underpass or crossing;

(2) That indemnifies an architect, engineer or surveyor for injury or damage arising out of:

  (a) Preparing, approving, or failing to prepare or approve, maps, shop drawings, opinions, reports, surveys, field orders, change orders or drawings and specifications; or

  (b) Giving directions or instructions, or failing to give them, if that is the primary cause of the injury or damage; or

(3) Under which the insured, if an architect, engineer or surveyor, assumes liability for an injury or damage arising out of the insured's rendering or failure to render professional services, including those listed in **(2)** above and supervisory, inspection, architectural or engineering activities.

10. "Leased worker" means a person leased to you by a labor leasing firm under an agreement between you and the labor leasing firm, to perform duties related to the conduct of your business. "Leased worker" does not include a "temporary worker".

11. "Loading or unloading" means the handling of property:

  a. After it is moved from the place where it is accepted for movement into or onto an aircraft, watercraft or "auto";

  b. While it is in or on an aircraft, watercraft or "auto"; or

  c. While it is being moved from an aircraft, watercraft or "auto" to the place where it is finally delivered;

  but "loading or unloading" does not include the movement of property by means of a mechanical device, other than a hand truck, that is not attached to the aircraft, watercraft or "auto".

12. "Mobile equipment" means any of the following types of land vehicles, including any attached machinery or equipment:

  a. Bulldozers, farm machinery, forklifts and other vehicles designed for use principally off public roads;

  b. Vehicles maintained for use solely on or next to premises you own or rent;

  c. Vehicles that travel on crawler treads;

  d. Vehicles, whether self-propelled or not, maintained primarily to provide mobility to permanently mounted:

    (1) Power cranes, shovels, loaders, diggers or drills; or

    (2) Road construction or resurfacing equipment such as graders, scrapers or rollers;

  e. Vehicles not described in **a., b., c.** or **d.** above that are not self-propelled and are maintained primarily to provide mobility to permanently attached equipment of the following types:

    (1) Air compressors, pumps and generators, including spraying, welding, building cleaning, geophysical exploration, lighting and well servicing equipment; or

    (2) Cherry pickers and similar devices used to raise or lower workers;

  f. Vehicles not described in **a., b., c.** or **d.** above maintained primarily for purposes other than the transportation of persons or cargo.

  However, self-propelled vehicles with the following types of permanently attached equipment are not "mobile equipment" but will be considered "autos":

    (1) Equipment designed primarily for:

      (a) Snow removal;

      (b) Road maintenance, but not construction or resurfacing; or

      (c) Street cleaning;

    (2) Cherry pickers and similar devices mounted on automobile or truck chassis and used to raise or lower workers; and

    (3) Air compressors, pumps and generators, including spraying, welding, building cleaning, geophysical exploration, lighting and well servicing equipment.

  However, "mobile equipment" does not include land vehicles that are subject to a compulsory or financial responsibility law or other motor vehicle insurance law in the state where it is licensed or principally garaged. Land vehicles subject to a compulsory or financial responsibility law or other motor vehicle insurance law are considered "autos".

13. "Occurrence" means an accident, including continuous or repeated exposure to substantially the same general harmful conditions.

14. "Personal and advertising injury" means injury, including consequential "bodily injury", arising out of one or more of the following offenses:

  a. False arrest, detention or imprisonment;

  b. Malicious prosecution;

  c. The wrongful eviction from, wrongful entry into, or invasion of the right of private occupancy of a room, dwelling or premises that a person occupies, committed by or on behalf of its owner, landlord or lessor;

d. Oral or written publication, in any manner, of material that slanders or libels a person or organization or disparages a person's or organization's goods, products or services;

e. Oral or written publication, in any manner, of material that violates a person's right of privacy;

f. The use of another's advertising idea in your "advertisement"; or

g. Infringing upon another's copyright, trade dress or slogan in your "advertisement".

15. "Pollutants" mean any solid, liquid, gaseous or thermal irritant or contaminant, including smoke, vapor, soot, fumes, acids, alkalis, chemicals and waste. Waste includes materials to be recycled, reconditioned or reclaimed.

16. "Products-completed operations hazard":

a. Includes all "bodily injury" and "property damage" occurring away from premises you own or rent and arising out of "your product" or "your work" except:

(1) Products that are still in your physical possession; or

(2) Work that has not yet been completed or abandoned. However, "your work" will be deemed completed at the earliest of the following times:

(a) When all of the work called for in your contract has been completed.

(b) When all of the work to be done at the job site has been completed if your contract calls for work at more than one job site.

(c) When that part of the work done at a job site has been put to its intended use by any person or organization other than another contractor or subcontractor working on the same project.

Work that may need service, maintenance, correction, repair or replacement, but which is otherwise complete, will be treated as completed.

b. Does not include "bodily injury" or "property damage" arising out of:

(1) The transportation of property, unless the injury or damage arises out of a condition in or on a vehicle not owned or operated by you, and that condition was created by the "loading or unloading" of that vehicle by any insured;

(2) The existence of tools, uninstalled equipment or abandoned or unused materials; or

(3) Products or operations for which the classification, listed in the Declarations or in a policy schedule, states that products-completed operations are subject to the General Aggregate Limit.

17. "Property damage" means:

a. Physical injury to tangible property, including all resulting loss of use of that property. All such loss of use shall be deemed to occur at the time of the physical injury that caused it; or

b. Loss of use of tangible property that is not physically injured. All such loss of use shall be deemed to occur at the time of the "occurrence" that caused it.

For the purposes of this insurance, electronic data is not tangible property.

As used in this definition, electronic data means information, facts or programs stored as or on, created or used on, or transmitted to or from, computer software, including systems and applications software, hard or floppy disks, CD-ROMS, tapes, drives, cells, data processing devices or any other media which are used with electronically controlled equipment.

18. "Suit" means a civil proceeding in which damages because of "bodily injury", "property damage" or "personal and advertising injury" to which this insurance applies are alleged. "Suit" includes:

a. An arbitration proceeding in which such damages are claimed and to which the insured must submit or does submit with our consent; or

b. Any other alternative dispute resolution proceeding in which such damages are claimed and to which the insured submits with our consent.

19. "Temporary worker" means a person who is furnished to you to substitute for a permanent "employee" on leave or to meet seasonal or short-term workload conditions.

20. "Volunteer worker" means a person who is not your "employee", and who donates his or her work and acts at the direction of and within the scope of duties determined by you, and is not paid a fee, salary or other compensation by you or anyone else for their work performed for you.

21. "Your product":

a. Means:

(1) Any goods or products, other than real property, manufactured, sold, handled, distributed or disposed of by:

(a) You;

(b) Others trading under your name; or

(c) A person or organization whose business or assets you have acquired; and

(2) Containers (other than vehicles), materials, parts or equipment furnished in connection with such goods or products.

b. Includes:

(1) Warranties or representations made at any time with respect to the fitness, quality, durability, performance or use of "your product"; and

(2) The providing of or failure to provide warnings or instructions.

c. Does not include vending machines or other property rented to or located for the use of others but not sold.

22. "Your work":

a. Means:

(1) Work or operations performed by you or on your behalf; and

(2) Materials, parts or equipment furnished in connection with such work or operations.

b. Includes:

(1) Warranties or representations made at any time with respect to the fitness, quality, durability, performance or use of "your work" and

(2) The providing of or failure to provide warnings or instructions.

THIS ENDORSEMENT CHANGES THE POLICY. PLEASE READ IT CAREFULLY.

NUCLEAR ENERGY LIABILITY EXCLUSION ENDORSEMENT
(Broad Form)

This endorsement modifies insurance provided under the following:

COMMERCIAL AUTOMOBILE COVERAGE PART
COMMERCIAL GENERAL LIABILITY COVERAGE PART
FARM COVERAGE PART
LIQUOR LIABILITY COVERAGE PART
OWNERS AND CONTRACTORS PROTECTIVE LIABILITY COVERAGE PART
POLLUTION LIABILITY COVERAGE PART
PRODUCTS/COMPLETED OPERATIONS LIABILITY COVERAGE PART
PROFESSIONAL LIABILITY COVERAGE PART
RAILROAD PROTECTIVE LIABILITY COVERAGE PART
UNDERGROUND STORAGE TANK POLICY

1. The insurance does not apply:

   A. Under any Liability Coverage, to "bodily injury" or "property damage":

      (1) With respect to which an "insured" under the policy is also an insured under a nuclear energy liability policy issued by Nuclear Energy Liability Insurance Association, Mutual Atomic Energy Liability Underwriters, Nuclear Insurance Association of Canada or any of their successors, or would be an insured under any such policy but for its termination upon exhaustion of its limit of liability; or

      (2) Resulting from the "hazardous properties" of "nuclear material" and with respect to which (a) any person or organization is required to maintain financial protection pursuant to the Atomic Energy Act of 1954, or any law amendatory thereof, or (b) the "insured" is, or had this policy not been issued would be, entitled to indemnity from the United States of America, or any agency thereof, under any agreement entered into by the United States of America, or any agency thereof, with any person or organization.

   B. Under any Medical Payments coverage, to expenses incurred with respect to "bodily injury" resulting from the "hazardous properties" of "nuclear material" and arising out of the operation of a "nuclear facility" by any person or organization.

   C. Under any Liability Coverage, to "bodily injury" or "property damage" resulting from "hazardous properties" of "nuclear material", if:

      (1) The "nuclear material" (a) is at any "nuclear facility" owned by, or operated by or on behalf of, an "insured" or (b) has been discharged or dispersed therefrom;

      (2) The "nuclear material" is contained in "spent fuel" or "waste" at any time possessed, handled, used, processed, stored, transported or disposed of, by or on behalf of an "insured"; or

      (3) The "bodily injury" or "property damage" arises out of the furnishing by an "insured" of services, materials, parts or equipment in connection with the planning, construction, maintenance, operation or use of any "nuclear facility", but if such facility is located within the United States of America, its territories or possessions or Canada, this exclusion (3) applies only to "property damage" to such "nuclear facility" and any property thereat.

2. As used in this endorsement:

"Hazardous properties" includes radioactive, toxic or explosive properties.

"Nuclear material" means "source material", "Special nuclear material" or "by-product material".

"Source material", "special nuclear material", and "by-product material" have the meanings given them in the Atomic Energy Act of 1954 or in any law amendatory thereof.

"Spent fuel" means any fuel element or fuel component, solid or liquid, which has been used or exposed to radiation in a "nuclear reactor".

"Waste" means any waste material **(a)** containing "by-product material" other than the tailings or wastes produced by the extraction or concentration of uranium or thorium from any ore processed primarily for its "source material" content, and **(b)** resulting from the operation by any person or organization of any "nuclear facility" included under the first two paragraphs of the definition of "nuclear facility".

"Nuclear facility" means:

(a) Any "nuclear reactor";

(b) Any equipment or device designed or used for **(1)** separating the isotopes of uranium or plutonium, **(2)** processing or utilizing "spent fuel", or **(3)** handling, processing or packaging "waste";

(c) Any equipment or device used for the processing, fabricating or alloying of "special nuclear material" if at any time the total amount of such material in the custody of the "insured" at the premises where such equipment or device is located consists of or contains more than 25 grams of plutonium or uranium 233 or any combination thereof, or more than 250 grams of uranium 235;

(d) Any structure, basin, excavation, premises or place prepared or used for the storage or disposal of "waste";

and includes the site on which any of the foregoing is located, all operations conducted on such site and all premises used for such operations.

"Nuclear reactor" means any apparatus designed or used to sustain nuclear fission in a self-supporting chain reaction or to contain a critical mass of fissionable material.

"Property damage" includes all forms of radioactive contamination of property.

THIS ENDORSEMENT CHANGES THE POLICY. PLEASE READ IT CAREFULLY.

SUPPLEMENTAL
EXTENDED REPORTING PERIOD ENDORSEMENT

This endorsement modifies insurance provided under the following:

COMMERCIAL GENERAL LIABILITY COVERAGE FORM (CLAIMS-MADE VERSION)

SCHEDULE

Premium _____

(If no entry appears above, information required to complete this endorsement will be shown in the Declarations as applicable to this endorsement.)

A. A Supplemental Extended Reporting Period Endorsement is provided, as described in Section **V** – Extended Reporting Periods.

B. A Supplemental General Aggregate Limit and a Supplemental Products-Completed Operations Aggregate Limit apply, as set forth in Paragraphs **C.** and **D.** below, to claims first received and recorded during the Supplemental Extended Reporting Period. These limits are equal, respectively, to the General Aggregate Limit and the Products-Completed Operations Aggregate Limit, if any, entered on the Declarations in effect at the end of the policy period.

C. Paragraph **2.** of **Section III – Limits Of Insurance** is replaced by the following:

2. The General Aggregate Limit is the most we will pay for the sum of:

   a. Medical expenses under Coverage **C**;

   b. Damages under Coverage **A**, except damages because of "bodily injury" and "property damage" included in the "products-completed operations hazard"; and

   c. Damages under Coverage **B**.

   However, the General Aggregate Limit does not apply to damages for claims first received and recorded during the Supplemental Extended Reporting Period.

The Supplemental General Aggregate Limit is the most we will pay for the sum of damages under:

   a. Coverage **A**, except damages because of "bodily injury" and "property damage" included in the "products-completed operations hazard"; and

   b. Coverage **B**,

for claims first received and recorded during the Supplemental Extended Reporting Period.

D. Paragraph **3.** of **Section III – Limits Of Insurance** is replaced by the following:

3. The Products-Completed Operations Aggregate Limit is the most we will pay under Coverage **A** for damages because of "bodily injury" or "property damage" included in the "products-completed operations hazard", except damages for claims first received and recorded during the Supplemental Extended Reporting Period.

   The Supplemental Products-Completed Operations Aggregate Limit is the most we will pay under Coverage **A** for damages because of "bodily injury" or "property damage" included in the "products-completed operations hazard" for claims first received and recorded during the Supplemental Extended Reporting Period.

E. Section **III** – Limits Of Insurance, as amended by Paragraphs **C.** and **D.** above, is otherwise unchanged and applies in its entirety.

F. The first paragraph of Paragraph **4.b.** of **Section IV – Commercial General Liability Conditions** is replaced by the following:

4. Other Insurance

b. Excess Insurance

This insurance is excess over:

(1) Any of the other insurance, whether primary, excess, contingent or on any other basis:

(a) That is effective prior to the beginning of the policy period shown in the Declarations of this insurance and applies to "bodily injury" or "property damage" on other than a claims-made basis, if:

(i) No Retroactive Date is shown in the Declarations of this insurance; or

(ii) The other insurance has a policy period which continues after the Retroactive Date shown in the Declarations of this insurance;

(b) That is Fire, Extended Coverage, Builders' Risk, Installation Risk or similar coverage for "your work";

(c) That is Fire Insurance for premises rented to you or temporarily occupied by you with permission of the owner;

(d) That is insurance purchased by you to cover your liability as a tenant for "property damage" to premises rented to you or temporarily occupied by you with permission of the owner; or

(e) If the loss arises out of the maintenance or use of aircraft, "autos" or watercraft to the extent not subject to Exclusion **g.** of Section **I** – Coverage **A** – Bodily Injury And Property Damage Liability;

(f) Whose policy period begins or continues after the Supplemental Extended Reporting Period begins; or

(2) Any other primary insurance available to you covering liability for damages arising out of the premises or operations for which you have been added as an additional insured by attachment of an endorsement.

G. This endorsement will not take effect unless the additional premium for it, as set forth in Section **V,** is paid when due. If that premium is paid when due, this endorsement may not be cancelled.

CG 27 10 07 98

THIS ENDORSEMENT CHANGES THE POLICY. PLEASE READ IT CAREFULLY.

EXCLUSION OF SPECIFIC ACCIDENTS, PRODUCTS, WORK OR LOCATION

This endorsement modifies insurance provided under the following:

COMMERCIAL GENERAL LIABILITY COVERAGE FORM (CLAIMS-MADE VERSION)

SCHEDULE

Date of Accident	Location of Accident	Description of Accident
"Location"	Address	Description of "Location"
"Your Product" or "Your Work" (Description)		Date of _____ (Manufacture, Sale, Distribution, Disposal, or Completion) (Specify Date and one of above acts)

(If no entry appears above, information required to complete this endorsement will be shown in the Declarations as applicable to this endorsement.)

A. COVERAGE A – BODILY INJURY AND PROPERTY DAMAGE LIABILITY (Section I – Coverages) does not apply to "bodily injury" or "property damage" arising out of:

1. The accidents or "locations", if any, described above; or

2. The products or work, if any, described above, if the "bodily injury" or "property damage" is included in the "products-completed operations hazard";

even if other causes contribute to or aggravate the "bodily injury" or "property damage".

B. **Extended Reporting Periods**

The following applies when this Endorsement takes effect, but only if:

1. This insurance is a renewal of an immediately preceding policy issued by us providing claims-made coverage for Bodily Injury and Property Damage Liability; and

2. That coverage applies to "bodily injury" and "property damage" arising out of any of the accident(s), products, work or "location(s)" described above.

In this case, we will provide an Extended Reporting Period under that preceding policy, but only for such "bodily injury" and "property damage" that occurred before the end of the policy period of that preceding policy (but not before any applicable Retroactive Date).

We will issue the Amendment of Section **V** – Extended Reporting Periods for Specific Accidents, Products, Work or Locations endorsement on that preceding policy, amending paragraphs **1.** and **2.** of EXTENDED REPORTING PERIODS (Section **V**) accordingly. The Extended Reporting Period will then be as set forth in that Section.

C. For the purposes of this endorsement, the following definition is added to DEFINITIONS (Section **VI**):

"Location" means premises involving the same or connecting lots, or premises whose connection is interrupted only by a street, roadway, waterway or right-of-way of a railroad.

THIS ENDORSEMENT CHANGES THE POLICY. PLEASE READ IT CAREFULLY.

AMENDMENT OF SECTION V – EXTENDED REPORTING PERIODS FOR SPECIFIC ACCIDENTS, PRODUCTS, WORK OR LOCATION

This endorsement modifies insurance provided under the following:

COMMERCIAL GENERAL LIABILITY COVERAGE FORM (CLAIMS-MADE VERSION)
PRODUCTS-COMPLETED OPERATIONS LIABILITY COVERAGE FORM (CLAIMS-MADE VERSION)

SCHEDULE

Date of Accident	Location of Accident	Description of Accident
"Location"	**Address**	**Description of "Location"**
"Your Product" or "Your Work" (Description)		**Date of _____ (Manufacture, Sale, Distribution, Disposal, or Completion) (Specify date and one of above acts)**

(If no entry appears above, information required to complete this endorsement will be shown in the Declarations as applicable to this endorsement.)

We have issued a renewal of this insurance excluding "bodily injury" and "property damage" arising out of the accident(s), products, work or "location(s)" described above. When that renewal takes effect, this insurance is amended as follows:

A. Paragraph **1.** of EXTENDED REPORTING PERIODS (Section **V**) is replaced by the following:

  1. One or more Extended Reporting Periods are provided as set forth below.

B. Paragraph **2.** of EXTENDED REPORTING PERIODS (Section **V**) is replaced by the following:

  2. Extended Reporting Periods do not extend the policy period or change the scope of coverage provided. They apply only to claims for "bodily injury" or "property damage" that occurred before the end of the policy period (but not before the Retroactive Date, if any, shown in the Declarations), and only if such "bodily injury" or "property damage":

    a. Arose out of the accident(s) or "location(s)", if any, described above; or

    b. Arose out of the products or work, if any described above and is included in the "products-completed operations hazard".

  Once in effect, Extended Reporting Periods may not be cancelled.

C. Paragraphs **3.**, **4.**, **5.** and **6.** of EXTENDED REPORTING PERIODS (Section **V**) remain unchanged. But the Supplemental Extended Reporting Period endorsement referred to in paragraphs **5.** and **6.** will be the Supplemental Extended Reporting Period Endorsement for Specific Accidents, Products, Work or Locations.

D. For the purposes of this endorsement, the following definition is added to DEFINITIONS (SECTION **VI**):

  "Location" means premises involving the same or connecting lots, or premises whose connection is interrupted only by a street, roadway, waterway or right-of-way of a railroad.

THIS ENDORSEMENT CHANGES THE POLICY. PLEASE READ IT CAREFULLY.

SUPPLEMENTAL EXTENDED REPORTING PERIOD ENDORSEMENT FOR SPECIFIC ACCIDENTS, PRODUCTS, WORK OR LOCATIONS

This endorsement modifies insurance provided under the following:

COMMERCIAL GENERAL LIABILITY COVERAGE FORM (CLAIMS-MADE VERSION)

SCHEDULE

Premium _____

(If no entry appears above, information required to complete this endorsement will be shown in the Declarations as applicable to this endorsement.)

A. The Supplemental Extended Reporting Period Endorsement described in Extended Reporting Periods (Section **V**), as amended by the Amendment of Section **V** – Extended Reporting Periods For Specific Accidents, Products, Work Or Locations Endorsement, is provided.

B. A Supplemental General Aggregate Limit and a Supplemental Products-Completed Operations Aggregate Limit apply, as set forth in Paragraphs **C.** and **D.** below, to claims first received and recorded during the Supplemental Extended Reporting Period. These limits are equal, respectively, to the General Aggregate Limit and the Products-Completed Operations Aggregate Limit, if any, entered on the Declarations in effect at the end of the policy period.

C. Paragraph **2.** of **Section III – Limits Of Insurance** is replaced by the following:

2. The General Aggregate Limit is the most we will pay for the sum of:

a. Medical expenses under Coverage **C**;

b. Damages under Coverage **A**, except damages because of "bodily injury" and "property damage" included in the "products-completed operations hazard"; and

c. Damages under Coverage **B**.

However, the General Aggregate Limit does not apply to damages for claims first received and recorded during the Supplemental Extended Reporting Period.

The Supplemental General Aggregate Limit is the most we will pay for the sum of damages under:

a. Coverage **A**, except damages because of "bodily injury" or "property damage" included in the "products-completed operations hazard"; and

b. Coverage **B**,

for claims first received and recorded during the Supplemental Extended Reporting Period.

D. Paragraph **3.** of **Section III – Limits Of Insurance** is replaced by the following:

3. The Products-Completed Operations Aggregate Limit is the most we will pay under Coverage **A** for damages because of "bodily injury" or "property damage" included in the "products-completed operations hazard", except damages for claims first received and recorded during the Supplemental Extended Reporting Period.

The Supplemental Products-Completed Operations Aggregate Limit is the most we will pay under Coverage **A** for damages because of "bodily injury" or "property damage" included in the "products-completed operations hazard" and for claims first received and recorded during the Supplemental Extended Reporting Period.

E. Section **III** – Limits Of Insurance, as amended by Paragraphs **C.** and **D.** above, is otherwise unchanged and applies in its entirety.

F. The first paragraph of Paragraph **4.b.** of **Section IV – Commercial General Liability Conditions** is replaced by the following:

4. Other Insurance

b. Excess Insurance

This insurance is excess over:

(1) Any of the other insurance, whether primary, excess, contingent or on any other basis:

(a) That is effective prior to the beginning of the policy period shown in the Declarations of this insurance and applies to "bodily injury" or "property damage" on other than a claims-made basis, if:

(i) No Retroactive Date is shown in the Declarations of this insurance; or

(ii) The other insurance has a policy period which continues after the Retroactive Date shown in the Declarations of this insurance;

(b) That is Fire, Extended Coverage, Builders' Risk, Installation Risk or similar coverage for "your work";

(c) That is Fire Insurance for premises rented to you or temporarily occupied by you with permission of the owner;

(d) That is insurance purchased by you to cover your liability as a tenant for "property damage" to premises rented to you or temporarily occupied by you with permission of the owner; or

(e) If the loss arises out of the maintenance or use of aircraft, "autos" or watercraft to the extent not subject to Exclusion **g.** of Section **I** – Coverage **A** – Bodily Injury And Property Damage Liability;

(f) Whose policy period begins or continues after the Supplemental Extended Reporting Period begins; or

(2) Any other primary insurance available to you covering liability for damages arising out of the premises or operations for which you have been added as an additional insured by attachment of an endorsement.

G. This endorsement will not take effect unless the additional premium for it, as set forth in Section **V,** is paid when due. If that premium is paid when due, this endorsement may not be cancelled.

Copyright, Insurance Services Office, Inc., 1997   **CG 27 11 07 98**   ☐

THIS ENDORSEMENT CHANGES THE POLICY. PLEASE READ IT CAREFULLY.

EMPLOYMENT-RELATED PRACTICES EXCLUSION

This endorsement modifies insurance provided under the following:

COMMERCIAL GENERAL LIABILITY COVERAGE PART

A. The following exclusion is added to Paragraph **2.**, **Exclusions** of **Section I – Coverage A – Bodily Injury And Property Damage Liability:**

This insurance does not apply to:

"Bodily injury" to:

   (1) A person arising out of any:

      (a) Refusal to employ that person;

      (b) Termination of that person's employment; or

      (c) Employment-related practices, policies, acts or omissions, such as coercion, demotion, evaluation, reassignment, discipline, defamation, harassment, humiliation or discrimination directed at that person; or

   (2) The spouse, child, parent, brother or sister of that person as a consequence of "bodily injury" to that person at whom any of the employment-related practices described in Paragraphs **(a), (b),** or **(c)** above is directed.

This exclusion applies:

(1) Whether the insured may be liable as an employer or in any other capacity; and

(2) To any obligation to share damages with or repay someone else who must pay damages because of the injury.

B. The following exclusion is added to Paragraph **2.**, **Exclusions** of **Section I – Coverage B – Personal And Advertising Injury Liability:**

This insurance does not apply to:

"Personal and advertising injury" to:

   (1) A person arising out of any:

      (a) Refusal to employ that person;

      (b) Termination of that person's employment; or

      (c) Employment-related practices, policies, acts or omissions, such as coercion, demotion, evaluation, reassignment, discipline, defamation, harassment, humiliation or discrimination directed at that person; or

   (2) The spouse, child, parent, brother or sister of that person as a consequence of "personal and advertising injury" to that person at whom any of the employment-related practices described in Paragraphs **(a), (b),** or **(c)** above is directed.

This exclusion applies:

(1) Whether the insured may be liable as an employer or in any other capacity; and

(2) To any obligation to share damages with or repay someone else who must pay damages because of the injury.

THIS ENDORSEMENT CHANGES THE POLICY. PLEASE READ IT CAREFULLY.

AMENDMENT OF LIQUOR LIABILITY EXCLUSION

This endorsement modifies insurance provided under the following:

COMMERCIAL GENERAL LIABILITY COVERAGE PART

Exclusion c. of COVERAGE A (Section I) is replaced by the following:

c. "Bodily injury" or "property damage" for which any insured may be held liable by reason of:

  (1) Causing or contributing to the intoxication of any person;

  (2) The furnishing of alcoholic beverages to a person under the legal drinking age or under the influence of alcohol; or

  (3) Any statute, ordinance or regulation relating to the sale, gift, distribution or use of alcoholic beverages.

This exclusion applies only if you:

  (1) Manufacture, sell or distribute alcoholic beverages;

  (2) Serve or furnish alcoholic beverages for a charge whether or not such activity:

    (a) Requires a license;

    (b) Is for the purpose of financial gain or livelihood; or

  (3) Serve or furnish alcoholic beverages without a charge, if a license is required for such activity.

THIS ENDORSEMENT CHANGES THE POLICY. PLEASE READ IT CAREFULLY.

AMENDMENT OF LIQUOR LIABILITY EXCLUSION – EXCEPTION FOR SCHEDULED ACTIVITIES

This endorsement modifies insurance provided under the following:

COMMERCIAL GENERAL LIABILITY COVERAGE PART

SCHEDULE

Description of Activity(ies):

(If no entry appears above, information required to complete this endorsement will be shown in the Declarations as applicable to this endorsement.)

Exclusion c. of COVERAGE A (Section I) is replaced by the following:

c. "Bodily injury" or "property damage" for which any insured may be held liable by reason of:

(1) Causing or contributing to the intoxication of any person;

(2) The furnishing of alcoholic beverages to a person under the legal drinking age or under the influence of alcohol; or

(3) Any statute, ordinance or regulation relating to the sale, gift, distribution or use of alcoholic beverages.

This exclusion applies only if you:

(1) Manufacture, sell or distribute alcoholic beverages;

(2) Serve or furnish alcoholic beverages for a charge whether or not such activity:

    (a) Requires a license;

    (b) Is for the purpose of financial gain or livelihood; or

(3) Serve or furnish alcoholic beverages without a charge, if a license is required for such activity.

However, this exclusion does not apply to "bodily injury" or "property damage" arising out of the selling, serving or furnishing of alcoholic beverages at the specific activity(ies) described above.

THIS ENDORSEMENT CHANGES THE POLICY. PLEASE READ IT CAREFULLY.

TOTAL POLLUTION EXCLUSION ENDORSEMENT

This endorsement modifies insurance provided under the following:

COMMERCIAL GENERAL LIABILITY COVERAGE PART

Exclusion **f.** under Paragraph **2., Exclusions** of **Section I – Coverage A – Bodily Injury And Property Damage Liability** is replaced by the following:

This insurance does not apply to:

f. Pollution

(1) "Bodily injury" or "property damage" which would not have occurred in whole or part but for the actual, alleged or threatened discharge, dispersal, seepage, migration, release or escape of "pollutants" at any time.

(2) Any loss, cost or expense arising out of any:

(a) Request, demand, order or statutory or regulatory requirement that any insured or others test for, monitor, clean up, remove, contain, treat, detoxify or neutralize, or in any way respond to, or assess the effects of "pollutants"; or

(b) Claim or suit by or on behalf of a governmental authority for damages because of testing for, monitoring, cleaning up, removing, containing, treating, detoxifying or neutralizing, or in any way responding to, or assessing the effects of, "pollutants".

THIS ENDORSEMENT CHANGES THE POLICY. PLEASE READ IT CAREFULLY.

LIMITED POLLUTION LIABILITY
EXTENSION ENDORSEMENT

This endorsement modifies insurance provided under the following:

COMMERCIAL GENERAL LIABILITY COVERAGE PART

SCHEDULE

Limited Pollution Liability Extension Aggregate Limit	$ _____
Premium $ _____	

(If no entry appears above, information required to complete this endorsement will be shown in the Declarations as applicable to this endorsement.)

I. Exclusion **f.** under Section **I** – Coverage **A** is replaced by the following:

2. Exclusions

This insurance does not apply to:

f. Pollution

(1) "Bodily injury" or "property damage" arising out of the actual, alleged or threatened discharge, dispersal, seepage, migration, release or escape of "pollutants":

(a) At or from any premises, site or location which is or was at any time used by or for any insured or others for the handling, storage, disposal, processing or treatment of waste;

(b) Which are or were at any time transported, handled, stored, treated, disposed of or processed as waste by or for:

(i) Any insured; or

(ii) Any person or organization for whom you may be legally responsible;

(c) At or from any premises, site or location on which any insured or any contractors or subcontractors working directly or indirectly on any insured's behalf are performing operations if the operations are to test for, monitor, clean up, remove, contain, treat, detoxify or neutralize, or in any way respond to, or assess the effects of, "pollutants"; or

(d) At or from a storage tank or other container, ducts or piping which is below or partially below the surface of the ground or water or which, at any time, has been buried under the surface of the ground or water and then subsequently exposed by erosion, excavation or any other means if the actual, alleged or threatened discharge, dispersal, seepage, migration, release or escape of "pollutants" arises at or from any premises, site or location:

(i) Which is or was at any time owned or occupied by, or rented or loaned to, any insured; or

(ii) Which any insured or any contractors or subcontractors working directly or indirectly on any insured's behalf are performing operations if the "pollutants" are brought on or to the premises, site or location in connection with such operations by such insured, contractor or subcontractor.

Subparagraph **(d)** does not apply to "bodily injury" or "property damage" arising out of heat, smoke or fumes from a "hostile fire".

(2) Any loss, cost or expense arising out of any:

(a) Request, demand, order or statutory or regulatory requirement issued or made pursuant to any environmental protection or environmental liability statutes or regulations that any insured test for, monitor, clean up, remove, contain, treat, detoxify or neutralize, or in any way respond to, or assess the effects of, "pollutants"; or

(b) Claim or suit by or on behalf of a governmental authority for damages because of testing for, monitoring, cleaning up, removing, containing, treating, detoxifying or neutralizing or in any way responding to or assessing the effects of, "pollutants".

However, this paragraph does not apply to liability for those sums the insured becomes legally obligated to pay as damages because of "property damage" that the insured would have in the absence of such request, demand, order or statutory or regulatory requirement, or such claim or "suit" by or on behalf of a governmental authority.

II. With respect to "bodily injury" or "property damage" arising out of the actual, alleged or threatened discharge, dispersal, seepage, migration, release or escape of "pollutants":

A. The "Each Occurrence Limit" shown in the Declarations does not apply.

B. Paragraph **7.** of **Limits Of Insurance** (Section **III**) does not apply.

C. Paragraph **1.** of **Section III – Limits Of Insurance** is replaced by the following:

1. The Limits Of Insurance shown in the Schedule of this endorsement, or in the Declarations and the rules below fix the most we will pay regardless of the number of:

a. Insureds;

b. Claims made or "suits" brought; or

c. Persons or organizations making claims or bringing "suits".

D. The following are added to **Section III – Limits Of Insurance:**

8. Subject to **2.** or **3.** above, whichever applies, the Limited Pollution Liability Extension Aggregate Limit shown in the Schedule is the most we will pay for the sum of:

a. Damages under Coverage **A;** and

b. Medical expenses under Coverage **C**

because of "bodily injury" or "property damage" arising out of the actual, alleged or threatened discharge, dispersal, seepage, migration, release or escape of "pollutants".

9. Subject to **8.** above, the Medical Expense Limit is the most we will pay under Coverage **C** for all medical expenses because of "bodily injury" sustained by any one person arising out of the actual, alleged or threatened discharge, dispersal, seepage, migration, release or escape of "pollutants".

 CG 24 15 10 01 □

THIS ENDORSEMENT CHANGES THE POLICY. PLEASE READ IT CAREFULLY.

FUNGI OR BACTERIA EXCLUSION

This endorsement modifies insurance provided under the following:

COMMERCIAL GENERAL LIABILITY COVERAGE PART

A. The following exclusion is added to Paragraph **2. Exclusions** of **Section I – Coverage A – Bodily Injury And Property Damage Liability:**

2. Exclusions

This insurance does not apply to:

Fungi Or Bacteria

a. "Bodily injury" or "property damage" which would not have occurred, in whole or in part, but for the actual, alleged or threatened inhalation of, ingestion of, contact with, exposure to, existence of, or presence of, any "fungi" or bacteria on or within a building or structure, including its contents, regardless of whether any other cause, event, material or product contributed concurrently or in any sequence to such injury or damage.

b. Any loss, cost or expenses arising out of the abating, testing for, monitoring, cleaning up, removing, containing, treating, detoxifying, neutralizing, remediating or disposing of, or in any way responding to, or assessing the effects of, "fungi" or bacteria, by any insured or by any other person or entity.

This exclusion does not apply to any "fungi" or bacteria that are, are on, or are contained in, a good or product intended for bodily consumption.

B. The following exclusion is added to Paragraph **2. Exclusions** of **Section I – Coverage B – Personal And Advertising Injury Liability:**

2. Exclusions

This insurance does not apply to:

Fungi Or Bacteria

a. "Personal and advertising injury" which would not have taken place, in whole or in part, but for the actual, alleged or threatened inhalation of, ingestion of, contact with, exposure to, existence of, or presence of any "fungi" or bacteria on or within a building or structure, including its contents, regardless of whether any other cause, event, material or product contributed concurrently or in any sequence to such injury.

b. Any loss, cost or expense arising out of the abating, testing for, monitoring, cleaning up, removing, containing, treating, detoxifying, neutralizing, remediating or disposing of, or in any way responding to, or assessing the effects of, "fungi" or bacteria, by any insured or by any other person or entity.

C. The following definition is added to the **Definitions** Section:

"Fungi" means any type or form of fungus, including mold or mildew and any mycotoxins, spores, scents or byproducts produced or released by fungi.

THIS ENDORSEMENT CHANGES THE POLICY. PLEASE READ IT CAREFULLY.

LIMITED FUNGI OR BACTERIA COVERAGE

This endorsement modifies insurance provided under the following:

COMMERCIAL GENERAL LIABILITY COVERAGE PART

SCHEDULE

Fungi And Bacteria Liability Aggregate Limit $

A. The following exclusion is added to Paragraph **2. Exclusions** of **Section I – Coverage B – Personal And Advertising Injury Liability:**

2. Exclusions

This insurance does not apply to:

a. "Personal and advertising injury" arising out of a "fungi or bacteria incident".

b. Any loss, cost or expense arising out of the abating, testing for, monitoring, cleaning up, removing, containing, treating, detoxifying, neutralizing, remediating or disposing of, or in any way responding to, or assessing the effects of, "fungi" or bacteria, by any insured or by any other person or entity.

B. Coverage provided by this insurance for "bodily injury" or "property damage", arising out of a "fungi or bacteria incident", is subject to the Fungi and Bacteria Liability Aggregate Limit as described in Paragraph **C.** of this endorsement. This provision **B.** does not apply to any "fungi" or bacteria that are, are on, or are contained in, a good or product intended for bodily consumption.

C. The following are added to **Section III – Limits Of Insurance:**

1. Subject to Paragraphs **2.** and **3.** of Section **III –** Limits of Insurance, as applicable, the Fungi and Bacteria Liability Aggregate Limit shown in the Schedule of this endorsement is the most we will pay under Coverage **A** for all "bodily injury" or "property damage" and Coverage **C.** for Medical Payments arising out of one or more "fungi or bacteria incidents". This provision **C.1.** does not apply to any "fungi" or bacteria that are, are on, or are contained in, a good or product intended for bodily consumption.

2. Paragraphs **5.**, the Each Occurrence Limit, Paragraph **6.**, the Damage To Premises Rented To You Limit, and Paragraph **7.**, the Medical Expense Limit, of Section **III –** Limits Of Insurance continue to apply to "bodily injury" or "property damage" arising out of a "fungi or bacteria incident" but only if, and to the extent that, limits are available under the Fungi and Bacteria Liability Aggregate Limit.

D. The following definitions are added to the **Definitions** Section:

1. "Fungi" means any type or form of fungus, including mold or mildew and any mycotoxins, spores, scents or byproducts produced or released by fungi.

2. "Fungi or bacteria incident" means an incident which would not have occurred, in whole or in part, but for the actual, alleged or threatened inhalation of, ingestion of, contact with, exposure to, existence of, or presence of, any "fungi" or bacteria on or within a building or structure, including its contents, regardless of whether any other cause, event, material or product contributed concurrently or in any sequence to such injury or damage.